CALLED

EDITED BY Nikolaus Satelmajer AND Ivan L. Williams Sr.

CORE QUALITIES FOR MINISTRY

Contributors:

Kyoshin Ahn, J. Harold Alomia, BJ Boles, John Brunt, Alex Bryan,
Michael W. Campbell, Steve D. Cassimy, Roger Hernandez,
Dan Jackson, Marquis D. Johns, Abraham J. Jules, C. Wesley Knight,
Esther R. Knott, Evan Knott, Macy McVay, Jiří Moskala, Gary Patterson,
Calvin B. Preston, Stephen Reasor, Ángel Manuel Rodríguez,
Nikolaus Satelmajer, Rollin Shoemaker, Diane Thurber, Ivan L. Williams Sr.

Cover design by Steve Lanto
Cover design resources supplied by the authors
Inside design by Aaron Troia
Inside art supplied by the North American Division Ministerial Association

The authors assume full responsibility for the accuracy of all facts and quotations as cited in this book.

You can obtain additional copies of this book by calling toll-free 1-800-765-6955 or by visiting http://www.adventistbookcenter.com.

Library of Congress Cataloging-in-Publication Data:
Called : core qualities for ministry / editors, Nikolaus Satelmajer and Ivan L. Williams, Sr.
    pages cm
 ISBN 13: 978-0-8163-5840-3 (pbk.)
 ISBN 10: 0-8163-5840-0 (pbk.)
 1. Pastoral theology—Seventh-day Adventists. I. Satelmajer, Nikolaus, 1944- editor.
 BV4011.3.C35 2015
 253'.2—dc23

2015015195

May 2015

Table of Contents

Introduction

This book is for ministers—pastors, chaplains, specialized ministries leaders (such as youth, family life, etc.), professors, teachers, and administrators. It is released in conjunction with the 2015 North American Division of Seventh-day Adventists (NAD) ministerial convention in Austin, Texas. The Seventh-day Adventist Church is a worldwide movement with a common mission. Yet, while our ministry colleagues around the world will find this book helpful, it was written specifically for the ministers in North America.

Ministry covers so many responsibilities and functions that it is nearly impossible to address them all in one book. We will discuss several aspects of the seven core qualities that the NAD Ministerial Department has identified as benchmarks. These benchmarks are critical for an effective ministry. The core qualities are identified at the end of the introduction and listed in greater detail at the beginning of each section.

We carefully chose contributors throughout North America. Some writers have extensive experience while others are just embarking on their ministry. Some are pastors in a *multichurch district*, while others are pastors in a *multipastor church*. They are as diverse as our church is diverse. The writers also represent a broad spectrum of ministries to reflect what ministers in North America are doing.

The writers deserve collective thanks for participating in this undertaking. We appreciate the time from their busy schedules to share from their spiritual insights and professional experience.

The ministerial leadership team of the North American Division of Seventh-day Adventists, Brenda Billingy, Jose Cortes Jr., Dave Gemmell, Donna Jackson, and Esther R. Knott, deserve our thanks for their participation in the project. We also thank Jerry Thomas and his team at Pacific Press® Publishing Association for enthusiastically working on this project. Sheryl Beck and Ruth I. Satelmajer were valuable in the editing process and we thank them.

Our God does not change and our mission is always the same, but the way we accomplish the mission does change. Ministers are constantly challenged to meet the needs of the community and congregation. Our prayer is that this book will help our colleagues find and experience fulfillment in ministry while meeting the challenges faced in our ever-changing world.

Nikolaus Satelmajer and Ivan L. Williams Sr.
Silver Spring, Maryland

Corequalities

Core Qualities of the Effective Pastor:

The mission of the Ministerial department of the North American Division of Seventh-day Adventists is to empower the ministerial community in leading churches to reach their world for Christ with hope and wholeness. Pastors who are the most effective in this mission are proficient in identifiable core qualities of ministry. These qualities serve as benchmarks for professional growth from the initial call, through undergraduate study and master of divinity education, internship, and continuing education.

CHARACTER
The foundational quality is allowing the character of Christ to be formed in us and modeled through personal integrity that aligns with biblical ideals.

EVANGELISM
Pastors are skilled and passionate about making disciples, helping people accept, internalize, and share in a vibrant relationship with Jesus Christ and the Seventh-day Adventist message.

LEADERSHIP
Pastors build a church vision and equip members to learn, grow, and serve.

WORSHIP
Pastors facilitate an enriching corporate worship experience that brings people into the presence of God.

MANAGEMENT
Pastors execute responsibilities in a timely and well-organized fashion.

SCHOLARSHIP
Pastors diligently and carefully study the Bible and professional resources for continual personal growth in Christ.

RELATIONSHIP
Pastors relate well to others regardless of faith, age, ethnicity, personality, or gender.

♥ CHARACTER

The foundational quality is allowing the character of Christ to be formed in us and modeled through personal integrity that aligns with biblical ideals.

Descriptors of Character include:
- senses call from God
- passionate for God
- follows God's leading
- loyal to the mission and foundational beliefs of the Church
- humble
- impartial
- disciplined in health, fitness, and self-care
- inspires a climate of trust
- emotionally mature
- stands firm for biblical, moral, and ethical principles
- open to counsel
- uses discernment
- honest
- takes initiative
- faithful to family
- good reputation
- sacrificial spirit

The Paradox of the Call

IVAN L. WILLIAMS SR.

A call from God demands total commitment on our part. God's call is personal, and you may experience what Jeremiah did when he proclaimed, "His [God's] word was in my heart like a burning fire shut up in my bones; I was weary of holding it back, and I could not" (Jeremiah 20:9, NKJV).

When God calls us, even if we resist, it is difficult to ignore the call. In fact, if we choose to ignore God's call and go in another direction, we will never experience the fulfillment that ministry would have brought us.

The call from God is very specific. We are told, "a call to the gospel ministry is a call not to be a sociologist or public performer, but an ambassador for Christ. A call to anything less is not a call to ministry. This call demands a full-time, life-consuming devotion."[1] The call to full-time ministry is specific, and our response needs to be wholehearted. Although several wanted to follow Jesus but needed to do other things first, as mentioned in Luke 9, His response to them is just as valid today to those called to ministry. Jesus tells those called by Him, "No one who puts a hand to the plow and looks back is fit for service in the kingdom of God" (Luke 9:62, NIV). When God calls us, we need to enthusiastically respond.

The call from God is very specific.

The Bible is filled with examples of God calling individuals to service for Him. God called Moses (Exodus 3), Miriam (Exodus 15:20, 21), Isaiah (Isaiah 6), Huldah (2 Kings 22; 2 Chronicles 34), the apostles (Mark 3:13–19), Anna (Luke 2:36), Paul (Acts 9), and Priscilla (Acts 18:26). God not only calls a variety of individuals, He also calls us in different ways. Individuals may receive the call in response to their prayers or reading the Scriptures. God's call may be sensed through the influence of a godly example. It may come in response to a person showing interest in the spiritual well-being of others, or from a desire to teach and preach the Word of God. It may also be confirmed by the recognition of other spiritual individuals, who see the person as a candidate for ministry.

Why the call to pastoral ministry?

In addition to calling all Christians to follow Christ's example and to walk in His footsteps (1 Peter 2:21), the Bible also confirms God's calling and gifting on some to be pastors (Ephesians 4:11). While the Bible is clear that God calls individuals to pastoral ministry, we have to ask why He would do that. There are several reasons that the apostle Paul gives. First, the manifestation of the Spirit is given to each one for the profit *of all* (1 Corinthians 12:7). Second, Paul says that God gave pastors "for the equipping of the saints for the work of ministry, for the edifying of the body of Christ, till we all come to the unity of the faith and of the knowledge of the Son of God, to a perfect man, to the measure of the stature of the fullness of Christ" (Ephesians 4:12, 13, NKJV).

The call to be a pastor is a "special calling because of its strategic and unique importance for the spiritual well-being of Christ's flock."[2] Yet, God is not only concerned for those who are part of "Christ's flock." David asks God a pointed question about humanity: "What is man that You are mindful of him, and the son of man that You visit him?" (Psalm 8:4, NKJV).

No sooner does David ask the question than God provides the answer through David: "For You have made him a little lower than the angels, and You have crowned him with glory and honor" (verse 5, NKJV).

God calls us to serve "Christ's flock," but the call is much broader—He wants us to serve all—even those who are not yet a part of the flock. God holds men and women in high esteem, for they are only "a little lower than the angels."

Paradox

Yet, the idea of God calling is somewhat of a paradox—"a seemingly contradictory statement that may nonetheless be true."[3] Imagine, a Holy God inviting flawed, sinful human beings to do His sacred work. That is a paradox, yet that is what God has done and is still doing. The Bible has a number of examples of this paradox.

Why did God call Abraham to move to an unnamed city and be the father of a great nation, and promise to bless the world through him? Why did God say Abraham was faithful even though the man was not always truthful? Or choose Abraham even though he accepted his wife's suggestion to have his firstborn child through another woman? Nevertheless, God called Abraham (Genesis 12; Galatians 3:9; Hebrews 11:8–19).

Why did God choose Moses, a killer, to receive and deliver the commandments written in God's own finger? From our perspective, it seems that God could have found more suitable candidates (Exodus 3; 20).

Why did God choose Peter to preach on the Day of Pentecost? Was this not the same Peter who denied his relationship with Jesus and denied that he even knew Jesus? Why did God choose Peter to confront Ananias and Sapphira, an untruthful husband and wife team? Surely God could have chosen someone more qualified than Peter (Acts 2; 5:1–11).

Imagine, a Holy God inviting flawed, sinful human beings to do His sacred work.

Why did God call David "a man after His own heart" (1 Samuel 13:14, NKJV), even though David was an adulterer and murderer? How could God say, through the voice of Paul, that David "will do all My will" (Acts 13:22, NKJV)? Was David worthy of God's confidence in him? Why was Samson one of the judges in Israel? In spite of his personal failures and acts of rebellion, God still used Samson (Judges 16).

These are just a few of the biblical paradoxes—God calls people to do His holy work even though they have exhibited major flaws in their lives. These paradoxes not only exist in the Bible, they are found throughout history. Even now, God seems to call individuals who seem unsuited for the holy calling. You and I may have a sense of unworthiness and wonder if God has really called us. It is tempting to get discouraged, but the apostle Paul writes words of inspiration: "But we have this treasure in earthen vessels, that the excellence of the power may be of God and

These are just a few of the biblical paradoxes—God calls people to do His holy work even though they have exhibited major flaws in their lives.

not of us" (2 Corinthians 4:7, NKJV). In spite of our weaknesses, God is willing to use us. This paradox should drive "the called ones" to a sense of great need and dependence on the Lord. In other words, because we are clay and broken vessels, we need to constantly lean on the Potter who can put us back together again and use us to serve His people. "Therefore we also, since we are surrounded by so great a cloud of witnesses, let us lay aside every weight, and the sin which so easily ensnares us, and let us run with endurance the race that is set before us" (Hebrews 12:1, NKJV).

When we recognize that it is God who initiated the call and gives us the will and desire to act or do His good pleasure (Philippians 2:13), we will see it is not a right to be called, but a privilege. Yet, it is a challenging call—something that we cannot fulfill on our own.

Jesus makes it possible for us to not only accept but also complete God's call. He is not only our Example (Philippians 2:6–8); He is also our Enabler. When we accept Him as our Lord and Savior, we also invite Him to make our call complete.

Yet, to what does God call us? Honor, glory, or greatness? Certainly those are desirable human goals. Jesus beckons us, however, to another kind of life: "Jesus taught that true spiritual leaders are servants—first of God, then of His people. That is a paradoxical and revolutionary concept because normally servants do not lead and leaders do not serve. But servant-leaders operate on a spiritual plane, not a natural plane. Therefore they must forsake the world's model of leadership and embrace Christ's, which places character above function, motives above activities, humility above promotions, faithfulness above success, and others above self."[4]

Distinctive roles

Ministers are called to perform a distinctive role because what they do in their profession should match who they are as individuals. "People in other vocations can at least escape into their religious faith when the pressure is on,"[5] but pastors must face the pressure with their work and faith wrapped together. The minister has to continually live with and remember the call to ministry is a call that impacts not only the level of work, but also the level of living. Ellen White summed this up when she said, "The fitting up for your work is a life business, a daily, laborious, hand-to-hand struggle

Pastors, for example, need to both understand and balance expectations.

with established habits, inclinations, and hereditary tendencies. It requires a constant, earnest, and vigilant effort to watch and control self, to keep Jesus prominent and self out of sight."[6]

Pastors must also be aware that their roles change over time. For example, the role of the Seventh-day Adventist pastor is significantly different today than it was in the formative period of the denomination. Pastors, for example, need to both understand and balance expectations. On the one hand, the conference that employs them usually has specific expectations. At the same time, they work with congregations. The expectations of the conference and the congregation may not always be the same. How does a pastor balance them? At the same time, there is the ever-present question, What does God expect from me?[7] While these expectations may weigh heavily on pastors, they need to take comfort in the fact that God not only has expectations—God also enables (Ephesians 3:20).

> *With input from a variety of groups and individuals, we have identified core qualities or competencies for pastors.*

What is it that God enables us to do? The Ministerial Department of the Adventist Church in North America is focused on clarifying the role of the pastor and the qualities for excellence. With input from a variety of groups and individuals, we have identified core qualities or competencies for pastors. These core groups are the following:

- Character
- Evangelism
- Leadership
- Worship
- Management
- Scholarship
- Relationship

These seven qualities are broadly stroked categories that entail many additional details.[8] Each quality clarifies and supports our role as a spiritual one. By focusing on the spiritual aspect, it does not mean that we diminish the value of these identified competencies—it actually means we put even greater value on them. Because ministry is a spiritual role, it means that these competencies are more than outward performances—these qualities are part of our motivation as we serve in God's ministry. These qualities are basic to the spiritual life of the minister, church member, and congregation. These qualities govern how we relate to our community and the individuals who are not yet part of God's kingdom.

While pastoring is a spiritual role, the fact is that we work in an ever-changing environment. Some of the issues we face today were either totally ignored or did not exist in previous generations. We are challenged to provide spiritual solutions in a world that is less and less familiar with the Word of God. As pastors, we need to obtain the best education possible, continue learning, and, at the same time, realize we need to daily depend on God for spiritual guidance.

God has given us a prophetic understanding of the future, and the final outcome is humbling because we are privileged to bear a message of hope to a dying world.

Imagining the future

We are influenced by the past and face the challenges of the present. As if that is not enough, we are called to imagine the future. Yet, at the same time, our Seventh-day Adventist theology gives us a sense of hope. Our heavenly Father is also the God of the future and He has graciously given us a message of hope for that future. God has given us a prophetic understanding of the future, and the final outcome is humbling because we are privileged to bear a message of hope to a dying world.

Building bridges

Finally, I believe Seventh-day Adventist pastors are called to be consensus builders. We are called upon to build bridges, instead of tearing them down. We live in a divisive time, where the church is increasingly polarized. Some members see themselves as "true believers," and view others as on "the other side." Pastors can either contribute to this division, by taking firm sides in the debates, or be solution-oriented and faithful shepherds of the flock. Pastors can lead by calling for civility and grace, regardless of their point of view.[9] We need to invite church leaders into fuller collaboration, so that pastors and church leaders create an atmosphere of transparency, love, forgiveness, and support for each other. Bridge building is a challenging task, and some of us will need to seriously

We need to invite church leaders into fuller collaboration, so that pastors and church leaders create an atmosphere of transparency, love, forgiveness, and support for each other.

review our skills in this area. We may need to either acquire the needed skills or sharpen the ones we have.

You and I, as Seventh-day Adventist pastors, have a distinctive role—full of challenges and opportunities. We are invited to walk with boldness and courage and face the paradoxes of ministry. Our confidence is not in our training or abilities—as important as they are. Our confidence is in the promise God gives us: "being confident of this very thing, that He who has begun a good work in you will complete it until the day of Jesus Christ" (Philippians 1:6). We trust God because the outcome is in His hands.

1. *Seventh-day Adventists Minister's Manual* (Silver Spring, MD: The Ministerial Association of the General Conference of Seventh-day Adventists, 1992), 17.

2. Derek Prime and Alistar Begg, *On Being a Pastor: Understanding Our Calling and Work* (Chicago, IL: Moody Publishers, 2004), 19.

3. *The American Heritage Dictionary of the English Language* (1970).

4. Dennis McBride, *The Biblical Model of Spiritual Leadership: A Paradoxical Style of Leadership,* http://www.yoyomaster.com/ministry.file/Servantleadership.html.

5. Dennis Wallstrom, *Role Conflict and Burnout in the Ministry,* Ph.D. diss., Fuller Theological Seminary, 1990 (Ann Arbor, MI: UMI, 1991), 3.

6. Ellen G. White, *Testimonies for the Church* (Mountain View, CA: Pacific Press® Publishing Association, 1948), 4:376.

7. Jesus' parable of the talents (Matthew 25:15–28) has to be applied in this context. It is not always just avoiding mistakes, but exploring possibilities and doing more with what we have been given than merely doing what is traditionally seen as appropriate.

8. See the book for core qualities and descriptors.

9. I want to emphasize that I am not arguing that we should not take a stand on moral issues, or on our clarity concerning the gospel. But there are far fewer issues on which we should "stand up and be counted" than many of us would assert. The shepherd brings sheep together instead of separating them. Pastors need to pull their congregations together, rather than allowing them to tear themselves apart.

Rebranding the Faith I Love: Why I Want to Be a Minister

EVAN KNOTT

G rowing up as a pastor's kid (PK) is rarely easy. Inevitably, as hundreds of other PKs have learned before me, friends and teachers often compared me to my father. Usually, the similarities were pointed out when I did something perceived as positive; the differences were made crystal clear when I got into mischief or underperformed.

One of the constant questions asked of me was whether I was going to be a pastor "like my dad." During my early teenage years, I hated this question because I felt like I was being steered down a predetermined path toward a career that was beyond my control. I did not want to be put into a box and labeled—I wanted to be my own person.

In hindsight, I think part of the reason I disliked such comparisons was because I always knew God was calling me to full-time ministry. I felt the strengths that God had gifted me and the life experiences and opportunities He had sent my way were preparing me for a life of service. It is one thing to be teased about growing up to be "just like your dad," but another thing entirely to recognize traits and skills in yourself that seem to suggest Someone has a plan for your life. The combination of both at times felt unbearable.

I tried to persuade myself that I was going to do something else. In high school, I became the editor of the school newspaper and discovered that I had a passion for journalism and communication—I still do. I decided that journalism was my chance to pursue something else with my life, and when it came time to select a major as a freshman at Andrews University, I decided to seek a degree in communication.

The impression that God was calling me into ministry did not diminish or disappear. However, I had an unshakable feeling that I would be making a mistake to ignore His still, small voice. Reviewing my freshmen academic bulletin, I discovered that a communication degree at Andrews required a minor or a second major. I was not yet ready to completely embrace a calling to full-time ministry, but I decided to add a second major in religion, "just in case."

It did not take long for God to make clear to me His will for my life. During my first semester in my freshman year, the theme of happiness kept emerging in my classes. This was across multiple disciplines, in very unrelated environments. This naturally caused me to reflect upon my own life. I gradually realized that I was not genuinely happy because I knew I was running away from what God was calling me to do.

> *It did not take long for God to make clear to me His will for my life.*

During this interval, I had a conversation with my dad that I will never forget. I explained to him my dilemma and uncertainty about deciding what I wanted to do with my life. My dad told me that while it is true that one can make a lot more money working in other professions, there is something special about knowing at the end of every day that you have been doing God's work. This struck a chord with me. True happiness is being in a loving and intimate relationship with God. Truthfully, my relationship with God had been suffering because of my unwillingness to fully surrender to His leading. I realized that despite what I was telling myself, I would never find deep satisfaction in my life, if I resisted God's calling.

By the end of that first semester, I had finally decided to acknowledge what I had known for some time—that God was calling me into ministry. I have always believed that God continually makes His will clear by opening and closing doors to confirm or alter our course in relation to His will. Time and again, God has shown me that He is "with" me. For the past six years, I have been preparing myself for full-time ministry, and while I am undeniably excited, I am also humbled and even fearful about some of the challenges I will face.

Fears

Growing up in Adventist churches and schools meant attending hundreds of hours of youth programming where I was often told by pastors, teachers, and youth leaders that my peers and I were in "danger" of leaving the church. We were reminded that there was an invisible, but very real, spiritual battle raging all around us. Speakers and teachers employed a variety of methods to keep us grounded in our faith, ranging from Bible studies to seminars to outreach activities. Informed about the dismal retention rates for Adventist youth and witnessing the best efforts of these dedicated men and women, it was disheartening to see so many of my peers either formally or functionally sever their ties with their Adventist faith—many while attending Adventist universities.

Roger Dudley, in his now fifteen-year-old study of Adventist adolescents over a ten-year period, estimated that it was reasonable to believe that at least 50 percent of Seventh-day Adventist teenagers in North America are leaving the church by their mid-twenties: he noted the percentage could very well be higher.[1] A study by the Barna Group examining the larger context of American Christianity mostly confirmed Dudley's finding: 61 percent of young adults had been churched at one time but were spiritually disengaged by their twenties.[2]

> *As a young pastor just moving into ministry, I am terrified at the prospect of my entire generation disappearing from Adventist pews.*

As a young pastor just moving into ministry, I am terrified at the prospect of my entire generation disappearing from Adventist pews. If present trends continue, the millennial generation may very well go down as the "lost generation." While some might believe that it is nearly impossible to reach the postmodern-millennial mind without compromising the truths of the Adventist message, acquiescing to the loss of an entire generation raised in households of faith must tear at the heart of God even more than it saddens me.

The Seventh-day Adventist Church in North America is even now witnessing the beginning of its own demise. Adventism is staring at its own impending death, if the bleeding does not stop soon. The "graying of Adventism"—much talked about and lamented—is a legitimate threat to the future of the North American church. In 2008, the median age of the general North American population was thirty-six: the median age among North American Adventists was fifty-one.[3] The disparity between these two numbers will only increase if trends continue their current trajectory.

This is the disturbing scenario that deeply troubles me as someone on the verge of beginning a career in ministry. It is temptingly easy to feel defeated and pessimistic about the future even before living it. What is the point of entering a career that could be obsolete or reduced to a geriatric chaplaincy in twenty years?

I have wrestled with these issues both personally and professionally. As a millennial myself, immersed in the culture and mind-set of my peers, I have also actively participated in ministry initiatives during the past six years aimed at securing university students in the Adventist faith. The shape of the emerging paradox is becoming clear: Adventist teens and young adults have likely never been more willing to discuss spiritual matters than they are now, but have also never cared less about how Scripture might inform and shape their beliefs.

The theology of "What I Think" is alive and well among a generation of young adults in North American Adventism. Think I am wrong? Sit in on a general education ethics class on any Adventist college campus. What has long been true of the general public has now become true of Adventism's own children: you cannot assume the Bible as a starting point for establishing objective truth.

The idea that anyone could know absolute truth or hold any kind of moral certainty is both foreign and appalling to many Adventist young adults. Persons claiming to have a greater or more important truth are viewed with skepticism and hostility. Relativism—in a beguiling Adventist frame—is the philosophical "king of the hill"—an opponent completely at odds with Jesus' claim to be the Way, the Truth, and the Life (John 14:6).

Like many of my peers now also just entering Adventist ministry, I struggle with doubts about whether I can be an effective pastor to those who actively disbelieve the fundamental premises of my own spirituality—that God reveals Himself in an accessible, knowable manner, through both invitations and commandments designed to inform and enrich my life.

There is no shortage of competitors vying for the attention of Adventist teens and young adults. While the centrifugal pull of secular culture and the allure of worldly wisdom has challenged every generation, the Internet revolution has meant that Millennials and those of the as-yet-unnamed generation following them have faced a challenge unique in human history. Millennials were the first generation to grow up with Google—the first generation to have easy and immediate access to music, games, movies, and even pornography via the digital portal of a smartphone they could hold in their hands.

The next generation is even more immersed in this world than are the millennials. Many preschool kids today appear to understand the uses of a tablet or smartphone before they can even speak in sentences. Current children's television instills "good" postmodern values at an early age. Advertisers target them from birth, creating appetites for products and experiences unimagined a generation ago. Television and video games have become frighteningly more realistic in their depictions of violence. By the time today's typical child graduates from high school, he or she will have viewed more than thirteen thousand violent deaths on television.[4] A narrative that focuses on the sacrificial death of one superhero can seem somehow mundane among so much destruction and loss. How are ministers supposed to preach the gospel in a world saturated with multiple painful narratives?

Both formal studies and anecdotal evidence point to the fact that the faith of the majority of Adventist teens and young adults is vaguely Christian at best. The spirituality embodied by young adults who have grown up in the Adventist Church has been aptly described as "Moralistic Therapeutic Deism"—a phenomenon observed among millennials throughout North American Christianity. This worldview restricts God to only those moments when He is needed to resolve a problem. Life's purpose seems more about being perceived as "nice" and being happy with oneself than living in any focused direction or for any greater cause.[5]

More than seventy years ago, one Adventist leader saw both his moment and our own with prescient accuracy.

The challenge Adventism faces in North America requires convincing millions who feel no need of a Savior to organize their lives as though He was, in Paul's phrase, the One in whom "all things hold together" (Colossians 1:17, NIV). How do we convince seventy-five million peers that there is a substantive—and eternal—difference between believing in Buddha and believing in Jesus Christ? When "decency" becomes the highest cultural norm, deep spirituality will seem eccentric, counter-cultural, and unattractive.

In their sociological analysis of Seventh-day Adventists in North America, Malcolm Bull and Keith Lockhart perceptively argue that Adventism's eschatology has provided a reason for replicating state institutions—and actually accelerated the loss of adherents raised in the faith. Through the power of Adventist institutions (particularly in education), converts of lower economical status are actually put on a fast track to experiencing material prosperity. Once converts or their descendants reach a comfortable level of affluence, they leave the church—either formally or functionally—in a chartable phenomenon Bull and Lockhart label the "revolving door."[6]

Bull and Lockhart have correctly identified one of the primary problems facing the young adults of Adventism today. In an era when the organized church can only employ a fraction of those graduating from its tertiary educational institutions, Adventist universities are experiencing great success in preparing Adventists for the public workplace. The increasing national recognition paid to several Adventist universities is powerful testimony to this. The bad news, however, is that this success appears to have arrived at an unacceptably high cost—the loss of tens of thousands of well-educated and faith-fatigued young adults. There is blame enough to go around, and in the present environment, no shortage of pointing fingers. Some blame the young adults themselves—for secularity, inattentiveness, and distractedness. Others point to a loss of mission focus by those elected to lead. But finger pointing does not allow us to grasp the needed tools to actually remedy the situation. If the majority of students graduating from Adventist colleges and universities are becoming successful CEOs, doctors, engineers, multimillionaires, or important public figures but no longer understand themselves as committed disciples of Jesus Christ, we may have done much to enrich the culture, but little to build the kingdom.

More than seventy years ago, one Adventist leader saw both his moment and our own with prescient accuracy. F. D. Nichol, often identified as a fixture of the twentieth-century Adventist establishment, nonetheless understood how the ground was even then moving beneath the Adventist Church. On the centennial of the Great Disappointment of 1844, Nichol wrote:

> We believe that the hour has come when a voice should be raised in warning against the deadly heresy of apathy which leads on to the even more deadly heresy of thinking that we are simply one more denomination in the world. This, we believe, is the most terrifying danger that ever confronted the Advent movement. . . .
>
> First, we forget the past. We have ever been warned against this by the messenger of the Lord. Yet today there are multitudes in our ranks who for one reason or another seem to have only the most vague ideas concerning the historical, as well as the prophetic facts that constitute the background and the beginnings of this movement. No people can long maintain a proper sense of direction if they are not absolutely clear with regard to their point of departure, that point at which they turned on their distinctive path from that of other people. We have halfway cut from under ourselves the foundation on which rests the reason of our existence as a distinct movement when we forget the history of our beginnings, the causes which brought us forth."[7]

As Nichol so cogently asserted, Adventism began as a *movement* and not a denomination. As a millennial myself, I can testify that *movements* appeal to contemporary young adults. Even a casual examination of recent history reveals that young adults have been at the forefront of mainstream popular

> *The loyalty that drove six generations of Adventists to give their time and treasure for the building of institutions is evaporating more rapidly than the froth atop a Starbucks cappuccino.*

movements on issues ranging from gay rights to police brutality protests to Occupy Wall Street. Movements have enormous appeal to idealistic young adults, and if Adventism is to persist and thrive among younger demographics, it must rediscover its true identity as a God-ordained *movement*—an organism capable of traveling, flexing, reimagining, and repurposing. The loyalty that drove six generations of Adventists to give their time and treasure for the building of institutions is evaporating more rapidly than the froth atop a Starbucks cappuccino.

The difficult truth is that pastors are becoming increasingly irrelevant to a generation uncontent to sit in rectangular spaces and listen to solitary voices for forty-five minutes at a stretch. As long as we see ourselves and are perceived by young adults as being a denomination or an "organized religion," pastors will find themselves struggling to win the respect of both the wider public and the specific audience they are committed to serve.

Hope

Despite these fears about entering into ministry, I am also immensely hopeful. When God calls you to ministry and puts a burden on your heart to reach the lost, you cannot help but be drawn to it. One major reason for my hope is that I see an opportunity to reach millennials because of their fascination with searching for lasting happiness. Where previous generations defined success in terms of financial stability and independence, millennials are significantly more interested in priorities relating to holistic well-being and community.[8] These are areas in which Adventism as a movement has been historically strong. Embracing Adventism's roots in emphasizing the health of the whole person—spiritual, emotional, and physical—should be extremely appealing to the millennial generation.

Those engaged in personal or public evangelism in the North American context have long acknowledged that success and prosperity often cause individuals to become less interested in God because they do not feel as great a need as those at economic rock bottom. What is great—and hope-inspiring—about reaching millennials with Adventist values is that even though they are as materialistic (if not more) than any previous generation, their prioritization on happiness, regardless of social or economic status, should make them receptive to Adventism, presented in the right manner.

More than anything else, this is what excites me about Adventist ministry—being part of an intentional "rebranding" of Adventism. Every time I stand behind a pulpit, present a Bible study, share a meal with someone, or even talk to a stranger in a grocery store aisle, I am presenting (some would say "selling") Adventism as a brand. Such rebranding is obviously much more complex than introducing the uninitiated to the Seventh-day Adventist Church's logo. The Adventist Church is not merely a weekly social gathering, comparable to going to the movie theater with friends or enjoy-

The rebranding of Adventism is not a task or process that can ever be finished.

ing a free concert in the park. Adventism, at its inspired best, is not reducible to either a building or even a set of theological beliefs. Adventism is nothing less than a Christ-called and Spirit-directed way of life that is on display every second of every day in our moment-by-moment interactions.

What excites me about ministry is the opportunity I have to influence how others, especially my millennial peers, understand what it means to be an Adventist and a follower of Christ. I am eager to present Adventism as a better way of life to people who are searching for holistic happiness and who may well think that religion is the last place they should look to find it. I want to show dozens of my friends and millions of my millennial peers that Adventism is a movement that embraces relationships and builds strong and meaningful communities. I want to do everything I can to build the kingdom of God by being His hands and feet in this world, pointing those who may not even know their "lostness" to the Savior who is always searching for them.

The rebranding of Adventism is not a task or process that can ever be finished. There will be no leadership fly-ins to aircraft carriers where banners proclaim "Mission Accomplished." Adventism as a brand must never be allowed to grow dated or stagnant: like the generations it seeks to serve, it must always keep moving. Adventism moves by neither avoiding or succumbing to culture, but by engaging individuals and groups at their perceived point of need and offering them a better way. It keeps moving by motivating confirmed Adventists to stronger and deeper interactions with everyday people in everyday life.

I am comforted by the knowledge that this God-ordained movement is bigger than me and even my enthusiasm. With all my best wishes and best efforts, I cannot solve the serious and seemingly intractable challenges that confront the Adventist Church today. But I can make a difference in the spheres of influence that God grants me by presenting a brand of Adventism that is contagious, portable, loving, and always on the move.

And yet I move forward with hope.

God rarely calls men and women to single-handedly clear all obstacles or knock down every wall that stands in the way of His movement. Instead, God calls individuals to make dents in their own contexts. Sometimes it feels discouraging to realize that the dent is miniscule in comparison to the walls that loom ahead of us. And yet I move forward with hope. Green and new to ministry as I am, I have already learned that there are no more satisfying moments in life than discovering that God has simultaneously been recruiting other "wall-busters." We are collectively part of a greater plan to "destroy strongholds. We destroy arguments and every proud obstacle raised up against the knowledge of God, and we take every thought captive to obey Christ" (2 Corinthians 10:4, 5, NRSV).

1. Roger Dudley, *Why Our Teenagers Leave the Church: Personal Stories From a 10-Year Study* (Hagerstown, MD: Review and Herald® Publishing Association, 2000).

2. George Barna, "Most Twentysomethings Put Christianity on the Shelf Following Spiritually Active Teen Years," in *The Barna Report,* September 11, 2006.

3. David Beckworth and S. Joseph Kidder, "Reflections on the Future of the Seventh-day Adventist Church in North America: Trends and Challenges (Part 1 of 2)," in *Ministry,* December 2010.

4. Larry Gross, "Television & Violence," in *Television Awareness Training: The Viewer's Guide for Family & Community* (New York: Media Action Research Center, 1979).

5. Kenda Creasy Dean, *Almost Christian: What the Faith of Our Teenagers Is Telling the American Church* (Oxford: Oxford University Press, 2010).

6. Malcolm Bull and Keith Lockhart, *Seeking a Sanctuary: Seventh-day Adventism and the American Dream* (Bloomington, IN: Indiana University Press, 1989), 360–362.

7. F. D. Nichol, "A Deadly Heresy That Threatens the Church," *The Advent Review and Sabbath Herald,* January 20, 1944.

8. Lisa Curtis, "Happiness is the New Success: Why Millennials are Reprioritizing," Forbes, January 23, 2012, http://www.forbes.com/sites/85broads/2012/01/23/happiness-is-the-new-success-why-millennials-are -reprioritizing/.

The Minister as a Professional and the Ethos of Ministry

ABRAHAM J. JULES

For centuries the debate has raged concerning whether ministry is a vocation or an occupation. Eugene Peterson dealt with this question in his book *For the Beauty of the Church: Casting a Vision for the Arts,*[1] and concluded that there is sufficient ambiguity within our culture for concern. In other words, the way in which others perceive us, whether in the community or church, and our self-perception are critical factors in defining the terms in question. I begin here because what seems clear is that the options of "either/or" in the twenty-first century are superficial in that they fail to take into account the complexities of society and the church. Whether we consider ministry a vocation or an occupation (or both), *how* we view *what* we do, for *whom* we do it, and *why* we do it has significant implications for the ethos in which we do it.

Ethos describes the character that we engage—ministry in this case—and speaks to our core guiding beliefs and principles. So, while we may not resolve the debate in this chapter, I hope to inspire sufficient introspection as to evoke reflection on how we have done ministry and how we can improve.

In this chapter, I will focus on three areas—our relationships, responsibilities, and personal conduct. It is through the experiences that grow out of this triumvirate that we shape and reshape ourselves in order to fulfill our conceptions of the ideal person. Poet Jose Marti declared, "Every human being has within him an ideal man, just as every piece of marble contains in a rough state a statue as beautiful as the one that Praxiteles the Greek made of the god Apollo."[2] This insight, I believe, is particularly applicable to ministry.

Our conceptions of ministry are often shaped by those whom we have emulated: those whose substance, style, energy, compassion, and other virtues struck a chord with us.

Whether it was how they preached or how they conducted a baptism, evangelistic meetings, baby dedication, or business meeting, or just their personal demeanor, something resonated with us that we deemed worthy of emulation. Something gave impetus to our determination to cultivate the skills, manner, and means with which to achieve the "ideal" person, and specifically—for our purposes—the ideal minister. With this in mind, let us begin with relationships.

Relationships

Four relationships define our vocational or occupational ethos: our relationships to our families, the local church, the local community, and the church organization. The family circle is the place where we are most likely to be our unvarnished selves. It is the one place where we can retreat from our ministerial responsibilities and be free from the scrutiny and expectations that come with our occupational responsibilities. This retreat is important because there are times when our labors can be especially taxing, and, without a safe place—a place where our relationships function on the principle of unconditional love—we run the risk of becoming casualties of stress.

A healthy family circle keeps us grounded and contributes balance to our perspective. Family mealtimes, recreation, projects, and worship cannot be underestimated for their value in providing opportunities of respite from the never-ending work of ministry. But more than that, the family circle provides the primary context for the cultivation of our ethos. I believe that this is what the apostle Paul had in mind in his exhortation to Timothy when he wrote, "But if anyone does not provide for his own, and especially for those of his household, he has denied the faith and is worse than an unbeliever" (1 Timothy 5:8).[3] Our primary relationships are in our own homes where we are charged with the responsibility of providing. Then there is the local church.

> *The family circle is the place where we are most likely to be our unvarnished selves.*

The local church is the arena in which people, mostly church members, are exposed to the limits and extremes of what we do vocationally. For this reason, it is imperative that we discipline ourselves in developing competencies in the basic functions of ministry. The competencies, while appearing task-oriented, are essentially relational; they convey our care, or lack thereof, for the individual member and the congregation in general. How we go about executing them speaks to the scope or limitations of our expertise. It is entirely possible that the way we learned or emulated a competency—a baby dedication, for example—may be, by comparison to other approaches, inadequate. In other words, there could be a better or more effective way to conduct it, and the difference between what we have done and what we might otherwise do may simply be exposure. It is not that we should be driven by a quest to be novel, but, rather, we should seek to develop a mind-set of excellence by exposing ourselves to different options that enable us to minister more effectively. In fact, by exposing ourselves to a variety of options, we learn not only what to do but also what not to do.

I remember visiting a church where twins were being dedicated. The well-meaning pastor presented a beautiful homily before he invited the father and mother to kneel in a prayer of dedication. The prayer went on and on and on, and it became evident to me—through slightly opened eyes—that the poor mother was struggling with her back and knees. Unable to bear the agony any more, I went over and helped the couple up, as the pastor, with his eyes tightly closed and his gaze transfixed toward the heavens continued to implore the Lord for the health of the parents. I vowed that I would never ask a couple to kneel for a baby dedication.

It is quite possible for us to fulfill traditions or follow procedures at the expense of people, simply because we sacrifice the substance for the form. This was especially true as I reflect back on growing up in church as a youth. At that time many of us dreaded the Communion service because we could not appreciate the substance of it. Its substance was obscured by the long drawn out form, which seemed almost interminable and came complete with deacon and deaconess miscues. When a new pastor came, he streamlined the service by serving the emblems together, thus allowing for a greater focus on the substance of the Communion rather than the form due to the reduction in the service's length. As a result of this one change, the new pastor was endeared to the youth and the Communion service was no longer dreaded. There was a change in relationship because the pastor, I assume, was sensitive to our needs and did not confuse the form of the Communion service with its substance. A healthy change usually results when the pastor understands that relationship is what ultimately lies at the root of our pastoral competencies. This, among other things, distinguished Jesus' ministry from that of the scribes and the Pharisees; and though we might not characterize Jesus' ministry as professional, the major difference in His ministry was His genuine care for people beyond the accepted forms and traditions. His ethos, the character of His engagement, reflected a genuine love and compassion for people. Jesus' orientation to the people is characterized in Matthew's Gospel when he writes,

"Seeing the people, He felt compassion for them, because they were distressed and dispirited like sheep without a shepherd" (Matthew 9:36). Though our members may, at times, be distressed and dispirited, they will sense our love and compassion for them by the way we minister.

Along with our family circle and church members, we also relate to our communities. Whether we are actively and intentionally or passively engaged, we are creating an impression that community members associate with our place of worship and members,

Though our members may, at times, be distressed and dispirited, they will sense our love and compassion for them by the way we minister.

particularly those who live in close proximity to the church. For this reason, it is imperative that we consciously endeavor to reach out and communicate with people in the community, in an altruistic way, about their needs and concerns. They are fully aware as to whether our motives are simply to proselytize or to contribute meaningfully to the community. Getting to know the community and city officials and in an *apolitical* way providing support through giving encouragement, voicing your concerns, or simply acknowledging their work, as is appropriate, can be helpful in fostering meaningful relationships.

Ultimately, we learn from these relationships that genuine love and compassion for people form the basis of how we are to go about doing what we do—how we minister. Once we are thoroughly convinced of God's love for us, we will be able to love others, as we should.

Responsibilities

Our responsibilities are defined, in great measure, by the expectations of our employer. But, fulfilling the expectations of our employer does not necessarily mean that we are meeting all of our responsibilities. If we believe that God still speaks to those whom He has called and that God still provides a vision for ministry, then our obligations are more broadly defined. Aside from our regular weekly, monthly, and annual tasks, we must be open to the promptings of the Holy Spirit, who impresses us—through a variety of means—to respond "in season and out of season." Clarity concerning who we serve ultimately allows us to be open and helps us to fully engage in our responsibilities. The apostle Paul reminded the Colossian believers, "Whatever you do, do your work heartily, as for the Lord rather than for men, knowing that from the Lord you will receive the reward of the inheritance. It is the Lord Christ whom you serve" (Colossians 3:23, 24). God expects us to be responsive to Him, but not without promise. Notice how Paul exhorts and provides encouragement to us: "Therefore, my beloved brethren, be steadfast, immovable, always abounding in the work of the Lord, knowing that your toil is not in vain in the Lord" (1 Corinthians 15:58). Paul understood the challenges of ministry and that our vision for ministry is most successful when the results are guaranteed. In other words, our personal ethos, how we do what we do, can evolve as we embrace the truth that success is built into, or is a by-product of, our labors.

Given the long list of our pastoral responsibilities, it is encouraging to know that even in the areas where we may not be especially gifted, our labors are not in vain. I have many colleagues for whom hospital visitation comes easily, but I have never considered it my strength. In fact, it has only been in the last decade of nearly thirty years of ministry that hospital visitation has transcended a duty. While I have never failed to go when called on to do so, it was never with a sense of eager anticipation, as the hospital environment brought up unpleasant memories and reminders of ailing loved ones. I had to literally pray my way into the facilities, but once there I was reconnected to my burden for ministry. Books and seminars helped me confront my concerns and focus on the one hospitalized. They also helped me cultivate a supportive bedside manner, a skill that helped me build confidence in my abilities and resulted in compassionate interactions with the ailing.

It is natural for us to gravitate to our specific areas of gifting.

A healthy personal ethos leads us to challenge and confront our deficits so that we can confidently minister more effectively. It is natural for us to gravitate to our specific areas of gifting, but given the diverse skill sets required for ministry, in the absence of a ministry team or staff, time must be allocated to working. This is especially true with respect to conducting special services: weddings, dedications, funerals, baptisms, and groundbreakings. The way in which we officiate conveys the quality of our care and has significant implications for our relationship with our church members and the community. Because we may not conduct such services regularly, it is advisable that we review them from time to time. A brief quarterly review in which you visualize the service as it unfolds can be done in less than an hour and can help prevent anxiety, especially if we collect and file resources that will assist us.

Some time ago, I was asked to conduct the dedication of a home for a church member. I promised to conduct the dedication but was called away the week before the event and did not have time to prepare. My plan was that on my return, I would go straight to the new home from the airport and conduct the dedication. On the flight back, I went into my iPad, pulled up the folder labeled "Dedications," read through several, and selected what seemed most appropriate. The only anxiety that I had was my concern for a flight delay, but it was short-lived as the plane left the gate and arrived at my destination on time.

> *In a system of ministry where one is, in great measure, self-directed, it is imperative that we are clear about the nature of our responsibilities and their connection to our personal ethos.*

My responsibility for the home dedication had strictly to do with ministry; it was vocational, but I would like to think that my advance preparation reflected professionalism. And the amalgamation of the two resulted in fulfilling the dedication in a way that built all of the relationships represented in that home. Almost without exception, our ministerial responsibilities ultimately build or devalue relationships, and the more thought and preparation we invest, the more apt we are to build. The years have also taught me that time often provides an opportunity for us to grow into an appreciation of those "less appealing" aspects of ministry, especially as we understand how they affect relationships and contribute to the whole.

In a system of ministry where one is, in great measure, self-directed, it is imperative that we are clear about the nature of our responsibilities and their connection to our personal ethos. This is especially true when it comes to the third and final area: personal conduct.

Personal conduct

Many areas—behavior, health, appearance, interpersonal relationships, time management, and finances—are part of personal conduct, which, in turn is part of our personal spiritual nurture and development. Our relatively high visibility makes us akin to public figures and means that our public and private lives matter. What we do in both spheres has the potential to impact and influence others because we represent God, our families, our communities, and the church. At the core of this is how we do what we do—our personal ethos.

Rather than pontificate where the lines are drawn with respect to all of the elements of personal conduct, I must assume that if you have gotten this far in ministry, you have some measure of understanding about the godly living to which we have been called. The apostle Peter, extolling the benefits of God's precious promises, reminds the believers that by partaking of the divine nature, they have escaped "the corruption that is in the world through lust." He then adds these carefully selected words of exhortation: "Now for this very reason also, applying all diligence, in your faith supply moral excellence, and in your moral excellence, knowledge, and in your knowledge, self-control, and in your self-control, perseverance, and in your perseverance, godliness, and in your godliness, brotherly kindness, and in your brotherly kindness, love. For if these qualities are yours and are increasing, they render you neither useless nor unfruitful in the true knowledge of our Lord Jesus Christ" (2 Peter 1:5–8). This is written to individuals who have undergone a personal transformation as a result of having received Jesus as Lord and Savior. Peter assumes that the readers or hearers of his letter are partakers of the divine nature as a result of their encounter with Jesus. It is safe to say that the motivation at the heart of one's personal conduct is not the threat or fear of losing one's employment, nor even the anxiety that might result from disappointing those who hold us in high regard or depend on us; rather, it is the knowledge of and respect for a privileged relationship that we have with the Father through the Son. Os Guinness isolates this truth when he writes of the nineteenth-century Christian soldier General Charles Gordon: "[The] peerless military strategist, legendary commander, and mostly all-conquering victor, lived so closely before the Audience of One. . . . Like all for whom God's call is decisive, it could be said of him, 'I live before the Audience of One. Before others I have nothing to prove, nothing to gain, nothing to lose.' "[4]

Additionally, in living before the Audience of One, we are compelled to relate to our employer with ethical integrity.

Guinness articulates the driving force of motivation for our personal conduct: our awareness of living before the Audience of One. When our personal conduct is exercised from this vantage point, we are able to live and serve with freedom and confidence. We are likely to have a healthy respect for the integrity of our word, keeping our appointments, being timely, dressing and being appropriately groomed, being above reproach in our personal business dealings, treating people with respect, being good stewards of our resources and those resources over which we have charge, and maintaining and advancing our competencies and skill sets in ministry. Additionally, in living before the Audience of One, we are compelled to relate to our employer with ethical integrity.

The Seventh-day Adventist Church has an organizational vision and a mission that are clearly articulated throughout each level of its structure from the local church to the world headquarters. As members and employees of the church, we have ethical obligations to the organization. Our financial remuneration is the result of the faith that individuals invest in the Lord and the organization. They return their tithes because they believe in the mission of the church and honor God by providing the financial resources for the spreading of the gospel. Hence, there is a series of relationships that are inextricably linked by faith. The member returns tithe in faith, the organization provides remuneration in faith, and the employee fulfills the vision and the mission of the organization in faith . . . and works. The apostle James reminds us that "faith, if it has no works, is dead" (James 2:17).

As members and employees of the church, we have ethical obligations to the organization.

I highlight these relational connections because it is easy to miss how central ethos is to all that we do. We rise or fall on our personal ethos. It defines our identity and conveys—with great transparency—where our hearts are and, by extension, where our treasures are. It is both visible and invisible in the sense that our families, our members, the community, and the church organization form perceptions of us not only by what we do but also by what we do not do. Genuine care and concern, whether for our tasks or those affected by them, is seldom successfully fabricated. For the most part, people get a sense of "how we are." They generally know whether we care, and often the degree to which we care because our care is conveyed by our ethos. So while for some, ministry is simply a vocation that should be undertaken organically, without particular attention to dress, deportment, or demeanor, and for others there ought to be specific standards that convey an "objective" professionalism, when the binary poles converge in specific cultural contexts and are exercised as an outgrowth of a healthy ethos, ministry is then defined by Christ's redemptive example and engaged relationally.

Some years ago, I was traveling across the country to preach at a large convention in Phoenix, Arizona. I arrived at the airport dressed casually with a carry-on in tow. As I waited at the gate for my connecting flight, a boy, maybe about ten or eleven years of age, sitting across from me with his mother, called out to me, "You're a preacher!" I said, "Yes! How do you know?" The boy replied, "I just know!" His mother interjected, "How do you know?" To which he responded, "I just know." I was not reading my Bible. I was not in a posture of prayer. I was not humming a hymn. I was seated quietly awaiting the announcement to board my flight. Ten to twelve years later, I am still humbled by that experience because it gave me a new appreciation for the ethos, to which, for some reason, God opened the eyes of this young man. There are people who are sensitive to our ethos whether we are aware of it or not, not simply because of what we do but because of whose we are; and so it will never hurt us to be intentional about cultivating our ethos to the honor and glory of God.

1. Eugene Peterson, *For the Beauty of the Church: Casting a Vision for the Arts* (Grand Rapids, MI: Baker Books, 2010).

2. José Martí, *Reader: Writings on the Americas* (North Melbourne, Australia: Ocean Press, 2006).

3. Unless otherwise noted, all Scripture is from the New American Standard Bible.

4. Os Guinness, *The Call: Finding and Fulfilling the Central Purpose of Your Life* (Nashville, TN: Zondervan Bible Publishers, 2003).

The Development of the Role of the Seventh-day Adventist Minister

MICHAEL W. CAMPBELL

Seventh-day Adventists affirm the Protestant Reformation principle of the priesthood of all believers.[1] At the same time, this does not and should not negate the need for full-time ministers, something affirmed by Martin Luther, John Calvin, and other Reformers. These ministers devoted their lives to proclaiming the gospel message and played a vital role in the formation of the Seventh-day Adventist Church. In order to better appreciate such contributions, it is necessary to identify and understand what an Adventist minister is and to trace the development of ministerial identity.

Seventh-day Adventist clergy typically prefer to describe themselves as a "minister" or "pastor." Early on, other terms like "reverend" were eliminated as being too pretentious. Within early Adventism, the most common designation among church members, both laity and clergy alike, was "brother" and "sister." This reflected the Restorationist[2] heritage of Adventism in what they understood to be a return to the primitive purity of the New Testament church. Later, Adventist ministers after ordination adopted the term "elder" to designate an ordination.

In North America, an Adventist pastor typically has two to three churches. A few belong to a church with multiple pastoral staff, but these have always remained a minority. Regardless of the size of the church or the pastoral district, Adventist pastors have had a sacred role in the life of the local church. At the very heart of such ministry is the need to balance both church ministry and evangelism. Both are vital to the success of the Adventist pastor and are essential aspects of Adventist ministerial identity. In order to appreciate the role of Adventist ministers, we will trace the historical development of the minister's role and function.

Early beginnings, 1844–1863

The Seventh-day Adventist Church formed in the wake of the Great Disappointment when Christ did not return, as anticipated, on October 22, 1844. Just like the Millerite movement, early Adventists came from a wide variety of denominations. Studies of early Adventist converts indicate that the largest percentage came in almost equal proportions from the Baptist or Methodist traditions, with a significant minority coming from the Christian Connexion, a loose confederation of Restorationist congregations. Thus, it is not surprising that as Sabbatarian Adventism coalesced during the late 1840s and through the 1850s, Adventist clergy mirrored these demographics.

It is also significant that, as the theological pillars of the Seventh-day Adventist Church were being formulated during a series of Bible Conferences, a few Sabbatarian Adventist ministers, most notably James White and Joseph Bates, played a prominent role in orchestrating these meetings. While a significant number of lay people also participated, what is also clear is that there was a joint sense of conviction that all must work together in studying and sharing "present truth." There does not appear to have been tension between clergy and laity because they were firmly united through their theological convictions. Not everyone was able to leave behind their family and employment, but those who did after hearing God's calling were viewed with a sense of respect. During this time, there was no formal church organization, which basically meant that the earliest pastors who joined the emerging group had no regular source of income.

Ministerial work from 1844 to 1863 necessitated commitment coupled with a willingness to sacrifice. James White, for his part, worked in hard labor (hauling rock, cutting wood, or mowing hay) during the daytime in order to save enough money to attend these early Bible Conferences. Joseph Bates, who had been better off, quickly spent his entire savings account (meant for retirement) sharing the message. He was known for walking to speaking appointments in order to reduce costs. Both men were moved when early believers gave them funds to defray their expenses as they shared the Adventist message. In other cases, Adventist ministers, out of necessity, took periodic breaks from ministry in order to attend to family farms or other business. Some examples include J. N. Andrews and J. N. Loughborough, both with young families, who became discouraged from the lack of ministerial funds. This lack of systematic funds to sustain Adventist pastors was one of the factors in the push for church organization in 1863.

Distinctive identity, 1863–1881

The Seventh-day Adventist Church formally organized in 1863. A key focus during those meetings was the need to provide consistent funding for ministers. A related matter was the need to certify or credential ministers so that church members would know who was legitimate. The challenge came from a few charlatans who masqueraded as genuine Seventh-day Adventist clergy. They solicited donations from unsuspecting church members, but in reality, they were scam artists. Church members were afterward more reluctant to support the needs of genuine ministers. Another challenge came from ministers who defected. For example, Moses Hull, who became a spiritualist, as well as B. F. Snook and W. H. Brinkerhoff, formed the offshoot "Marion party." And still yet others, such as J. B. Frisbie, did not defect at all but simply became discouraged and gave up the ministry for a time. Such losses diminished the ranks of ministers.

Church organization therefore played a crucial role in the formation of early Seventh-day Adventist ministerial identity. Part of the purpose of the local conference was to provide a mechanism for aspiring ministers to receive a "ministerial license." Typically, an aspiring minister was expected to raise up a congregation. They functioned chiefly in an itinerant role returning to visit that congregation on a periodic basis. By 1869, there were enough ministers that a two-tier system was noticeable. Initially, a minister received a "ministerial license," but an experienced minister received "ministerial credentials" in conjunction with the ordination service.

Church organization therefore played a crucial role in the formation of early Seventh-day Adventist ministerial identity.

As the church grew, so did its need for ministers. During the 1860s, frequent letters in the *Review and Herald* appealed for ministers to visit isolated church members. It was not uncommon for church members to go many months, or even years, without a visit. When a minister did show up, often in conjunction with a "monthly" or "quarterly" meeting (as regional gatherings of believers), these meetings reflected earlier Pietistic gatherings within Evangelicalism stemming from the eighteenth century. A typical gathering focused on alternating seasons of prayer, singing hymns, Bible study, and testimonies. These "testimonies" were to be short (two to three minutes) and a "good" testimony meeting was one in which everyone gave their testimony multiple times. Such meetings were truly spiritual "high points" that mirrored the "holy fairs" of Scotland. Typically, a minister was featured who was allowed to preach as much as possible, and the services concluded with the administering of church ordinances—baptism and the celebration of the Lord's Supper. The Lord's Supper became a special "Advent ordinance" expressing faith in the effica-cious blood of Jesus Christ along with the command to continue to observe this sacred rite until the second coming of Jesus. Early Adventists appropriated this church ordinance as a way of af-firming their conviction about the soon return of Jesus Christ. It is also due to this connection with quarterly meet-ings that Adventist ministers continue to lead out in Communion.

The primary work of the Adventist minister was twofold: the first and primary objective was to pursue evangelistic objectives and, closely related, to make sure that each local church functioned properly.

Another aspect of the daily life of ministers was officiating for funerals and weddings. A random selection of obituaries from the 1870s indicates that approximately 80 percent of church members died from tuberculosis. Even the adoption of the health message did little to slow the ravages of this disease. In fact, in some locations Adventist ministers were so difficult to come by that church members were advised to seek ministers from other denominations.[3] Weddings were much easier to plan in advance but did not generally necessi-tate an Adventist minister. Many early Adventists, including James and Ellen White, went to a justice of the peace. During the 1870s, a number of weddings were held in the homes of early Adventist believers. Thus, early on funerals and weddings became a significant part of ministerial responsibilities.

The primary work of the Adventist minister was twofold: the first and primary objective was to pursue evangelistic objectives and, closely related, to make sure that each local church functioned properly. The first was ac-complished by making sure that the local church was organized. During the 1860s, two officers were elected at the local church level: an elder to lead in worship and the spiritual welfare of the congregation, and the deacon, who was responsible for the physical welfare. Early on a third church office, the church clerk, was elected to keep track of finances and official church records, especially the official list of membership for the congregation and to take minutes at church business meetings. Unless the church was partic-ularly large, only one person for each church office was necessary. From an early period, the elder and deacon were both set apart through ordination, which sometimes included women.[4]

The earliest job description for an Adventist minister dates to 1873. The minister is admonished to examine church records, check the list of members, ascertain their spiritual condition, take action about those who are backslidden, send letters to those who are absent, learn who should join the church, and inquire after those keeping the Sabbath but not at church. They were expected to celebrate church ordinances, examine the financial books to make sure they were accurate, encourage people to contribute for the support of the church, sign up local members for church publications, encourage members to support other institutional endeavors (during this formative period this often meant contributing funds for collective projects such as the "Dime Tabernacle" built in 1879), look after family prayers, supply publications, and provide relief for the poor.[5]

Ministers were also admonished to make sure they conducted a nominating committee when they visited the local church. When there was a "church trial," the minister was a neutral individual who could settle squabbles between members. According to the earliest guidelines, the minister selected the nominating committee by appointing "two brethren of good judgment who with him shall act as a nominating committee to nominate candidates . . . and their nomination is to be ratified by a threefourths [sic] vote provided that no valid objection is raised by those not voting in the affirmative."[6] Church members were encouraged to nominate and vote by secret ballot.

While this was an option, it appears that most early Seventh-day Adventists recognized the ordination given by another denomination as still valid.

The rapid expansion of ministers during the 1870s brought with it new challenges. One such problem was the title to give ministers. As already indicated, the title of reverend was quickly repudiated. James and Ellen White both referred to clergy as "ministers" and less frequently as "pastors." Ultimately, both were more concerned that such clergy be "workers" or "laborers." James White frequently referred to the role of *minister* when he described himself as the "pastor" of the Battle Creek church—even if he was often absent due to his leadership roles.

Another interesting practice that developed during this period was ordination. The earliest ministers were previously ordained ministers. James

White argued in 1867 that just like baptism, "when this is done and by the proper persons, once is sufficient, if the candidate does not apostatize." In my survey of this period, only two early Seventh-day Adventist ministers were re-ordained. While this was an option, it appears that most early Seventh-day Adventists recognized the ordination given by another denomination as still valid. It typically took between four and five years (in a time before systematized theological education) for an aspiring minister to gain enough experience. The earliest ordinations that I found occurred in 1872, the same year in which Ellen White is first listed with other ministers as having ministerial credentials. In the 117 ordinations from 1872 to 1881, a fairly uniform practice developed. All records describe the service as a solemn and sacred event. It entailed an "ordination sermon" with admonition to be faithful, followed by prayer, and the laying on of hands (including all ordained ministers present), and concluded with a charge that uniformly mentions "the right hand of fellowship" in recognition of their special role.

Thus, from 1863 through 1881, ministerial identity was connected to both evangelism and the local church. The primary task of the minister was outreach: ministers should preach the gospel and hold evangelistic meetings. This was especially true of young aspiring ministers. At the same time, the role of the minister was closely connected to ecclesiology and the life of the local church. As ministers traveled, they were responsible for making sure that order was maintained.

A professional ministry

During the late 1870s, a series of educational endeavors led the way for ministerial training. In 1872, Goodloe Harper Bell started a school that formed in 1874 into Battle Creek College. The editor of the *Review and Herald,* Uriah Smith, developed a series of Bible lectures to supplement the curriculum. This developed into short Biblical Institutes where area ministers and their spouses could come for brief intensives. These were so popular that James White encouraged Smith to travel to California and New England to train pastors. In fact, Smith's book *Biblical Institutes* was the first theological textbook for this early generation of Seventh-day Adventist ministers and served as a reference about Adventist beliefs. Although these biblical institutes started in the late 1870s, they really took off as a significant phenomenon during the 1880s and 1890s. During the 1890s, as Adventist education underwent a revolution after the famous Harbor Springs, Michigan, Conference,[7] the Adventist component, especially Bible classes, became an integral part of the curriculum.

By the early twentieth century, then General Conference president A. G. Daniells sensed the need to increase the proficiency and effectiveness of Adventist clergy. "I think brethren," he noted to history and Bible teachers at the 1919 Bible Conference, "that among all the vocations in the world, that of the minister is the highest and most sacred, and calls for the greatest care on the part of those who enter it."[8] Daniells cast a vision about the importance of training Adventist pastors. Part of the reason for this, he observed, was that he was perturbed about the poor quality of some of the ministerial graduates coming from Adventist institutions. As things stood then, ministers were poorly prepared for the grueling task of ministry.

The blame for the lack of preparation of Adventist pastors, according to Daniells, was due to several reasons. Adventist educators needed to model core values to students, especially honesty, sincerity, integrity, and good judgment. This was both a responsibility as well as an opportunity as the teacher can mentor students to go beyond sheer theoretical knowledge to impress upon the ministerial student the vital importance of a godly life. Students should learn to be studious and work hard. It went without saying, according to Daniells, that teachers should recommend quality books. In order to balance all of this, ministerial students should learn "regularity in their habits of study, working, and living" (or as he later put it, "value of time") that was "essential." The Bible should be "supreme" in ministerial education. It is a book that "contains greater power" and students must have through their understanding of Scripture a "revolutionizing and regenerating influence" upon minds and hearts. The denomination in 1919, according to Daniells, was not doing "all that they can do along this line." Students must move beyond the theoretical into a deeper and more practical understanding of God's Word so that their sermons focus on God's Word.

Daniells was supported by W. W. Prescott during the conference. He supported Daniells's focus on expository sermons but also indicated that ministers needed a more Christ-centered approach for Adventist theology. This was the real power behind Adventist preaching and an opportunity for Adventist preachers to share God's Word.

After the 1919 Bible Conference, plans were laid for a graduate school, but because of "certain contingencies" the plans were only realized fifteen years later in the form of the Advanced Bible School. By 1932, the General Conference Committee began to consider plans for graduate level ministerial training. Such training was clearly needed lest Adventist ministers feel compelled to study outside in other seminaries or universities. Such a school, they envisioned, would be led by six to ten Bible teachers "of outstanding promise and ability" who could guide students during a one-year graduate program. The curriculum included courses on the Bible, Ellen White's life and writings, doctrines, and evangelism. Minors could be offered in church history, secular history, Greek and Hebrew, and "spoken and written" English. In 1933, the General Conference set up a committee to consider locations, and the first summer session started on June 6, 1934, on the campus of Pacific Union College in Angwin, California.

> *The crucial point is that Adventist pastors are needed to make sure new church members become committed Christian believers in their local churches.*

The sending organization was responsible for transportation. The matriculation fee was five dollars, and tuition was three dollars per semester hour of credit. M. E. Kern was appointed the first dean, and when the school opened its doors, forty students showed up. After the first session, the positive response paved the way for three successive sessions.[9]

In 1937, the seminary moved to Takoma Park, Maryland, in the portion located in the District of Columbia where it later became a part of Potomac University. It soon became a part of Andrews University when the seminary moved yet a third time to Berrien Springs, Michigan. At this point, Adventist ministerial education received respected status. The dream of Daniells to see a more intentional plan for ministerial education evolved from a series of Bible Institutes in the late 1870s through the 1890s, into a regular bachelor's degree in theology at most Adventist colleges by the 1910s and 1920s. Then Daniells and other church leaders pushed for the development of more advanced graduate level training that culminated with the Advanced Bible School in 1934. Today this institution is the Seventh-day Adventist Theological Seminary, a part of Andrews University. Most Seventh-day Adventist pastors in North America, thanks to this vision, attend the Seminary at Andrews University at some point.

Perspective

Today the Seventh-day Adventist Church, with some twenty million members, is the fifth largest Christian denomination in the world. One of the greatest challenges facing the denomination is the need for Adventist pastors who can achieve balance by focusing on both church health as well as evangelism, the two original tasks of the Adventist pastor. Individuals such as Russell Burrill are calling for Adventist pastors to become more evangelistically focused.[10] Pastors must remember that the primary responsibility of the Adventist pastor is to lead the church and train its members to effectively proclaim the gospel to the world.

At the same time, there is a danger of going to the opposite extreme by focusing solely on evangelism. This is especially relevant in portions of the world where Adventist pastors focus so much on evangelism that they often neglect discipleship and church health. While this approach may yield impressive numbers, usually this does not contribute to long-term health and church growth. In some parts of the world, some are baptized repeatedly by different denominations, and there can be a tendency to count the same church member

A new generation of pastors must focus on discipleship and evangelism.

multiple times. The crucial point is that Adventist pastors are needed to make sure new church members become committed Christian believers in their local churches. The challenge is to focus on church health as a higher priority instead of focusing on statistics regarding baptisms, visits, and so forth. Dedicated pastors are needed to focus on the health of the whole church.

The Seventh-day Adventist Church is a global church, and it is essential to provide an adequate number of trained, quality pastors. Within North America, if current projections continue as the baby boomer generation retires, there will be a shortage of Adventist pastors. A new generation of pastors must focus on discipleship and evangelism. As the Seventh-day Adventist Church continues to grow, it will be imperative that pastors have opportunities for training so that they can faithfully proclaim God's Word.

1. This chapter is an expansion of two previous articles: "Seventh-day Adventists and the Formation of Ministerial Identity: Lessons From Our Past," *Ministry,* October 2014, 6–10, and "A High and Sacred Calling: A Look at the Origins of Seventh-day Adventist Ministerial Training," *Ministry,* April 2007, 20, 21.

2. The Restorationist movement, broadly defined, was a historical movement within American religion that was especially prominent during the nineteenth century. The movement coalesced around several leaders, most notably Elias Smith (1769–1846) and Abner Jones (1772–1841) in the north, and Alexander Campbell (1788–1866) in the south. Such a diverse movement included a host of other lesser-known preachers, many of whom were itinerant. Altogether the movement, also known as Christian primitivism, shared a fundamental conviction that the Christian church needed to return to the primitive purity of the early Christian church.

3. This is based upon a survey of early Adventist obituaries from the 1860s where ministers of other denominations are frequently listed as officiating the service in the absence of a Seventh-day Adventist minister.

4. Cf. Brian E. Strayer, *J. N. Loughborough: The Last of the Adventist Pioneers* (Hagerstown, MD: Review and Herald®, 2013). The author documents a series of early female deaconesses whom Loughborough set apart through ordination.

5. "Pastoral Responsibilities," *Review and Herald,* June 24, 1873, 13.

6. "Answers to Correspondents," *Review and Herald,* October 28, 1873, 160.

7. The Harbor Springs Conference was a meeting held in Harbor Springs, Michigan, in July and August 1891. The meeting represented a turning point in Adventist education by creating a distinctively Adventist curriculum. See G. R. Knight, *A Brief History of Seventh-day Adventists* (Hagerstown, MD: Review and Herald®, 1999), 96.

8. "Report of Bible Conference," August 1, 1919, 1261.

9. Shirley Annette Welch, "History of the Advanced Bible School, 1934-1937," Term Paper, Andrews University, 1977.

10. Russell Burrill observes that he does not "advocate a total return to this model [of early Adventism] as some think. My concern . . . [is] that we get back [to] the evangelistic/pastoral balance." Russell Burrill e-mail to the author, January 19, 2015. See also Blake Jones, "An Apostle or Elder? Defining the Role of the Ordained Adventist Minister," Paper presented to the Adventist Theological Society, November 22, 2014.

I Did Not Plan to Be Here: Ministry Continues

GARY PATTERSON

The celebration of anniversaries includes a host of memorable events such as marriage, the opening of a business, the founding of a city or country, and even major traumatic occurrences. I have also been invited to many church anniversaries, and it is always with mixed emotions that I participate in such events. Long-standing friendships and memories that are renewed at times like these are delightful, but something in the back of my mind keeps saying, "I didn't plan to be here." But I am getting ahead of the story.

My call to ministry

It is hard to say when my call to ministry occurred. My first memory of an indication of a call occurred in the mid-1940s near the end of World War II. My father was serving as a pastor in Albany, Oregon, which was a few miles from Camp Adair, a military base that processed new inductees and recruits for overseas service.

My parents opened our little house on First Street to the Seventh-day Adventist soldiers on weekends to observe the Sabbath and attend our church. I remember seeing twenty or thirty soldiers a weekend sleeping in rows on the living room and dining room floors, happy to be in a home on the Sabbath. On one of those Sabbaths, I recall my first words of commitment to ministry. As was my custom after services, I was standing on the church porch beside my father, who was shaking hands with the worshipers who were leaving. One of the soldiers going out shook my hand and asked, "Gary, what are you going to be when you grow up?" And the answer—unrehearsed and unplanned—sprang from my lips, "I am going to be a minister."

As I attended camp meetings and other large gatherings through the years,

I heard of dramatic calls to ministry others had experienced. There was the evangelist who, as a young man, was playing drums in a dance band when he felt a sudden paralysis in his hand and received the impression of his call. Another was the farmer plowing in his field when he was impressed that farming was not his calling. There were those who saw signs in the sky or heard a distinct voice directing them to ministry. And then there were soldiers who came back from the horrors of war, promising God that they would enter the ministry if they got back alive. Somehow my unrehearsed and unplanned words did not seem to rise to the level of such dramatic calls.

But the call persisted. Through my high school years I toyed with other options. Playing my saxophone in the band and singing in the touring choir drew me to consider a career teaching music. I enjoyed algebra, geometry, and physics and considered being a math and science teacher. But when college induction for freshmen came around in the fall of 1955, I found myself at the theology registration table. The die was cast—ministry was my calling. But one thing still bothered me. I was sure the Lord would come in the next five years or so, and I would not even be done with seminary training before that great event. Yet, just maybe by being in the process of training for ministry, my life would count for something.

The call to ministry is uniquely God's doing, but its perception is as varied and personal as are those He calls.

It was a notion not out of keeping with the times. Richard Fearing, in his memoirs of a life in ministry, recalls, "When I graduated from college in 1950 along with a large number of World War II soldiers, it seemed that all of us thought that we were going to 'finish the work.' There were scores, even hundreds of young men and women who graduated after being involved in global warfare and felt certain that our Lord would come during their ministry."[1]

Reluctant to rejoice

I entered ministry in the Idaho Conference in 1960. Now fifty-five years later, I must confess, I did not plan to be here. I assumed the Lord would return long before this. And as with my hesitance about participating in church anniversaries, I am reticent to rejoice at being here.

The call to ministry is uniquely God's doing, but its perception is as varied and personal as are those He calls. As the *Minister's Handbook* states,

"Ministers for God do not consider themselves 'self-called.' As with the apostle Paul, the initiative is not the individual's, but the Lord's. Paul did not choose the ministry of the gospel; rather, God chose him for that ministry. Paul's choice was whether or not to respond to God's call. A call to the gospel ministry is a call to become an ambassador for Christ. This call demands the full commitment of one's being to this high calling."[2]

It is easy to confuse a calling to ministry with one's employment by a church entity. Yet, a distinction must be maintained between the two. As John Killinger puts it, "Ministers don't work for their churches, they work for God. The church always thinks they work for them, because they provide them with office space and pay their salaries. But such thinking is mistaken, whether it is the church that thinks it or the ministers who occupy their office space. If this is not borne in mind, it will lead to all kinds of distortions of the minister's self-image and the church's authority in the total scheme of things. Part of the confusion stems from the nomenclature we use. We say that God calls a minister, but we also say that a church calls its ministers. In a way, both are true. But the two callings are very different."[3]

Ellen White observes that "God calls for workers . . . who, placing themselves in the hands of the Lord as humble learners, have proved themselves workers together with Him . . . . Let them step into the ranks of workers, and by patient, continuous effort prove their worth. . . . Let them fill with fidelity the place to which they are called, that they may become qualified to bear still higher responsibilities. God gives all opportunity to perfect themselves in His service."[4]

Much can be learned about leadership and administration, both from seminary training and the secular world, which can be applied and used in one's ministry. In fact, it would be foolish to ignore or dismiss the abundance of ideas and material available to make the ministerial function more effective. Yet, there is something beyond training and skill sets that distinguishes a ministerial calling from a career. As C. E. Bradford observes, "The best thing that could happen to some of us would be to have every book in our libraries stolen for a while until we learned how to search the Scriptures."[5]

Harris W. Lee states, "Leadership in the church may use insights from the secular world, but it is rooted in the faith 'once delivered to the saints.' Church leaders may quote James Burns, Warren Bennis, Peter Drucker, and Tom Peters, but they are inspired by the Lord of the church, by the prophets and apostles, and by the fact that leadership is a gift, a calling, and a ministry."[6]

Seeking to fit into some preconceived role or context as to what a call to ministry is leads to frustration. We are not gifted alike, nor are we called to duplicate ministers. Learning from others is wise and a blessing, but seeking to be other than what God gifts us to be stunts what we may become by His grace. The apostle Paul makes it clear that these "gifts of the Spirit" are not ours, but rather, they belong to the church. Paul states, "To each one the manifestation of the Spirit is given for the common good" (1 Corinthians 12:7, NIV). Thus, these gifts, rather than being given to an individual, are given to the church through those called to ministry. John R. W. Stott observes that "we pastors have God-given responsibilities both to the congregation we serve and to the doctrine we teach, for both have been committed to us. Yet our prior responsibility is to ourselves, to guard our personal walk with God and our loyalty to Him. Nobody can be a good pastor or teacher of others who is not first a good servant of Jesus Christ."[7]

> *Learning from others is wise and a blessing, but seeking to be other than what God gifts us to be stunts what we may become by His grace.*

Congregations are blessed by the variety of ministerial gifts their pastors bring as they move from place to place. A minister must address many needs, but not all ministers are equipped to meet all these needs. It is this situation, if not addressed carefully, that leads to frustration and burnout. Donald P. Smith recognizes this potential, stating, "The cross fire of role conflicts that is perhaps the most intense for many ministers is the conflict between the person they understand themselves to be and the role they feel required to play. As can readily be imagined, this may be one of the most painful types of conflict because ministers visualize themselves especially as men of integrity."[8]

In extensive surveys of active pastors, Smith indicates that study, sermon preparation, and preaching are listed as primary objectives and favored activities of pastors, yet administration, which ranks as the least favored activity, takes up the bulk of a pastor's time. Such a conflict between preference and time demands becomes stressful. Often, personal life and family needs get shortchanged in the process of seeking to meet the demands of ministry. Ellen White observes, "There are hours in the day that call for severe taxation, for which the minister receives no extra salary, and if he chooses to chop wood several hours a day, or work in his garden, it is as much his privilege to do this as to preach. A minister cannot always be preaching and visiting, for this is exhaustive work."[9]

Strange as it sounds today, I can remember that in our Albany, Oregon, house, my mother cooked on a woodstove in the kitchen and I helped my father chop the wood in the backyard. We also grew a large garden in which he labored. Today not many of us are chopping wood, so we must seek exercise in other ways. But the point is still valid. Neglect of one's physical needs and family in the name of devoted service to ministry is neither wise nor godly. And in the bigger picture, it actually reduces the time one can devote to ministry as a result of illness and early death. We will benefit if we work "in harmony with the plan God has laid down for the perfect development of the physical, the mental, and the spiritual powers."[10]

What is next?

There is the call to ministry, the work of ministry, but how does retirement fit into the picture? Does a call to ministry terminate when one ceases to be employed by the church? And once again we are up against that misperception which conflates a call to ministry with a salary. I recall an incident when I was interviewing a large group of senior ministerial students for possible placement in our pastoral ranks. One of them pressed me with a question. "I have a call to ministry," he stated. "How can you refuse to call me into your conference?"

I tried to explain to him—rather unsuccessfully, I fear—that there were many students seeking employment and I was able to hire only two of them. I sought to explain that his call to ministry was between God and himself, and my inability to hire him did not negate that call. And now, in the same manner, I recognize that retirement does not cancel the call either.

Richard Fearing recalls a comment made by one of our colleagues who addressed the issue of retirement from employment in a unique way. "Jack Harris, a retired ministerial colleague . . . once remarked, I enjoyed every minute of my work, but I would not want to do it for another second."[11] The point was that he had ceased the demands of employment, but not the call to ministry. John Killinger, looking back over years of ministry, observes, "When all is said and done, what richer place could there be for us to live our lives? Imagine having a family of hundreds of people, all caring about you and the way you feel, inviting you into the inner sanctums of their lives, sharing their sorrows and joys with you, listening to your speeches, holding you up to God each day in prayer, and trying in their various ways to help you do your job. There is no other calling in the world quite like it. Where else could we feel as satisfied about the worth of what we are doing?"[12]

So, how does one continue to be "in ministry" following retirement? I have discovered there is yet much to do—things I never imagined even existed. For forty years, I worked within the system of the church, and although there were opportunities to touch lives outside the circle of members to which I was assigned, particularly when I was in evangelistic outreach, for the most part, it was within the confines of the church that I fellowshiped and served. Upon retirement, I embarked in a ministry for some five thousand employees of the home care division of Adventist Health System who were not members of the Seventh-day Adventist Church, leading them into the concept of what Adventist healthcare is about. Never before in my ministry did I have such a vast audience.

After five years in that ministry, I spent eight years recruiting senior ministerial students on our college and university campuses for service in chaplaincy ministry. I helped them develop a track in which they would receive a master of divinity degree and four units of Clinical Pastoral Education (CPE). Both of these ventures were unique ministries.

In addition, a dozen churches requested the assistance of an interim pastor in assignments that lasted six to twelve months. In fact, I ended up serving more congregations in these assignments than I did during my previous forty years of service. There were also guest speaking appointments and the writing of articles and books, which included both the *Minister's Handbook* and the *Elder's Handbook.* Such opportunities never even crossed my mind prior to retirement. Clearly, one may retire from employment, but not from the call to ministry.

> *The higher call to ministry is not a call to be right; it is a call to serve.*

In addition to these specific assignments, there is the opportunity to share one's counsel and experience with a new generation of church leaders. Yet, as much as experience may be valuable to pass on, times change. As James Russell Lowell's great hymn makes clear,

"New occasions teach new duties,
Time makes ancient good uncouth;
They must upward still and onward,
Who would keep abreast of truth."[13]

Several years ago, a young pastor friend told me of being railed upon by one of the old timers who was criticizing the younger generation for failing to do the work the way he thought it ought to be done. He held up the pioneers of the church as the model for finishing the work, stating that we should be returning to and following their ways in our approach to ministry. After listening to him for some time, my young pastor friend replied, "Maybe you are right, but remember, they didn't finish the work either." Certainly there is nothing wrong with being right, but I have often had to ask myself, "Would you rather be right or be helpful?" The higher call to ministry is not a call to be right; it is a call to serve.

Robert Webber, speaking of the younger evangelicals and their quest for ministry, observes, "Traditional evangelical leadership of the twentieth century is driven by the concerns formed out of the fundamentalist/modernist controversy. This traditional movement, its churches, publishing houses, mission boards, seminary and college education, have been and are now shaped by an apologetic Christianity that is fueled by the desire to be right." Webber then points out that there has been a shift. "The leadership of the younger evangelical is not shaped by being right, nor is it driven by meeting needs. Instead, it arises out of a missiological understanding of the church. . . . We do not define God's mission. It defines us. It tells us who we are, what our mission is, how to do ministry, worship, spirituality, evangelism. There is no aspect of the Christian life, thought, and ministry that is not connected with God's mission to the world."[14]

Yet, when the mission of the church becomes the preservation of the institution and past thinking, it closes off the ability of a new generation to hear the voice of God calling to new ventures and ways of doing things.

Without a doubt, the institution and structure of the church has made possible the spread and growth of our small community of believers in the late 1800s to some twenty million in 150 years. It is a miracle, indeed. Yet, when the mission of the church becomes the preservation of the institution and past thinking, it closes off the ability of a new generation to hear the voice of God calling to new ventures and ways of doing things.

Our pioneers lived by a concept of "present truth," recognizing that not all had been achieved or understood at any given point. And the same concept applies today. There are plenty of things for us "oldsters" to do in retirement, but one of them is not stifling the new generation by imposing our ideas and methods on them. Sharing wisdom, counsel, and experience with them, yes. But let them move ahead in new directions with new ideas and actions as God leads.

Ministry continues

My father lived a life of rich ministry, which in the latter part of his career included serving in the arena of public affairs and religious liberty. In this capacity, he spoke with and came to know personally a host of legislators, governors, and judicial leaders on the local, state, and national level. And although he frequently addressed such governmental assemblies, in his later years, Parkinson's disease robbed him of his ability to continue his formal ministry. But his call to ministry was not ended. In his nineties, as part of his local congregation, he became the great-grandfather of the little children of the church— and just maybe this was a

> *There are plenty of things for us "oldsters" to do in retirement, but one of them is not stifling the new generation by imposing our ideas and methods on them.*

more important work than standing before legislatures. While he was still able to get around on his feet, he would greet the children with a Sabbath blessing and hug. But even when it became more difficult for him to walk around, the children would not be denied the greeting. So, Sabbath after Sabbath, there would be a long line of them seeking him out at his accustomed seat on the aisle for their hug and blessing from the great-grandfather. And thus his call to ministry remained to his last breath.

In his final hours, as he reclined in a chair, eyes closed, his grandson, Geoff, who had followed in our footsteps in ministry, read from his grandfather's preaching Bible that had been presented to him: "I have fought the good fight, I have finished the race, I have kept the faith. Now there is in store for me the crown of righteousness, which the Lord, the righteous Judge, will award to me on that day—and not only to me, but also to all who have longed for his appearing" (2 Timothy 4:7, 8, NIV). Then my father rose up in his chair, placed his hand on his grandson's head, and passed the patriarchal blessing on to a new generation in a beautiful prayer. So the call to ministry never ended. It was passed on.

I did not plan to be here today. I thought the Lord would return long before this. But until He comes and calls us home, the call to service lives.

1. Richard Drew Fearing, *Lord, What Am I Doing Here?* (Caldwell, ID: Griffith Publishing, 1996), 163.

2. *Minister's Handbook* (Silver Spring, MD: Ministerial Association of Seventh-day Adventists, 2009), 16.

3. John Killinger, *Seven Things They Don't Teach You in Seminary* (New York, NY: Crossroad Publishing Company, 2006), 147.

4. Ellen G. White, *Gospel Workers* (Nampa, ID: Pacific Press®, 1915), 494, 495.

5. Charles E. Bradford, *Preaching to the Times* (Silver Spring, MD: Ministerial Association of Seventh-day Adventists, 1993), 26.

6. Harris W. Lee, *Effective Church Leadership* (Minneapolis, MN: Augsburg Fortress, 1989), 19.

7. John R. W. Stott, *Preaching Between Two Worlds* (Grand Rapids, MI: Eerdmans, 1982), 265.

8. Donald P. Smith, *Clergy in the Cross Fire* (Philadelphia, PA: Westminster Press, 1974), 45.

9. Ellen G. White, *Evangelism* (Nampa, ID: Pacific Press®, 1946), 660.

10. Ellen G. White, *Testimonies for the Church* (Nampa, ID: Pacific Press®, 1902), 7:281.

11. Fearing, *Lord, What Am I Doing Here?,*196.

12. John Killinger, *The Tender Shepherd* (Nashville, TN: Abingdon Press, 1985), 207.

13. James Russell Lowell, "Once to Every Man and Nation," no. 606 in *Seventh-day Adventist Hymnal,* (Hagerstown, MD: Review and Herald®, 1845).

14. Robert E. Webber, *The Younger Evangelicals* (Grand Rapids, MI: Baker Books, 2002), 240, 241.

✝ EVANGELISM

Pastors are skilled and passionate about making disciples, helping people accept, internalize, and share in a vibrant relationship with Jesus Christ and the Seventh-day Adventist message.

Descriptors of Evangelism include:
• promotes/models a life of prayer, Bible study, and personal worship
• effective teacher/mentor
• successful in leading and promoting small group ministries
• promotes community outreach
• advocates for the marginalized
• inspires every-member evangelism
• oversees well organized evangelistic operations
• effective in gaining decisions for Christ

Evangelism . . . Just Do It

BJ BOLES

The evangelistic challenges that confront a local pastor are varied and great. For many pastors, the realities of ministry can include the feeling of being overworked, under-resourced, and underfunded. Some have a sense that most of their time is absorbed keeping the church afloat rather than investing in growth. Beyond the pressures that are placed on the pastor to be "successful" in evangelism (get baptisms), there may also exist the additional stresses of generating local support, seeking funding, finding the needed energy, and creating the time in an already crowded schedule. Even the word *evangelism* can be charged with emotions from past experiences and external peer influences that impact our current perceptions. Defining evangelism may seem fundamental but, in reality, there are differences of view and perspective on what exactly "doing evangelism" means.

For many years, I was first in line to implement the latest strategy presented and promoted by church organizations. I "did" all the programs and yet

> *I sought new technology, bought the latest software, utilized the latest marketing strategy, and was ever seeking the missing link.*

was frustrated with the limited success I had compared to the glowing testimonies I had heard at pastors' meetings about the program. I sought new technology, bought the latest software, utilized the latest marketing strategy, and was ever seeking the missing link. There was "success" in my ministry, but not at the level I had expected. What was I doing wrong?

This chapter will share four foundational principles of evangelism I learned through the school of hard knocks. What is most needed is a re-evaluation and reframing of evangelism itself. I wish to share what I have learned, hoping it will give guidance to you, my fellow local district pastor. God has provided me with a clearer understanding of what I need to do *more* of and what I should do *less* of in order to be successful in God's call for evangelism. These four guiding principles have made a difference in my ministry.

Pray and unify

To say that prayer is a foundational principle for successful evangelism seems a bit obvious, especially to an audience of pastors. However, I realize from my own experience that acknowledging the importance of prayer and actually making prayer number one are very different things. I must painfully admit that, for much of my ministry, the percentage of time dedicated to prayer was miniscule compared to the time I actually spent "doing" evangelism. It was not that I did not believe in prayer, but rather there was just so much to do that time seemed to get away from me. After a church board meeting, where unity seemed to be a distant hope, the message of 2 Chronicles 7:14 hit me hard: "If my people, who are called by my name, will humble themselves and pray and seek my face and turn from their wicked ways, then I will hear from heaven, and I will forgive their sin and will heal their land" (NIV). I was moved to admit that prayer had not been foundational. I was moving forward with outreach plans and evangelistic strategies without deep prayer. We should have been investing in prayer to humble ourselves, bind us together in His purpose, and attune ourselves to His will. We needed the blessing that unified prayer brings.

God has provided me with a clearer understanding of what I need to do more *of and what I should do* less *of in order to be successful in God's call for evangelism.*

When I finally made prayer a priority, a fascinating thing began to happen. The more I prayed, the less I worried. When the church and I began praying earnestly, we came together in harmony. We grew together in spirit and spiritual direction. We spent less time arguing about what to do and more time asking God for guidance.

All that we do evangelistically as a church should be prefaced with prayer, bathed in prayer, and contemplated in prayer. Too often prayer is segmented to a mere introductory role at a church board meeting or serves as the way to conclude. Rarely is prayer the focus of the meeting. It is often relegated to a compartmentalized aspect of the plan rather than the backbone. It was not until the disciples at Pentecost were in one accord after much prayer that God blessed them in an incredible way. If the disciples had rushed out to "evangelize" the world without having had the upper room experience, the results would have paled compared to the mighty blessing given them through the Holy Spirit.

There is great pressure to be successful in evangelism. Sometimes the pastor takes on that stress, and sometimes others place it on the pastor. In either case, we want to succeed and conduct many baptisms for God's kingdom. It would seem with these internal and external pressures that we would need to utilize every drop of time to implement our strategy. However, how can we not have time for prayer? In short, prayer maximizes our efforts. Our prayers, we are told, need to be

> *The more I prayed, the less I worried.*

focused: "Solicit prayer for the souls for whom you labor; present them before the church as objects for the supplication. It will be just what the church needs, to have their minds called from their little, petty difficulties, to feel a great burden, a personal interest, for a soul that is ready to perish."[1]

Engage and involve

I find fascinating the things we "debate" regarding evangelism. Some believe evangelism itself is dead, antiquated, and no longer effective. This seems hard to fathom considering what Jesus said in the Great Commission of Matthew 28:19, 20: "Go therefore and make disciples of all the nations, baptizing them in the name of the Father and of the Son and of the Holy Spirit, teaching them to observe all things that I have commanded you; and lo, I am with you always, even to the end of the age."[2] This command of Jesus needs to be coupled with His prediction and promise in Matthew 24:14: "And this gospel of the kingdom will be preached in all the world as a witness to all the nations, and then the end will come." It is clear that sharing the gospel with the lost is to be the mission of the church until the end. The discussion gets blurry when we lump the commission with discussions of evangelistic implementation. The commission has not changed, but how we implement it can be varied and diverse. Everyone seems to have an opinion of how to do or not to do evangelism.

Other debates rage on whether evangelism should be exclusively public or personal, an event or a process, or traditional or creative. Jesus demonstrated both public and personal evangelism. The apostles demonstrated both traditional and creative manners of reaching the people. Both events and a process are needed and should walk hand-in-hand. One without the other will not be as effective. Public evangelism should not be done at the exclusion of personal evangelism—or vice versa.

In many ways, these "discussions" lead us to eliminate items from our evangelistic tools. This is not to mention the division these debates stir within the body of Christ. No wonder there are those who ignorantly make statements such as, "Evangelism doesn't work."

Furthermore, we often make excuses as to why we should not do evangelism. "We tried it before and it didn't work," or "This town is just too hard to evangelize," or "This church just doesn't support evangelism." These are created obstacles that can stall the progress of church evangelism.

> *The more we polarize ourselves regarding evangelism, the more we paralyze the work.*

Another excuse to stall evangelism is money. We think that if we do not have money, then we cannot do evangelism. Money is merely a means to accomplish God's will, not in itself the goal. Funding has never, does not, nor will ever stop the work of the Lord from moving forward. "Not having money" is therefore not a reason to not do evangelism—it is only an excuse. If money is needed in order to reach your community, God will provide it. If the funding does not come according to your plan, adjust your plan and move forward in faith.

The more we polarize ourselves regarding evangelism, the more we paralyze the work. In the story of David and Goliath, God's people were frozen before the giant. It took the simple faith of a boy to break the shackles of hesitation and get the army engaged in the battle. Romans 8:31 gives us a promise: "What then shall we say to these things? If God is for us, who can be against us?" It is time to rise up to the great task and take the gospel to the world. We need to stop debating and making excuses and start engaging on all fronts. Evangelism is an opportunity, not a burden.

Evangelism is an invitation for the whole body to be engaged. They may, however, need a pastor of faith, like a David, to lead the way and show them that all things are possible through Christ. Those of us who lack faith and have difficulty believing in God's ability to grant the victory will be encouraged by the father's response to Christ in Mark 9:24: "Immediately the father of the child cried out and said with tears, 'Lord, I believe; help my unbelief!' "

We must strive to involve every member in seeking to win people for Jesus. Perhaps, we are the greatest impediment to successful evangelism, for in the end there is nothing that can stop the Lord's work from being a success except not doing it. It is time we spend less time talking about evangelism and just do it. We are invited to be coworkers with Christ Jesus: "In the work for this time, it is not money or talent or learning or eloquence that are needed so much as faith graced with humility. No opposition can prevail against truth presented in faith and humility, by workers who willingly bear toil and sacrifice and reproach for the Master's sake. We must be co-workers with Christ if we would see our efforts crowned with success."[3]

Integrate and adapt

Rather than compartmentalizing evangelism so that it is just done once in a while, we must change our collective perception so that all we do in the church has an evangelistic goal. Sharing Jesus with others is not optional for the church, but rather the lifeblood that should course through all the actions of the body of Christ.

I like to call this approach "total evangelism," which engages all the willing in your congregation (the whole body) in an all-out commitment to evangelism. This does not exclude outreach events such as a traditional evangelistic series, felt-needs seminars, or some other creative forms of evangelistic events but integrates them into part of an ongoing strategy. This mission of total evangelism can only be done by changing and maintaining a new evangelistic attitude among your members. They must be continually reminded and reinforced that our mission is to share Jesus with others and bring them into the fellowship. I use a simple motto: "Bring them to Jesus and keep them in Jesus."

It is important to train leaders to speak from up front and in Sabbath School classes with the awareness that visitors are present.

One of the greatest opportunities for evangelism is Sabbath itself. Every week we have an opportunity to show Jesus by inviting people to church. This opportunity may require redesigning the Sabbath worship experience so that it is designed for guests and is visitor-friendly. Special effort should be made to ensure that guests are comfortable. Special bulletins, welcome bags, and instilling the concept that every member is a host are a great start.

It is important to train leaders to speak from up front and in Sabbath School classes with the awareness that visitors are present.

Ultimately, what will make the Sabbath evangelistic focus a success is to ensure Christ is seen throughout and in the congregation. God's love should flow through every conversation, action, and word spoken. Let your church be a place where Christ is seen. John 13:35 says, "By this all will know that you are My disciples, if you have love for one another." Create a safe place where the guest can encounter God and be moved by the Holy Spirit. As your members experience this positive environment, they will enthusiastically invite others to church. A loving positive environment is contagious.

A healthy evangelistic approach should be a multifaceted program for reaching others. There is no one-size-fits-all plan. We need to be willing to adapt and diversify to reach our specific culture and meet the unique dynamics of our community. Just as Paul became as a Jew that he might win Jews but yet adapted his approach when dealing with other groups, we also must be creative and flexible in our approach toward evangelism. This does not mean we compromise principles, nor are we ever ashamed of the gospel. We do not change the ingredients of the gospel but should be willing to change the recipe to reach the people we are connecting with for Jesus. The gospel is not out-of-date, and people still very much need the Lord. He is still the answer to their problems. We must, however, speak in a language and take an approach that is understood and is received by our target audience.

> *We do not change the ingredients of the gospel but should be willing to change the recipe to reach the people we are connecting with for Jesus.*

A total approach to evangelism is where all efforts of the church strive to win people for the kingdom. Do various things to meet various groups. Seek to understand your audience so you can better reach it for Jesus. So find an itch in your community and scratch it. Do not get stuck in a rut of doing the same things you have always done or fall into the trap of never trying something new. This is how we are encouraged to present Jesus: "Present Jesus because you know Him as your personal Saviour. Let His melting love, His rich grace, flow forth from human lips. You need not present doctrinal points unless questioned. But take the Word, and with tender, yearning love for souls, show them the precious righteousness of Christ, to whom you and they must come to be saved."[4]

Christ-centered and God-empowered

Evangelism is about uplifting Jesus to a lost world. Jesus must remain central in our message, manner, and approach. Jesus tells us in John 12:32, "And I, if I am lifted up from the earth, will draw all peoples to Myself." Evangelism is not about exalting the church or uplifting a person (i.e., the pastor or evangelist). We must maintain the focus on sharing Jesus at all times. This approach, according to John, will be irresistibly attractive to those seeking God.

There are no supermen in evangelism. Pastors who think they can do it all will find their efforts limited, and in the end, they will be less effective under the load. We must trust the Holy Spirit to do His job. Too often we seek to do God's job for Him. Unfortunately, there was a time in my ministry when I did not truly trust the Holy Spirit to do His work. I tried to do His job for Him by seeking to convict and convert the hearts of people. It was only when I got out of the way and let God work did the results change.

We need to understand our role and God's role. We are tools and not the talent. God convicts; God converts; God gives the increase! Let God work and give Him all the glory. I began publically praying for me to decrease and the Lord to increase. This constant reminder and acknowledgment to humble myself so God could be glorified was a converting moment. It was refreshing to realize I did not have to do it all.

The way I determined evangelistic success changed as well. I began to deem it successful to simply and faithfully do His will. Evangelism is successful, if you allow yourself to be used by God to reach others. I stopped worrying about numeric success (baptisms) and just wanted the church and myself to be the best conduits for His power. This is how Jesus deemed success. He did not count His efforts as success by the number of converts or baptisms He had but, rather, by if He was doing the will of the Father. Success is doing what God asks—numbers are the result, not the goal. When we focus on numbers, we then are tempted to force, press, stress, and cajole. Let God do His work on the heart of the hearer. "Sometimes ministers do too much; they seek to embrace the whole work in their arms. It absorbs and dwarfs them; yet they continue to grasp it all. They seem to think that they alone are to work in the cause of God, while the members of the church stand idle. This is not God's order at all."[5]

Conclusion

My parting charge to you is to enjoy evangelism and infuse it into your way of thinking. These four principles cannot be accomplished overnight or by quickly typing a letter to your leaders but, rather, is a committed ongoing process. My church is committed to these principles, and they have transformed the congregation. We did not chase baptismal numbers, but thank God that most Sabbaths two or three individuals are baptized. The various ministries in our 1,100-plus member congregation think and function evangelistically. All that we do is focused on the mission of the church. I encourage you, my colleague, to set the example of recognizing the importance of each principle as you continually remind, disciple, and encourage your members. Be perseverant and patient with your members. View evangelism as a wonderful opportunity to see God work.

The Lord who called you to this task is faithful and will empower you and show you great and wonderful things.

Be prayerful! Be creative! Be committed! Be encouraged! Be engaged! God would never ask us to do something and leave us abandoned. The Lord who called you to this task is faithful and will empower you and show you great and wonderful things.

1. Ellen G. White, *Medical Ministry* (Mountain View, CA: Pacific Press®, 1963), 244, 245.
2. Unless otherwise noted, all Scripture is from the New King James Version.
3. Ellen G. White, *Selected Messages* (Washington, DC: Review and Herald®, 1958), 1:118.
4. Ellen G. White, *Evangelism* (Washington, DC: Review and Herald®, 1970), 442.
5. Ibid., 113.

Retaining Young Adults

MARQUIS D. JOHNS

How do we retain our Seventh-day Adventist members, especially our young adults? In 2013, the North American Division of Seventh-day Adventists (NAD) approached the Barna Group, a Christian research firm, to study retention. The Barna Group was asked to focus on the largest generational group; a group that numbers almost eighty million[1] and that wears many names—Mosaics, Generation Y, Bridgers, and millennials to list a few. Barna focused its attention on the subset of the group of ages eighteen to twenty-nine. For the purpose of this chapter, we will focus on those born between 1980 and 2000. We will look at what it takes to retain millennials who are already either actively or somewhat actively involved in a church.[2]

Let us first turn our attention to Scripture—Numbers 20—where this familiar but often overlooked story provides a clear example of what we need to do to retain our millennials: equip, educate, and empower them. In the chapter, God tells Aaron that his time as a leader in Israel has come to an end and it is now time for Moses to "take Aaron . . . up to Mount Hor. . . . And Aaron shall be gathered to his people and shall die there" (Numbers 20:25, 26).[3]

Ellen White says, "Aaron's work for Israel was done. Forty years before, at the age of eighty-three, God had called him to unite with Moses in his great and important mission. He had co-operated with his brother in leading the children of Israel from Egypt. He had held up the great leader's hands when the Hebrew hosts gave battle to Amalek. He had been permitted to ascend Mount Sinai, to approach into the presence of God, and to behold the divine glory."[4]

Aaron is being called to die. He accomplished great things as a leader in Israel: leading the people for four decades, holding up the hands of another great leader and beholding the very presence of God. Nonetheless, his time was at its end. This is not to say that he had nothing else to offer Israel. This is not to suggest that God was sending him to die to make room for new leadership. Although we acknowledge his sin as the reason why his leadership had to come to such an abrupt end, this is not an attempt to characterize all older leaders as sinful.

Inherent in the text are two ideas: Aaron's time was up, and God had prepared someone else to lead—"Take . . . his garments and put them on Eleazar his son" (Numbers 20:25, 26). Aaron could have resisted handing over leadership to Eleazar. Besides the fact that he was literally being stripped of his position, earlier in his life, his two oldest sons had died. How did those two sons die, and why would this make him hesitate to see Eleazar in charge? Leviticus tells us, "Now Nadab and Abihu, the sons of Aaron, each took his censer and put fire in it and laid incense on it and offered unauthorized fire before the Lord,

> *If we are to retain Seventh-day Adventist young adults, four things need to happen.*

which he had not commanded them. And fire came out from before the Lord and consumed them, and they died before the Lord" (Leviticus 10:1, 2).

Not only were Nadab and Abihu's roles in the leadership and priestly duties of Israel significant, but they were also the sons of Israel's high priest and nephews of Moses. Notice God had called them, along with Moses, Aaron, and the seventy elders by name to come up the mountain and have a meal in His presence. Chosen and consecrated to the priesthood, they assisted Aaron in the first operations of the newly instituted sanctuary service. In all the camp of God's liberated children, only Moses and Aaron had higher honor than they. However, when they were given the opportunity to lead, what did these young adults do? They offered "unauthorized fire" and died for their sin. One can see how Aaron would have been justified, both as leader and parent, to exhibit a measure of hesitancy when the time came to relinquish his robe and role to another of his children.

This was not, however, Aaron's decision to make. Even though the Bible tells us that "all the house of Israel wept for Aaron" (Numbers 20:29), it was not the people's decision either. Although they may have preferred the steady hand of Aaron and were concerned that Eleazar might repeat the sins of Nadab and Abihu, once the Lord made His decision, Eleazar was to be Israel's high priest. Furthermore, they need not have been too distressed, because *both* "Moses and Eleazar came down from the mountain" (verse 28), signaling that there would still be, for at least a little while longer, someone to give Eleazar counsel and guidance.

Let us now discuss the key points from this biblical narrative that show how we can retain millennials in the church.

Eleazar was engaged in his church by virtue of the fact that he was born into not just the Levitical line, but more specifically into the Aaronic line. In

Numbers 20, we see him climbing Mount Hor with his father and uncle, where he was equipped and empowered to lead. Although Moses also died before entering the Promised Land, Eleazar benefited from having the guidance and experience of his uncle available to him when he started functioning as high priest. I believe that Adventist millennials are in a similar situation as Eleazar. If they are engaged, equipped, and empowered as Eleazar was, not only will we be able to retain them, but they will play pivotal roles in reclaiming their de-churched peers and reach their unchurched counterparts.

Engage

If we are to retain Seventh-day Adventist young adults, four things need to happen. First, they must be engaged. The Barna Group classified eighteen- to nineteen-year-old Adventist millennials as either "engaged" or "disengaged" from their local church. Engaged participants were those who attended services at least monthly and indicated that church is relevant to them. Disengaged participants did not meet one or both of the above criteria.

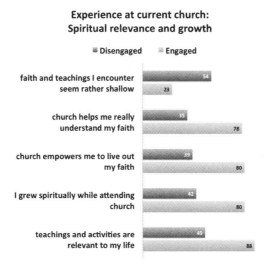

Experience at current church:
Spiritual relevance and growth

Experience at current church:
Relationships and a sense of belonging

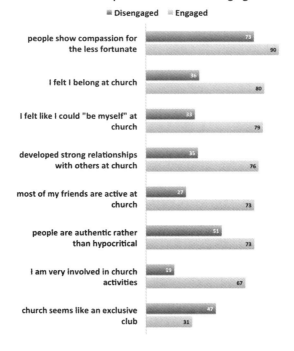

■ Disengaged ■ Engaged

people show compassion for the less fortunate	73 / 90
I felt I belong at church	36 / 80
I felt like I could "be myself" at church	33 / 79
developed strong relationships with others at church	35 / 76
most of my friends are active at church	27 / 73
people are authentic rather than hypocritical	51 / 73
I am very involved in church activities	19 / 67
church seems like an exclusive club	47 / 31

Experience at current church:
Rigidity/acceptance of others' beliefs

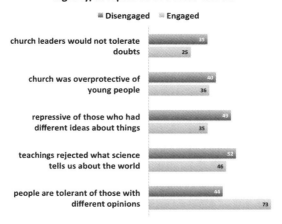

■ Disengaged ■ Engaged

church leaders would not tolerate doubts	35 / 25
church was overprotective of young people	40 / 36
repressive of those who had different ideas about things	49 / 35
teachings rejected what science tells us about the world	52 / 46
people are tolerant of those with different opinions	44 / 73

The findings show where our denomination is struggling and areas where we seem to be doing well. However, I believe for millennials to continue to be engaged, the church will have to carefully look at the areas where we see very little difference between the engaged and disengaged millennials. We need to look at areas where our young adults say they are disengaged and

RETAINING YOUNG ADULTS | 69

work toward strengthening these areas.

As previously stated, Eleazar was engaged because he was born into not just the Levitical line, but also into the Aaronic line. He was trained as a priest and knew how to carry out priestly duties. At the time of Aaron's death, he was ready to take a leadership position. Ideally, more young adults who are already engaged in the church need to be put into leadership.

Equip

Eleazar was equipped. All the necessary equipment that once belonged to his father Aaron—the garments that enabled Aaron to perform the duties of his office—were given to Eleazar. These garments and vestures were designed to inspire a reverential awe and respect. Each item, given by God, was very detailed and carried symbolic meaning. The reader familiar with the sanctuary service, and in particular with the garments of the high priest, knows that they include everything from a ceremonial head dress to consecrated undergarments. Although this exchange may have been sad for Aaron, it was also an exciting moment to know that God had allowed at least one of his sons to continue the priestly ministry.

The Adventist Church needs to equip its young adults to lead.

There was no power struggle, no confusion of roles, no need for anyone to be perplexed about whom to go to when it was time for the high priest's duties to be carried out. This is because everything needed to carry out the office was given to Eleazar, as it had been given his father. Even though he had all of the high priest's equipment, Eleazar at times needed guidance, particularly since his father was dead. God's people and Moses needed to trust that Eleazar was receiving direction and instruction from God.

The Adventist Church needs to equip its young adults to lead. More importantly, the church must be ready to place young adults in leadership roles. Once we have identified young adults who are engaged and have equipped them, when we place them into leadership, we must be willing to follow them. Former leaders should make themselves available for advice and consultation, but eventually, we must trust that God is working through these young adults.

Educate

In *You Lost Me,* David Kinnaman separates church-going millennials into three categories: nomads, prodigals, and exiles. Nomads are those who have drifted from active church involvement. Prodigals have given up on the faith of their childhood and describe themselves as ex-Christian. Exiles feel stuck between church and the "real world."[5]

Kinnaman then delineates six "cultural grievances" the millennials have with the church. The church is overprotective, shallow, anti-science, repressive, intolerant of doubt, and elitist when it comes to relating to those outside the church.[6] As you look at the chart below based on Barna's survey of our millennials, these grievances hold just as true when it comes to Adventist young adults' perceptions of their church. As a matter of fact, the percentages of Seventh-day Adventist participants who said their experiences fit these descriptions were actually higher than the national norms.

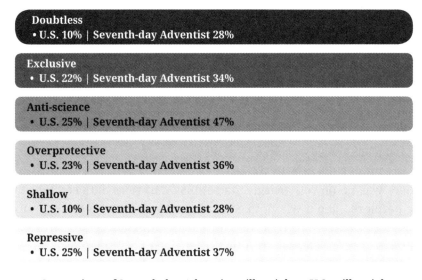

Doubtless
• U.S. 10% | Seventh-day Adventist 28%

Exclusive
• U.S. 22% | Seventh-day Adventist 34%

Anti-science
• U.S. 25% | Seventh-day Adventist 47%

Overprotective
• U.S. 23% | Seventh-day Adventist 36%

Shallow
• U.S. 10% | Seventh-day Adventist 28%

Repressive
• U.S. 25% | Seventh-day Adventist 37%

Comparison of Seventh-day Adventist millennials to U.S. millennials with a Christian background. Percentage of those who "agree strongly" that each characterizes their church experience.

Even though this data shows that the Seventh-day Adventist figures are higher than the U.S. national averages, all hope is not lost.

In *You Lost Me*, Kinnaman suggests a relational "turn" in order to meet the concerns that accompany each grievance. Doubting turns to doing, exclusion turns to embracing, being repressive turns to being relational, anti-science turns to stewardship, shallow turns to apprenticeship, and overprotectiveness turns to discernment. He gives several examples of how each grievance can be turned. He suggests that to turn overprotectiveness to discernment, the church should not "make strict rules about media consumption to save the kids from smut."[7] They should read "the Bible and the newspaper watching, listening and reading together while doing cultural exegesis."[8] Pop culture is not going to go away. Telling young adults to avoid watching, reading, and talking about current events is futile.

Educating our young adults helps them to be more like Daniel, Hananiah, Mishael, and Azariah. Ellen White tells us, "Daniel and his associates had been trained by their parents to habits of strict temperance. They had been taught that God would hold them accountable for their capabilities, and that they must never dwarf or enfeeble their powers. This education was to Daniel and his companions the means of their preservation amidst the demoralizing influences of the court of Babylon. Strong were the temptations surrounding them in that corrupt and luxurious court, but they remained uncontaminated. No power, no influence, could sway them from the principles they had learned in early life by a study of the word and works of God."[9]

> Gone are the days when you could just tell young people, "Because I said so," and that sufficed as an answer to a difficult question.

Gone are the days when you could just tell young people, "Because I said so," and that sufficed as an answer to a difficult question. In a day where within a millisecond anything presented as a fact can be Googled and produce many competing views, we have to be intentional about providing our young people with the type of education that will endure for a lifetime. As Roger Parrott puts it, "teach ideas and critical thinking" as opposed to just recalling facts.[10]

Empower

Empower your young adults by identifying areas they are passionate about and developing projects for them. Avoid pushing them into areas or projects where they demonstrate little to no passion, as doing so will greatly impact their ability to produce, as well as affect their self-confidence.

Next, listen to them. Pay close attention to their preferences and concerns. Listen to their suggestions and be sure to acknowledge their contributions. The importance of both public and private acknowledgment cannot be overstated or underestimated. Affirmation makes them feel empowered and creates an environment where they are willing to continue sharing their ideas and talents. It also boosts self-confidence.

Communication is very important to millennials; therefore, communicate, communicate again, and communicate once more. Thom and Jess Rainer tell us, "This young American generation is empowered by media"[11]; no form of media is more powerful than social media. Our churches should be, to the extent that they are comfortable, current on social media. This creates many opportunities to communicate with our young adults and also to be in tune with the things they are most interested in and concerned about. Since this is an area many young adults are passionate about, it presents a leadership opportunity—put them in charge of your church's social media presence.

As we saw with Eleazar, we can no longer be afraid to give significant responsibilities to young adults. I have identified two things that great leaders do. One, they identify leadership potential in others. Two, they willingly empower that leadership.

As leaders, we often recognize leadership potential in others but may fear empowering them. This fear leads to the suppression of potential and creates a lack of trust in leadership. It generates an environment in which millennials are not comfortable. Although church is not entirely about creating comfort, we need to foster environments where young adults feel comfortable sharing in the vision and mission of their churches. It could very well be the tipping point when it comes to reaching both the de-churched Adventists and the unchurched.

What is the tipping point? In his *New York Times* bestseller *Tipping Point*, Malcolm Gladwell describes three groups of people needed to create a tipping point (a series of small changes or incidents that are significant enough to cause a larger, more important change). He calls them connectors, mavens, and salesmen.

He describes connectors as "people with a special gift for bringing the world together."[12] The most important criteria for being a connector is knowing "lots of people."[13] The next group he feels can be instrumental in creating word-of-mouth epidemics are mavens. "Maven" he says, "comes from the yiddish, and it means one who accumulates knowledge."[14] The thing he finds most fascinating about them is not just the fact that they collect information but their willingness to share that information with people.[15] Finally, there are the salesmen. Salesmen are people "with the skills to persuade us when we are unconvinced of what we are hearing."[16]

In your congregation and among your millennials, you will find people who will fit one, two, or all three of these categories. They are invaluable to the retention of those already engaged, as well as to your projects for reaching those who may have walked away. Search for them. When you find them, acknowledge them and empower them.

Conclusion

Eleazar was the high priest who shepherded Israel into the Promised Land. When they crossed the Jordan River, with the ark, he was in front. When they marched around Jericho, with the ark before them, he was leading. As one of those "under forty" whom God identified as leaders, he stood with Joshua and Caleb as reminders that God wants and rewards people who have faith and obey Him.

Eleazar was able to lead because he demonstrated that he was engaged—he accepted the role of a "regular" priest and fulfilled his duties to the best of his ability. God noticed his work and indicated to the current leaders, Moses and Aaron, that Eleazar should take up the leadership role of the high priest. Moses and Aaron accepted God's decision and equipped and educated Eleazar to do the best possible job. They gave him the garments he needed to show that he was the high priest. They trained him in the duties he needed to perform. They ensured that he understood what he needed to do and was capable of doing it. Aaron, no doubt, reminded him of the reason for the untimely deaths of his older brothers. As a good leader, Aaron would have shared some of his own faults—the golden calf, expressing doubt with Miriam—as important lessons for Eleazar to learn.

After Aaron's death, Moses empowered Eleazar to lead. Moses did not try to take over the role of high priest. That was not his job. Nor did he try to tell Eleazar what to do—Moses died shortly after those events. Eleazar was empowered to do everything that the high priest was to do because he *was* the high priest. He was not *practicing* to be a high priest; he was not a high priest in training—he *was* the high priest.

> *They need to be trained; we need to have them "shadow" us.*

The pattern is clear for us to follow. Barna's research shows that there are millennials in our churches who are engaged. They have committed their lives to following Jesus and are active participants in church and community. They are fulfilling the Great Commission. We need to ask God to show us what roles He wants these young adults to fill in our churches.

Once God has revealed that to us, then we need to equip and educate them. They need to be trained; we need to have them "shadow" us. We need to ensure that they have everything they will need to lead capably. This is the time when we can use that sometimes dreaded "in training" title.

Finally, once they have gone through the training and education, we need to empower them—to place them in leadership positions. And we need to ensure that the church sees and understands that they are the leaders. Make yourself available, as did Moses, for consultation and guidance—but turn the leadership reins over to them, and trust that because God has selected them, and because they have a relationship with Him and a passion for His work, that they will lead successfully.

1.

	Seniors "Greatest Generation"	Builders "Silent or Swing Generation"	Boomers "Pig in the Python"	Busters "Generation X"	Generations Y & iY "Millennials"
Live births	59.6 million	55.4 million	75.9 million	51.5 million	77.9 million
Birth years	1900–1928	1929–1945	1946–1964	1965–1983	1984–2002
Life paradigm	Manifest destiny	"Be grateful you have a job"	"You owe me"	"Relate to me"	"Life is a cafeteria"
Attitude to authority	Respect them	Endure them	Replace them	Ignore them	Choose them
Role of relationships	Long term	Significant	Limited, Useful	Central, Caring	Global, 24/7
Value system	Traditional	Conservative	Self-based	Media	Shop around
Role of career	Loyalty	Means for living	Central focus	Irritant	Place to serve
Schedules	Responsible	Mellow	Frantic	Aimless	Volatile
Technology	What's that?	Hope to outlive it	Master it	Enjoy it	Employ it
Market	Commodities	Goods	Services	Experiences	Transformations
View of future	Uncertain	Seek to stabilize	Create it	Hopeless	Optimistic
Comments	A high school education was sufficient to find a good-paying, secure job with good benefits in their early years.	Caught between two potent and influential generations earned them the name "swing." No U.S. President came from this generation.	Until the millennials, this generation was the largest in American history. No generation had its own literary genre until the boomers.	Called busters due to the dramatic decline in live births from their predecessor generation. Referred to as slackers due to poor work ethic.	As the boomers shaped so much of American culture for most of the last half of the twentieth century, so they will for the first half of the twenty-first.

This table was created with information from Tim Elmore, *Generation Y: Our Last Chance to Save Their Future* (Atlanta, GA: Poet Gardener Publishing, 2010), 24, and Thom S. Rainer and Jess Rainer, *The Millennials: Connecting to America's Largest Generation* (Nashville, TN: B&H Publishing Group, 2011), 8–16.

2. The research cited in this chapter originated from a study conducted by the Barna Group. Four hundred eighty-eight online interviews were conducted among the population of young adults between the ages of eighteen and twenty-nine who currently attend or attended a Seventh-day Adventist church as a child. The survey was conducted between September 16, 2013, and September 24, 2013. The sampling error for 488 interviews is +4.3 percentage points, at the 95 percent confidence level.

The Seventh-day Adventist Church for North America sent an e-mail inviting the above-mentioned age group to participate in a study, with a hyperlink to the survey Web site embedded. A link was also posted on Facebook. Most (394) of the interviews were conducted with young adults who accessed the survey through Facebook with the remaining 91 taking the survey through the e-mail invitation. The surveys took an average of sixteen minutes and were conducted using Web-enabled survey software.

Subsequently, two discussion groups—one for ages eighteen to twenty-two and one for ages twenty-three to twenty-nine—lasting for three days were conducted during the month of September with twenty-four of the survey participants. Participants were recruited based on their survey answers in order to include a variety of spiritual histories.

3. Unless otherwise indicated, all Scripture quoted from the English Standard Version.

4. Ellen G. White, *Patriarchs and Prophets* (Nampa, ID: Pacific Press®, 2002), 425.

5. David Kinnaman, *You Lost Me* (Grand Rapids, MI: Baker Books, 2011), 317.

6. Ibid.

7. Ibid., 136.

8. Ibid.

9. Ellen G. White, *Prophets and Kings* (Nampa, ID: Pacific Press®, 2002), 482.

10. Roger Parrott, *The Longview: Lasting Strategies for Rising Leaders* (Colorado Springs, CO: David C. Cook, 2010), 14, Kindle ed.

11. Excerpt from Thom S. Rainer and Jess W. Rainer, *The Millennials: Connecting to America's Largest Generation* (Nashville, TN: B&H Publishing Group, 2011), 201.

12. Malcolm Gladwell, *The Tipping Point: How Little Things Can Make a Big Difference* (New York: Back Bay Books, 2002), 37.

13. Ibid., 38.

14. Ibid., 58.

15. Ibid., 61.

16. Ibid., 68.

The Challenge of the Second Generation

ROGER HERNANDEZ

My son, a second-generation Hispanic, was sitting next to me during a car ride home and asked me a simple Bible question. I replied by saying, "Jonathan, remind me when we get home to show you a text from Daniel that will answer that question." He looked at me and said, "Dad, who is Daniel and why did he send you a text?" This interaction describes part of the challenge of connecting with the second generation. They hear us; they just do not understand us.

Second generation is a term mostly used for young people that are born in this country to immigrant parents. This group has always been of interest to me, but once my children became teenagers, I developed a much deeper interest because it concerned my family members.

Challenges for the second generation

The second generation faces specific challenges, and their spiritual well-being is often compromised. I will review three of these challenges that occur in many congregations.

First of all, the second generation is treated as exiles in their own country. Daniel A. Rodriguez refers to Virgilio Elizondo, one of the most influential Latino theologians of the past twenty-five years, who summarizes the predicament of second-generation Latinos: "We have always been treated as foreigners in our own countryside—exiles who never left home."[1] They are not accepted in their ancestor's churches because they do not speak the language very well (among other things), and they do not fit well in an English-speaking church, because they feel outnumbered and out of place. Many attend but do not belong, so they leave.

In one church I pastored, we had more than sixty second-generation members, most of them youth. Every Sabbath the church service was translated simultaneously into English through headphones they received when they arrived at church. The person who was in charge of distributing the headphones told some of them, "Why don't you go to a church that speaks English?" Needless to say, we had to assign someone else to distribute the headphones. The harmful comment by the headphone distributer, unfortunately, is not an isolated incident—it happens too often. The message conveyed to this group is, "We are not changing. This is our church." This incident refers to language issues, but that is not the only challenge.

> *The result is disastrous— we keep the language and lose a generation.*

Secondly, in some churches a conflict between culture and the gospel develops. Too many church boards—and members in general—send the message to the second generation that culture is more important than people, and preserving language is paramount. The result is disastrous—we keep the language and lose a generation. Speaking Spanish, or any language, is a tradition—nothing more. I agree with Ed Stetzer who states that "churches that love tradition that way will choose their traditions over their children every time."[2]

How do congregations demonstrate that culture is more important than the gospel? Some, for example, insist that Sabbath School lessons must be taught in the native language, even though the youth cannot read it, or write it, and barely speak it. The resistance to English is also evident in the music selection, or any part of the church service. The lament for the native language of the older generation all too often ignores the needs of the younger generation.

Finally, often leadership positions are given to those who are proficient in the native language—those who can express ideas and exhort the congregation in the native tongue. Yet, often the second generation is better educated, holds higher paying jobs, and is often assigned to leadership roles in their professions. Keeping this group out of church leadership is harmful to both the individual and the congregation. The congregation may lose the ignored person, and the individual's spiritual life may be challenged.

What should we do?

These are some of the challenges faced by the second generation and the church. They are real, but a willing church, under the guidance of the Holy Spirit, can meet these challenges just as it meets many others. I propose several suggestions. Some of them are conceptual and directional, while others are more practical in nature. I will offer several suggested solutions and, while so doing, will reflect on the personal experiences I have had.

Recognize that the future is now

How many times have you heard—I hope we have not said it—that the youth are the church of tomorrow? If that is our position, we risk not having a church tomorrow. The question is this: Are we willing to trust younger members, including the second generation, to not only *attend* church but to lead the church? It seems to me that all too often the secular world has more confidence in youth than the church. In the American version of football, the key player is called the quarterback. Usually, the quarterback is an experienced player, but some players are young and given leadership roles in their starting years. They are not put on the sidelines to watch; they are given the opportunity to lead. Do we have the confidence in our second-generation youth to lead, or are they expected to sit on the sidelines?

Recently, I met with several young adults who were second-generation Hispanics and listened to their thoughts on the church. It was a very candid conversation. Some were faithful in attendance, while others were not. Some had rejected the church of their youth altogether. All wanted to talk. From the conversation, one clear lesson became evident, especially from the ones who attended church—they want to participate in church and not just watch others.

One of those who left the church more than ten years ago asked me a pointed question: "Do you have young people in leadership positions at all levels of the church?" I answered truthfully (and painfully)

> *Do we have the confidence in our second-generation youth to lead, or are they expected to sit on the sidelines?*

that we do not and then thought to myself, *Why do we not?* Maybe the reason is that we have equated youth with inexperience and think that age translates into effectiveness. The fact is, our age does not automatically mean we are capable, mature, or effective. The fact is that the Seventh-day Adventist Church in its early years gave the youth more responsibility than we now do. If God used capable youth in the early days of our church, surely God will use them now as well.

I invite my fellow ministers to focus on the youth, including the second-generation youth. Listen to them. Give them the opportunity to share their thoughts. Look at the talents they have and then place them in ministries in the church.

Grace alone

I grew up in the Seventh-day Adventist Church. Our family went to church at least three times a week, sometimes more. I liked going to church, but I, along with others, struggled with all the rules and regulations that did not make sense to a teenage boy. I have heard it said that rules without relationship lead to rebellion, and that is exactly what happened to me. I was shown the *what* without the *why*. I received *knowledge* without *power*. Max Lucado puts it succinctly: "It wasn't that the people didn't believe in grace at all. They did. They believed in grace a lot. They just didn't believe in grace alone."[3] The second generation and, for that matter, all youth need both. It is easier to focus on the *what,* but such a focus brings about several negative consequences.

One of the negative consequences includes the fact that knowledge without power is frustrating. The person who has knowledge but no power never feels secure because they do not know when they have done enough. Should you pray one or two hours? One works toward victory instead of from victory. There is never a finish line. It's like the song says, "Forever running, but losing the race."[4]

Another challenge is that knowledge without power is dangerous.

One of the most vivid memories of growing up is having a constant feeling of guilt. I knew what was right, yet I did not do it. That was very frustrating. I believe that many second-generation Adventists have a similar experience. Think about it for a moment—guilt is not a sufficient motivator for change. For example, millions know about the dangers of smoking, yet most smokers do not quit. Most know about the benefits of going to school, yet many drop out. Countless teens know about the consequences of premarital sex, yet teenage pregnancy is rampant. Often we know what to do, but we do not do it.

Another challenge is that knowledge without power is dangerous. It can make you feel superior and act superior. It can make you think that all you need to convert someone is to share information. I had no problem reciting the eschatological timeline. I could produce all the texts that proved why we were God's church and others were not. This is dangerous, not because prophetic information is not good, but because when conversion has not happened, knowledge can be used as a club, even if in your own private life you are struggling with sin. Ellen White writes what happens in an unconverted heart: "There need to be far more lessons in the ministry of the Word of true conversion than of the arguments of the doctrines. For it is far easier and more natural for the heart that is not under the control of the Spirit of Christ to choose doctrinal subjects rather than the practical. There are many Christless discourses given no more acceptable to God than was the offering of Cain. They are not in harmony with God."[5]

The final challenge we will look at is the fact that knowledge without power makes secondary issues primary. The greatest church battles I encountered growing up and that second-generation Adventists often still face in immigrant churches are secondary issues: hair length for guys, movie theater attendance, and whether jeans are appropriate attire for church. These were long battles and lively discussions, always followed by more rules and less freedom. When we make *everything* a sin, eventually *nothing* becomes a sin. It seems to me that the greatest questions of life are often left unattended, especially the most important one: how to develop a saving relationship with Jesus Christ. It was not until I was a junior in college that I understood that concept and gained the knowledge of a loving Savior.

> *When we make everything a sin, eventually nothing becomes a sin.*

One day when I was a kid, a well-intentioned parishioner gave me a bag of green army soldiers. The bag probably contained a hundred of them. As a young boy, that was heaven. I started playing war immediately. When my parents came home and saw what was happening, they were disappointed. They asked me to get some scissors and proceeded to lecture me on the evils of war, and they cut off all the guns from the soldiers. They encouraged me to become a medical missionary as they handed over all the green soldiers, with missing limbs. I am convinced my parents did what they thought was right. They loved me and wanted to see me in heaven, and went about it the best they knew how. Yet, the reality of the Christian experience teaches us that the key to conversion is to bring Jesus into our hearts. Our efforts should be dedicated to that end, because when that happens, real transformation takes place.

> *Grace is transformational.*

It seemed to me that people in my church (and sometimes in my house) were more interested in compliance, even if conversion did not happen. As long as you looked the part, you were accepted. Fear was used as a motivator to change. Jesus is after character transformation, not just compliance to the rules. Grace, thus, is not only a mental experience. Grace is transformational. God's grace frees us to be happy and healthy followers of Jesus Christ.

New worship approaches, or churches to reach the second generation

If we are serious about attracting and keeping the second generation, we need to look at a variety of approaches. In this section, we will examine three such approaches.

Incorporation churches: These are "country of origin" language churches that seek to incorporate this group in their present structure. For example, singing some of the songs in English, having the sermon translated via headphones, having a monthly youth day where they are responsible for the service. These churches are intentional in assigning leadership positions for people of the second generation. This works well as long as the pastor has that vision. When a pastoral change is made, the direction of the church can be affected.

Individualization churches: Another approach is to start an alternate worship service, sometimes called youth church. The youth have leadership responsibilities, and the whole service is in English. The risk for this approach is the pushback from members who prefer traditional services in both form and language. They have "spies" that go to the youth service and continually complain about what they experience, even though the service is not for them.

Independence churches: This, to me, is the most successful way of reaching this generation. In one of my previous assignments, we started three such churches. They quickly transitioned from being just second-generation churches to multicultural churches. There are a number of such Seventh-day Adventist congregations in the North American territory. Here is a sampling:

- Mosaic, Hillsboro, OR: http://mosaicadventist.com/
- Impact, Collegdale, TN: https://www.facebook.com/ImpactSDA Church?ref=br_tf
- Resurrection, West Covina, CA: http://resurrectionsda.org/
- Arise, Silver Spring, MD: http://www.arisesda.com/
- Zion, New York, NY: https://www.facebook.com/ZionSDA?fref=p -b&hc_location=profile_browser
- Epic, Chicago, IL: http://epicwiredsda.com/
- Ignite, Kendale Lakes, FL: http://www.myignitechurch.org/
- Remix, Portland, OR: http://remixadventist.com/

Two characteristics are common in all of these churches: They minister to a younger and multicultural crowd, and many of the congregations are less than ten years old.

Moving forward

Starting such churches takes planning, and often you will find resistance. If you want to have a successful plant, keep the following in mind.

Expect resistance: I have not come across many of these churches (or any church plants for that matter) that have been started with complete acceptance. It is safe to say that not only are they opposed, but they experience a higher level of opposition from church members that are concerned about music and their own youth leaving. Often the question is, "Why do we need another church?"

Expect lack of commitment: It is naïve to expect a generation that has been told for so many years to stay on the sidelines to suddenly understand what it takes to play the game. Most of these churches take years to develop leaders. Do not get frustrated by the lack of buy-in. Continue to train and empower.

Many of them have been hurt or neglected by the church of their parents.

Expect slower growth: Hispanic and other first-generation churches usually experience rapid growth. This diminishes in the second generation. I have been tracking them for over fifteen years and have not seen one explode with growth. Yet, most of them have grown, stabilized, and are winning their peers who count themselves in some of the least-reached demographics in North America. Keep looking for ways to do evangelism.

Expect mistrust: It takes time to gain their trust. Many of them have been hurt or neglected by the church of their parents. It takes longer to trust. Millennials have unprecedented access to information and believe they are as much of an expert as any adult in a particular topic. You do not get their trust; you must earn it by having patience and deep relationships, and by backing up what you say.

Expect conversions: Most of the churches I have been tracking have experienced real, unchurched conversions—not just biological or transfer growth. Seeing someone come to faith in Jesus is a wonderful experience, but time is needed.

Final thoughts

We have discussed ways to reach the second generation and also shared challenges of planting such congregations. Hopefully, you or someone close to you will get the vision to plant churches to reach this demographic. There are many reasons why to plant such churches; but before you do, here are five reasons why not to. Do not plant:

- in order to "show them" how it is supposed to be done;
- if you want to be the boss;
- if you think it would be nice to try this;
- if your spiritual life has been down for a while;
- if your personal life is strained at the moment.

I invite you to consider the second generation. If you have them in your church or community, listen to them. Ask them for their input and offer to partner with them. Once you have developed a relationship of trust, you can explore various possibilities. In some instances, their needs can be met in existing congregations. In other instances, it may be best to plant a new congregation.

---

1. Virgilio Elizondo quoted in Daniel A. Rodriguez, *A Future for the Latino Church: Models for Multilingual, Multigenerational Hispanic Congregations* (Downers Grove, IL: IVP Academic, 2011), 305, 306, Kindle.

2. Ed Stetzer, "Missing the Mission: Looking for the Right Results While Loving the Wrong Things," *Christianity Today*, May 9, 2013, http://www.christianitytoday.com/edstetzer/2013/may/missing-mission-looking -for-right-results-while-loving.html.

3. Max Lucado, *Grace: More Than We Deserve, Greater Than We Imagine* (Nashville, TN: Thomas Nelson, 2012), 45, Kindle.

4. Larnelle Harris, "Were It Not For Grace," from the Album *First Love* (Brentwood, TN: Brentwood, 1998), accessed January 7, 2015, http://youtu.be/ViuXiqNr94o.

5. Ellen G. White, *The Voice in Speech and Song* (Boise, ID: Pacific Press®, 1988), 342, 343.

Community Engagement: Fulfilling the Mission

CALVIN B. PRESTON[1]

Jesus Christ had a special sense of mission for the poor and oppressed. In His love and compassion, He embedded Himself in the midst of the poor, tending to their needs while teaching them God's love. He demonstrated sympathy, care, sensitivity to their needs, and urgency in responding to them. He is our truest and surest Example of how to serve the poor in urban outreach ministry and community service. His love beckons us into the activity of service in urban mission work.

How do we implement Jesus' care for the poor? The 2,500-member West End Seventh-day Adventist Church in Atlanta, Georgia, contemplated that question. Our method of facilitating outreach in the community needed to be reinvigorated with a focused and intentional method that was wholistic and empowering in its approach of providing services to the community. With a history of more than thirty years in the West End community, it has been the custom of our church to follow the traditional approach of delivering services to people perceived to be in need. That approach has worked in the past; however, now less than 1 percent of the congregation resided in a fifteen-mile radius of the church. We realized that, aside from the obvious visible clues of a community ravaged by urban blight, the West End church had to find a better way to gauge the pulse of the local community, whose current dynamics were quite different from when the church was built three decades ago.

A changing community

In order to fulfill our mission, we had to understand the nature of our community. The history of the West End community since the mid-twentieth century has been one of struggle and determination. It is a historic enclave nestled in the shadows of Atlanta, the ninth largest city in the United States, with an estimated population of 5.5 million people. And in this "city too busy to hate," a reference to Atlanta's eventual rise above racism, discrimination, and economic oppression after the Civil Rights Movement, there are tens of thousands of people who live in the midst of despair and hopelessness. Today, the West End community is rife with social decay that is evident to any passerby—vacant and abandoned properties, brownfields, food insecurity, high unemployment, crime, low-income and fragmented families, high rates of teenage pregnancy, high dropout rates among African American males, increased school closures, rampant drug use, and increasing concentrations of HIV/AIDS transmissions. And, situated in the heart of this demographic of poverty is the West End Seventh-day Adventist Church.

> *Our congregation had the option to continue with minimal involvement or consider other opportunities.*

What role had the West End church played in the life of this community? At best we had established a marginal relationship with our community. Our congregation had the option to continue with minimal involvement or consider other opportunities.

The biblical imperative

What is our church to do with the simple, yet profound, directive that Jesus Christ issued to the disciples, "A new command I give you: Love one another. As I have loved you, so you must love one another" (John 13:34, NIV)? While that may seem simple and easy to fulfill, the reality is that a church has to establish a solid spiritual foundation for its outreach ministry.

The theological framework that undergirds the West End church's community engagement strategy is the love of Christ in action. Love and compassion, if properly organized and implemented, become the transforming agenda for urban ministry. The urban landscape is changing, and urban ministries are at a crossroads. If the church is to be an effective agent of compassion and justice, Robert Lupton notes, we must change our strategies.[2]

Christ's love is the sword of the Spirit that goes before us in the treacherous battlefield. The enemy of God desires to find *the called* caught off guard and unmindful of his cunning debauchery, trickery, and vile wickedness, and he will make every attempt to prevent God's Word from entering the environments that need it most. Urban ministry may lead *the called* into some deep, dark, seedy places into which God's children usually do not go. Or there may be the one-on-one encounter with an individual whose life is so muddled with demonic spirits that almost nothing can penetrate the hopelessness surrounding the person.

Implementing the imperative

In the last three years, our congregation has focused on evangelism and community outreach as mandates of the Great Commission. God has given us the divine directive to use spiritual gifts of the church to fulfill His mission. We asked the Holy Spirit for guidance on how particular gifts should be utilized in the church to witness in the worldwide mission field as well as in local communities. When the mission involves service to the local community, leaders must seek divine guidance on how best to utilize those gifts to meet the community needs.

We acquired an adjacent three-acre property, formerly operated by the West End Salvation Army Boys' and Girls' Clubs, containing a tennis court and a 22,000-square-foot (2,400-square-meter) facility. We renamed the complex the West End Family Life and Community Center (also known as WE Center). The new community center's planning committee determined that the services to the community needed to be reevaluated and reinvigorated with a mission statement, a focused and intentional plan of action, and an organizational structure that allowed for the solicitation of funds from various sources. In order to fulfill the mission of the center, we established a board of directors with a diverse knowledge base. The board of directors

> *The concept of community engagement operating in the context of Christian love and compassion is simple, but far-reaching.*

included individuals gifted with teaching, charity, compassion, law, and administration. The board worked fervently and expeditiously over the course of a year to build a consensus among community constituents and business consultants regarding the types of programs the WE Center would offer. The board solicited administrative, technological, and program resources within and outside the church. The mission statement reflects the depth and breadth of the center's ministry: "West End Family Life and Community Center, known as the 'WE Center,' is a faith-based program sponsored by West

End Seventh-day Adventist Church. Our mission is to provide effective educational, social, spiritual, and recreational programs that enhance the quality of life for youth and adults of the West End and surrounding community."

The concept of community engagement operating in the context of Christian love and compassion is simple, but far-reaching. Church members who work in community outreach, particularly in urban settings, are essentially agents of change involved in the ongoing process of defining, assessing, and monitoring community needs while garnering resources to implement the necessary change in the community. The goal is to enrich the community by building internal and external relationships with entities or individuals who have access to resources.

The WE Center's community strategic plan includes the following steps:

- Determine the goals of the plan
- Establish a target audience and territory
- Develop engagement strategies with the familiar
- Develop engagement strategies with the unfamiliar
- Prioritize the engagement events
- Create an implementation plan
- Audit the progress
- Maintain all relationships

The process of community engagement is cyclical and demanding. It requires strenuous effort and time. It is high maintenance with a profit margin of nil. After all, the goal is not to make money but to embed the gospel on the urban battlefields for the Lord's glory.

How we proceeded

With the acquisition of the facility, our leaders needed to further determine how to meet the needs of the community. It was incumbent upon the church to build genuine relationships with individuals and families in the community; discover the specific needs of the community; provide common ground for creating solutions to those needs; and offer opportunities for restoration, renewal, and life-changing strategies for the poor, who quite often find themselves hungry, homeless, sick, imprisoned, vulnerable, lost, and alone. With the acquisition of the building, we had the opportunity of providing ongoing programs in the urban mission field of the West End community.

The WE Center offers a wholistic approach to ministering to community needs and seeking to nurture the whole person—physical, spiritual, and mental—of all ages. In a few years, we have made a large impact on the community. As with most large urban areas, the needs of the poor and downtrodden are often forgotten. However, in our community, the center is recognized as a caring institution that is vital to the health and well-being of local residents.

> *As with most large urban areas, the needs of the poor and downtrodden are often forgotten. However, in our community, the center is recognized as a caring institution that is vital to the health and well-being of local residents.*

Our center is mission driven, but we also recognize the need to seek community input. In order to hear from the community, the center organized a series of interactive neighborhood meetings and focus groups. We also did a community feasibility study to determine how best to serve the community's needs. The feedback from these sessions has proven beneficial on several levels.

First, the feedback and statistics regarding the community helped determine our target audience, and the specifics of our programming. Relying on a combination of community feedback and U.S. Census Reports, the committee concluded that our target audience would be seniors, youth, and families. Demographic data indicated important information about the majority of households within the center's region: the predominant racial group was African-American; most heads of households earned incomes that were at or below the national poverty level; many households that consisted of dependents under the age of eighteen years old were headed by single females; and, based on high school graduation rates, the education levels were low.

Second, the feedback from the community engagement sessions helped us understand that there were three basics we needed to address: education, health and wellness, and recreation. Community stakeholders expressed specific issues they believed pervade our community: gangs, drugs, school delinquency, property crimes, family violence, food shortage, and health disparities. The following programs were suggested:

- Senior citizen day program
- Summer camp
- After-school program
- Spanish classes
- Computer technology training classes
- Health and wellness seminars

- Fitness boot camp
- Soup kitchen
- Community food pantry
- Community garden
- Clothes closet

At our grand opening, we inaugurated several of these programs, keeping in mind that we would later expand into other areas.

Once we had a better understanding of the community's profile, we completed additional assessments. The church leadership and the center's board of directors utilized three important tools to gain an understanding of the compatibility of outreach services to community needs.

The first tool involved the preparation of the case study of the WE Center by an external consultant.[3] This assessment included research of the center's community development to be served by the center. In addition, it contained data about local feeder schools, businesses, funding, and the organization's programming. The final recommendations of the case study to the West End church and board of directors were (1) to fill the void of services to the community left open by the abrupt departure of Salvation Army Boys' and Girls' Clubs; (2) to ascertain input from community stakeholders to create short- and long-range plans; (3) develop programs germane to needs of the community; and (4) seek sufficient funding to avoid unpredictable economic collapse.

The second tool that provided insight on the needs of the community involved the collaboration of a focus group consisting of key members and constituents living or doing business in the community. Participants were primarily members of the Beecher Donnelly Neighborhood Association, a network of homeowners.

The third tool helped us understand the psychological and anthropological roots of just how pervasive poverty was in the community. It was to help us effectively interact with people of varying cultures and socioeconomic backgrounds, specifically in the context of human resources, nonprofit organizations, and government agencies whose staff interact with individuals of different cultures or ethnic backgrounds. The knowledge gained from this study was critical for many reasons. First, the West End church has a majority of upper-middle-class African American congregations where approximately more than 65 percent of the parishioners have attended and/or graduated from institutions of higher learning. Great care was taken not to assume specific characteristics based on shared racial identification. So, there were some clear educational, economic, and other cultural disparities between the church and the community that it aimed to serve. The cultural competence research offered particular dimensions for us to be attentive to in our planning and delivery of services:[4]

- A cognitive component that emphasized critical awareness of biases and knowledge pertaining to a group's history, religion, and beliefs
- A behavioral component that emphasized the ability to put skills into practice to build trust and effectively communicate with and serve diverse families and children
- An organizational component that emphasized contextual issues and support for culturally competent practices from an organization that is committed to diversity and innovation to meet the needs of diverse families and children

Ministry in action

It is important to understand the biblical imperative, study the community, listen to the community, and organize the church, but then we must ask, What has happened? How have we responded? Below is a snapshot of the progress that has occurred during a twelve-month period:

Youth served in the after-school program	270
Youth served in summer camp	120
Seniors served in the day program	350
Persons enrolled in computer training	70
Persons enrolled in the Spanish class	35
Food distributed	45,000 lbs.
Pieces of clothing distributed	5,000
Persons enrolled in fitness boot camp	75
Number of meals served	4,800
Persons attended health and wellness seminar	200

How well is the center doing? Statistics are an important indictor, but they are only one indicator. Behind each statistic is a story.

I recall a specific incident when a woman ran in to the center one Tuesday morning. It was the beginning of the school year, and parents needed food and clothes for school-age children. The staff presumed she came for food; however, from the moment she entered the building, a cloud of desperation surrounded her. She was panting and speaking so erratically that no one could make out what she was saying. She kept looking at the door, as if she were being chased. The staff and I realized that this desperate woman was not present for any of our offerings that day. I invited her into the family counseling office, where the executive director and a camp counselor prayed with her.

The staff and I realized that this desperate woman was not present for any of our offerings that day.

The mother was at her breaking point. Single, four children, unemployed, no health insurance, no income resources to pay the rent or restore her electricity, which had been terminated two weeks earlier. With no one to help, she left her house and started walking with no particular destination. Her oldest daughter followed the mother as she walked angrily and aimlessly through the crime-riddled neighborhood. When she reached the four-way intersection that converges at the center, she entered the building, not knowing what it was. She only knew that there were people there and maybe there was someone in the building who could help her.

She was desperate and had concluded that her parental role was hopeless and her children did not need her. A spirit of violence had overtaken the oldest daughter—fighting with her mother, siblings, and strangers who looked at her indifferently. In the last year, she had been suspended from school numerous times. Upon attempting to register her daughter for high

With no one to help, she left her house and started walking with no particular destination.

school, she was told by the school administrators that the daughter would not be able to register at any city public school without securing an assessment from a child psychologist. After one hour of talking and praying with this woman, I asked to schedule an appointment with her daughter. Unknown to the staff and me, the young girl sitting in the parking lot was her daughter. Her mother and I urged the girl to come inside. I spoke casually to the young girl, as if she was my own daughter, and I asked her about the fighting.

Eventually, the teenage girl, whose self-esteem was nonexistent, confessed that she believed they never had enough food and that fighting protected her from being picked on by children because she was so poor. All of this had driven her mother to the brink of giving up on life and her children.

Our team spent more than two hours with them. We provided clothes, school supplies, and food. But more importantly, when she left the center, there was a smile on her face. God is happy when we put smiles on His children's faces.

Conclusion

The success of our community outreach programs rests largely on the church's adherence to biblical principles. The Word of God tells us to "write the vision, and make it plain upon tables, that he may run that readeth it. For the vision is yet for an appointed time, but at the end it shall speak, and not lie: though it tarry, wait for it; because it will surely come, it will not tarry" (Habakkuk 2:2, 3, KJV). The West End Seventh-day Adventist Church is engaged in doing just that. We developed a strategy for evangelism through community outreach (plan of action), devised a means of implementation (execution), and coordinated a vitally important part of connecting the plan to the community: promoting the vision to the community at large. We operate the center in order to fulfill our mission, and God has blessed. With God's blessing, our church has become a "center of influence" where residents, schools, colleges and universities, entrepreneurs, business owners, city officials, and others seek to align with our core Adventist values and partner with us in accomplishing community outreach.

> *God is happy when we put smiles on His children's faces.*

No two communities are alike. Your community may be very different from ours, but your community has needs. What are those needs? And most importantly, how can your church fulfill those needs?

---

1. I want to thank Hermina Glass-Hill for her valuable assistance in writing this chapter.

2. Robert D. Lupton, *Compassion, Justice and the Christian Life: Rethinking Ministry to the Poor* (Ventura, CA: Regal Books, 2007).

3. David Mitchell, "Case Study for the West End Family and Community Center," presented October 2011.

4. Esther Calzada, *Enhancing Cultural Competence in Social Service Agencies: A Promising Approach to Serving Diverse Children and Families,* Office of Planning, Research, and Evaluation at the U.S. Department of Health and Human Services, March 31, 2014, http://www.acf.hhs.gov/opre.

 LEADERSHIP

Pastors build a church vision and equip members to learn, grow, and serve.

Descriptors of Leadership include:
• promotes a clear, written strategy for the church
• delegates effectively
• models servant-leadership
• inspires excellence
• makes wise decisions
• faithful in conference support
• assesses and nurtures local church leadership
• motivates members to use their best gifts
• fosters spiritual maturity
• champions Adventist education

Pastoral Leadership in the Large Congregation

ALEX BRYAN

The platform in the church where I am currently the pastor has as much square footage as the sanctuary of my first district. The choir loft in my current church holds more chairs than the auditorium of my first church. This past Sabbath during my sermon, I turned around to face a robed choir and looked into as many faces as I typically did facing forward into the congregation of my first pastorate. There is no getting around the fact that I now pastor in a very different environment.

The truth is, I have invested about half of my twenty-two-year pastoral career in a small church setting and the other half in a large church setting (my first church claimed fewer than 90 members; my current church greater than 2,400). There are many similarities in both contexts; there are also many differences. The purpose of this chapter is to consider the work of pastoral ministry in the larger church context. Having said that, I believe the challenges and opportunities described in the pages that follow provide lessons for all congregational life: large, medium, and small.

Before we explore pastoral leadership in a large church context, a couple things need to be said at the outset.

First, pastoral work in a large congregation is not more (nor is it less) important than in a small congregation. The common progression, where inexperienced ministers are placed in smaller contexts and then receive "calls" to larger and larger congregations over a career, may have something to do with growing maturity, pastoral skill, or preaching acumen. But it certainly does not mean a "move up" to a better or more significant responsibility. There are, in fact, seasoned, first-rate quality ministers who spend an entire career in smaller congregations. This should be appreciated, and celebrated.

Second, there are many professional functions that really *do not change* very much from small congregations to large: weddings, funerals, baptismal studies, grief counseling, conflict resolution, Bible study, and prayer, just to name a few. I think, too often, that those who minister in very large or very small congregations fail to appreciate just how much we all have in common. The tragedy of a fatal car accident, the loneliness of divorce, news of a cancer diagnosis, dark feelings of guilt or shame, persistent doubts about the existence of a good God, wavering hope that our children will turn out OK—human beings are all the same, whether they worship in a room of seventy or seven hundred.

Having established that ministry, large or small, has equal value and that all pastors hold much in common, we can now move to the unique pastoral work of ministry to the larger congregation. A colleague who once pastored a small church but now ministers in a "mega-church" environment once said, "Night and Day. The two assignments are dramatically different."

I agree.

So how is pastoral work in a large church so different? What makes it decidedly unique? There are, it seems to me, at least six particular and consequential realities of pastoral leadership in the large church setting. They are:

- Sermonic expectation
- Staffing requirement
- Communication complexity
- Member care limitation
- Operational sophistication
- Global participation

I will write about these from my own experiences, nourished, of course, by countless personal conversations with Adventist ministers who serve in similar arenas, and further fortified by two-and-a-half decades of reading about professional ministry.

Sermonic expectations

First, the work of preaching is *notably different* in a larger church. This all starts with a congregational expectation: for better or worse, congregations with a more numerous membership have come to expect (even demand) higher quality preaching. I do not simply mean that they anticipate good theology or doctrinal accuracy. This minimal standard is, of course, true. The *norm* I am referring to has to do with them requiring evidence—clear evidence in the pulpit on Sabbath mornings—of consequential, foundational study, careful theological preparation, substantial reading, and skillful, artistic design of a sermon manuscript, which produces a half-hour of *wow*.

I do not mean to say that the larger the congregation, the larger the expectation of *entertainment*. I do mean to say, however, that large churches anticipate that the weekly sermon will be well thought out, make logical sense, and include a story, with regular opportunities to think, laugh, cry, feel, and be challenged. Many such congregations have come to expect either a masterful manuscript, read with poetic eloquence, or a memorized sermon, free of notes. Let me repeat what I have said already: I do not believe these congregants are sinfully shallow, salivating over their rightful meal of thirty minutes of delicious religious entertainment. Sure, there may some unhealthy desires. But generally, I recognize that Adventist Christians in general appreciate effective public communication (*who*, not what, is the draw at camp meetings), and this is heightened on a weekly basis in the large membership church. We can judge this expectation as good, bad, or neutral; but what we *cannot say* is that this anticipation does not, in fact, exist. Big churches want big sermons.

> *Allow God to use you powerfully. Work to faithfully steward the precious minutes you have, standing before God's people with purpose and grace.*

What this means is that a preacher's homiletical labor is much more demanding in a church of many than in a church of few. All preachers experience significant stress related to the weekly demands of pulpit performance. But in my experience, enriched by many conversations with pastors of both small churches and large, those who stand in front of large crowds every seven days experience a level of parish pressure *unlike* that of the small congregation preacher.

So, what is the pastor of the five hundred-plus congregation to do with this considerable demand? Two words: *embrace it*. Allow God to use you powerfully. Work to faithfully steward the precious minutes you have, standing before God's people with purpose and grace. Demand a budget for resources. Insist upon at least sixteen to twenty hours for sermon-related preparation each week. Make it your best time. Guard it ruthlessly. Listen to other great preachers. Attend preaching seminars. Pace yourself. Figure out the Sabbaths you *must* be in the pulpit and the seasons you can and *must* regroup. Recognize that in the larger church settings many, if not most, will assume your role as preacher is most important, and it will certainly be true that the sermonic half-hour will be the largest and most consistent interaction you have with the vast majority of your members. Do not forget this: you will likely *never* invest thirty personal minutes in the lives of many of your congregation. But you can give them this investment every week, each Sabbath. So give it your best! Rise to the occasion, admitting the reality of the sermonic demand.

Staffing requirements

To many, the presence of a "church staff" may seem like a luxury, both for a congregation and for the senior pastor. It is true that having more than one pastor *spreads the load* of pastoral work, bringing relief to any one minister, and greater care to the parish. However, statistical analysis often shows that a "number of church members per pastor" ratio actually demonstrates that those who pastor larger congregations often hold a *greater burden*. In my present context, for example, the ratio of church member to pastor in the local conference is 360:1, while the ratio at our church is 480:1. This does not include the presence of some 1,400 college students, many of whom utilize our church for worship and fellowship and avail themselves quite liberally (to our joy) of pastoral life coaching, Bible study, and pre-marriage counseling.

There is an additional issue with a church staff that likely includes both trained pastors and also a number of locally employed support staff. This could include office manager, bookkeeper, custodian, facility director, communications coordinator, worship director, technology coordinator, and so on. It requires support, accountability, and coordination to work effectively as a team. In my current context, the church has about a dozen full-time employees and a number of additional part-time employees. What does this mean? It means *work.*

The senior pastor of a large congregation is a team leader. This, at a minimum, means administering a weekly staff meeting, where each person participates in review and planning of the considerable ministry operations of the church. But more than this, each member of the team requires one-to-one communication and support outside a formal collective staff meeting, where both encouragement and accountability are provided. I will be the first to confess failure in achieving the full possibilities of this work. Yet, I am continually reminded of the importance of a senior pastor's investment in associate pastors and general church staff. In recent days, I have committed more time to eating, playing, planning, and praying with the church staff with the intention of boosting their own satisfaction in ministry. In turn, the communal happiness and missional success of the congregation increases. The large church simply cannot be healthy without a healthy church staff, and this requires the purposeful and substantial intention of the lead pastor.

Communication complexity

Another challenge in the larger congregation is the ability of the church administration to effectively communicate with the members. The difficulty is twofold.

First, in a big church much more is going on. There are numerous weekends that so many events are happening that I am not even aware of them all. It is not unusual for twenty or thirty ministry gatherings of some sort to be going on within a forty-eight-hour window. This does not include twenty-plus Sabbath School classes and multiple worship services each week. When I pastored a small congregation, almost every event was church-wide. Everyone was invited and everyone knew about it. An event would be announced from the front with little else to clutter the airwaves. The large church is quite different. I can say with confidence that 95 percent of what we do is *never* included in a worship service announcement, and 50 percent of what we do is *never* included in the church bulletin. And, to be honest, much of what is placed in the church bulletin gets lost in the myriad of other items calling for the church's attention. Because a lot is going on, it is frequently a challenge to know if the right things are being communicated to the right people in the right way.

Second, in a big church you wish to connect with a sizable number of people. Communicating to such an expansive and diverse audience carries its own considerations. Where do people actually find out about this or that? I am often discouraged by ignorance to a particular initiative or opportunity on the part of a church member. Do people read the bulletin? Who is on Facebook? Twitter? Instagram? Who actually reads their e-mail or newsletter? Can we even afford such a mass mailing? What about posters, bulletin boards, flyers? Flat screens in the church? PowerPoint? What ought we to communicate in the small amount of time we have inside the worship hour? And, what should the senior pastor announce from the front?

Communication in the large congregation is complex: first, because so much is going on and, second, because there are so many ears to consider. I openly acknowledge that there is much work we need to do in this area. There are a couple of conclusions I have landed upon that may be of some use to you.

First, I am convinced that the way people receive information has changed dramatically in the past few years, and this impacts the large congregation much more than the small congregation. I believe printed bulletins, brochures, e-mails, mailed newsletters, literature racks, and the like are declining in value. I believe announcements at the very beginning of the worship service have always (but now even more so) been quite limited in their value. On the other hand, I believe that social media, text messaging, image-rich and text-light posters, and announcements made *later* in a worship service have growing impact. The bottom line: the large church needs to have a conversation with the congregation to determine how they hear and *want* to hear information. I also believe people make decisions about participation in events quite late, and this requires greater innovation to make certain that reminders and invitations are sent out less than seventy-two hours from the experience.

Second, I believe we should communicate *more* about *less*. What do I mean? There may be a dozen fund-raising projects going on in the large church at any one time. There may be a dozen outreach projects, small groups, and "who knows what" in process. *And this goes on all the time.* It seems to me that pastoral leadership, in consultation with key leaders, needs to figure out how to communicate what is most important *to the exclusion* of what is less important. I do not mean that there is not a time and place to communicate all that is going on in the church. Rather, I am arguing that only the most critical projects, events, and initiatives should receive airtime in the worship service and the most prominent place in the various vehicles of communication. I have come to the conclusion that people can handle a limited amount of information related to fund-raising and fun-raising, and we need as much absence of clutter as possible.

> *Second, I believe we should communicate* more *about* less.

Member care limitations

This may seem like an obvious point, but perhaps more so to pastors than church members: it is impossible for the senior pastor of the large congregation to be in every hospital room, at every birthday party, in every living room, in the tank at every baptism, at the altar at every wedding, and at the graveside of every funeral. It is impossible, quite frankly, to know every name. The scope and scale of pastoral care in a bigger church is just that: it is bigger. There are at least twenty church members receiving chemotherapy in every given season. Someone is going through divorce. Someone has lost their job. Someone has lost their mother. Our staff reserves the first thirty minutes to an hour of our weekly staff meeting reviewing the many serious and dark valleys where our members currently walk.

So, how should the pastor of the larger congregation approach all of this?

Here are some suggestions:

First, it is important to *publicly acknowledge* certain realities of how pastoral care works and does not work. The congregation should know that it is illegal for hospitals to release information about patients in their care. Inform the church: *The only way your pastoral team will know if someone is in the hospital is if you tell them.* Church members should also have access to a phone number they can call to reach a pastor, and they should understand how quickly that call will be heard and addressed. The congregation should understand that each church member processes grief and difficulty uniquely: some will want to be mentioned from the front of the church and some will not. Some are private and some are not. *Do not assume silence on the part of the pastoral team to necessarily mean absence of care.* And there are many other things that can and ought to be communicated as well. If pastors clearly set expectations and follow through on those expectations, good care can be given and appreciated.

Second, a solid plan for "pastoral coverage" is in order. Some large churches have each member of the pastoral staff take "calls" for a week or more, passing the responsibility from pastor to pastor. We have chosen a different model, where one pastor serves as the church chaplain, overseeing the needs of the church, and coordinates with the other pastors to deal with situations as needed. The church chaplain also organizes about a dozen elders, who are on call to make visits in homes and hospitals. What is important is not so much the particular plan but that a clear and effective approach is in place to meet the needs of the congregation.

Third, if the preaching expectation for the senior pastor *rises* with the size of the church, I believe the chaplaincy role, by necessity, *eases* a bit. In other words, a large

> *My first ministerial director told me that* all *congregations want, first and foremost, two things: a good preacher and* a pastor who actually likes them.

church basically understands that "the pastor" cannot be everywhere. This does not mean, however, that the senior pastor can afford to be viewed as aloof or removed from the congregation. My first ministerial director told me that *all* congregations want, first and foremost, two things: a good preacher and *a pastor who actually likes them.* I have made it a practice to make the rounds Sabbath mornings. That is, between our two major worship services, I visit every Sabbath School class, just walking around, connecting, saying

Hello. There is something about "being seen" that is important. Members of a large congregation generally understand the reality that you may never spend four hours with them at a dinner table. But they do want to have looked you in the eye, exchange greetings, see you with people, and serve—particularly in places where they live.

Operational sophistication

I have managed to write this chapter so far without talking about *management.* I confess a love-hate relationship with business language and practice as it relates to the church. On the one hand, I wish to scream, "This is not a business, it's a church!" But then I also recognize that the church can learn a lot from a well-run organization of any kind, including business. There is no avoiding the reality that *all churches* are businesses. We have budgets, buildings, and employees to which we must attend. We have systems and structures to manage. This reality is not secular; it is sacred. We are stewards of the resources God has given us.

The large congregation is, plain and simple, a small to medium-sized business operation. Nearly four million dollars passed through our accounting office last year. We have legal considerations ranging from taxes, insurance, employment, safety, and even (regretfully) sexual predator policies we have to write, review, and enforce. Our church is *a major convention center.* We hold more than two hundred events each year, ranging from several hundred to thousands of people. We have an equal number of additional gatherings with smaller numbers of people. Our facility is busy all the time. The operation of our physical plant includes complexities that rival many other denominational church facilities, including administrative offices, schools, media centers, publishing houses, and campgrounds. A small church may utilize their church building a day or two a week. The large church taxes its space seven days a week. My point is this: we must consider depreciation of equipment, renovation of physical space, landscaping, parking, utilities, and on and on. The senior pastor cannot ignore these considerations. The lead minister has an official, fiduciary responsibility to ensure the proper function of the church board, finance committee, church staff, and our relationship to the church at large. Pastoral work in a large church setting is deeply and persistently impacted by organizational considerations.

Global participation

We will review a final area of concern of the pastor of a large church. It is the considerable expectations and responsibilities that fall *outside the district.* I will speak briefly of these in two categories, leadership and preaching.

First, pastors of large congregations, not only senior ministers but also associate pastors, may be called upon to participate as leaders in the regional and global work of the Adventist Church. We are often called upon to sit on boards and committees. We are asked to serve the wider denomination with an investment of judgment, creativity, and care, not only in our areas but also in places beyond.

Large congregations also bare considerable responsibility in funding the work of the church through significant tithe contributions. This reality invites the large church to participate in shaping the future of the wider church. In my experience, it is important for the senior pastor to speak openly about the responsibility and joy of giving in this way. A large congregation can too easily feel "used" by the denomination. A lament I have heard is, "Pastor, they take our money and then they also take our pastor's time. How is this good or wise or fair?" We must respond to this concern. The pastor of the large congregation must articulate—at least once a year—the unique contribution their church makes to the global whole. I believe if the congregation understands the mission of the worldwide Adventist Church, they will embrace, with joy and unselfishness, the unique role they have been given.

> *Large congregations also bare considerable responsibility in funding the work of the church through significant tithe contributions. This reality invites the large church to participate in shaping the future of the wider church.*

Second, a pastor's preaching is a big part of this wider investment—one that takes considerable time and energy at the expense of the pastor's family. Pastors of large congregations are asked to speak for camp meetings and other convocations each year. We are invited to talk with other pastors at ministerial meetings, inspire teachers through our words at teacher conventions, and communicate with young people in a variety of worship and retreat settings. Here is the reality: *travel takes its toll.* It may well be an honor to be asked to preach for this event or that, but this does not remove the considerable investment that is made. Both the pastor and the local community share this sacrifice.

Pastoral work in the larger church context is almost always a calling to ministry both

> *The pastor of the large congregation must articulate—at least once a year—the unique contribution their church makes to the global whole.*

inside and outside the local parish. The pastor must be aware of the tension this creates in terms of time and energy resources, and also the communication required to inspire the church to its place in the sisterhood of Adventist fellowship.

Summary

Pastoral leadership in the larger church context is a rich blessing. In many important ways, it does not differ from ministry in the small congregation. There are significant differences. The demands upon the pastor of the large congregation are complex and many, the stressors are all too forceful and faithful, and the expectations are seemingly and systematically sky-high. All of this should create ample humility, calling upon God and my congregation for abundant and regular grace.

Pastors and Elders: Partners in Ministry

NIKOLAUS SATELMAJER

Today, church elders perform a pivotal function in Seventh-day Adventist churches. That was not so in the formative years: churches did not elect elders—only deacons were elected. In 1874, G. I. Butler, president of the General Conference of Seventh-day Adventists, defined in detail the work of the church elder. By 1885, the function of the elder was further clarified, and it has not changed much since then.[1]

Thousands of individuals function as church elders, and the denomination would suffer greatly without their leadership. Who are the elders? What expectations should we have of them? What do elders think their needs are? Once we explore these questions, we will focus on several functions of church elders that can greatly enhance the life and mission of a congregation.

Listening to elders

The work of the elder is just about as broad as that of a pastor. Similar to the pastor, they have responsibilities that cover most operations of the church. The breadth of these responsibilities may be one reason some elders get discouraged.

Elders can find what is expected from them in the *Church Manual* and *Elders Handbook*.[2] Various conferences also provide training seminars for elders, and many pastors tell elders what they expect from them. The church in North America also listened to the elders in an extensive survey conducted in 2014.[3] The survey showed that church elders are very interested in being effective in their role, and they welcomed training and resources. This survey will guide the development of resources for elders in the foreseeable future.

In this chapter, we will focus on selected roles of elders and how pastors and elders can work together to provide spiritual leadership to the congregation.

The focus will be on areas that can be implemented without extensive training or investment of funds but can be a positive impact on the congregation. What then can you, as pastor, do so that the elders will not only fulfill their responsibilities but also experience spiritual fulfillment in their lives?

Leadership

The exact leadership role of the elder depends on the church to some extent. Does the church have a full-time pastor, or does the pastor have several congregations? Whether the pastor has only one or more congregations, meetings between the pastor and elder or elders are necessary.[4] If such does not take place, most likely conflict will arise that will have a negative impact on the congregation.

Pastors and elders need to meet on a regular basis. Why even mention such meetings? Is it not done routinely? Surprisingly, I have found that in a significant number of congregations, it does not happen. All too often such meetings take place only when a problem arises. We will look at several kinds of meetings between the pastor and elders.

I accepted the invitation of a conference to relocate to a new church even though I knew in the recent past that the church had faced some serious issues. Once I arrived, it became obvious that the church was still experiencing challenges. What was I to do? How could we move forward? It was more out of desperation that I asked to meet with the elders. I decided to ask them three questions: In your opinion, what has happened in the church during the past five years? Where do you see the church five years from now? and What should be the presence of the denomination beyond the immediate area of our church? The responses from the elders were thoughtful and very helpful. Their input enabled us to deal with some of the issues from the past and, at the same time, look with positive anticipation to the future.[5] This discussion can be helpful at any time, but it is most helpful to have it near the start of your ministry in a church or district.

Regular meetings between the pastor and elders will enhance the ministry of both. Another time, my wife and I were elders of a large church with many elders. We met once a month on Sabbath morning. A group of elders was assigned to provide breakfast, and we usually had a presentation focusing on some aspect of elder ministry and also discussed ongoing events. We looked forward to these productive meetings and the fellowship with the group of elders.

Other churches find it helpful to have an elders meeting before a church board. Such meetings give the key leaders of the church an opportunity to discuss the agenda and be prepared for the church board meeting. If you have such meetings, the church board meetings will most likely be shorter—something that board members will appreciate. Some churches hold these elder meetings several days before the church board meeting, while others schedule them thirty or sixty minutes before the board.

Even if you have regular elder meetings, you will find that on each Sabbath items arise that need the attention of the pastor and elders. Early in my ministry, I was asked to be a guest speaker in a church. I noticed that before worship began the pastor had a very brief (about three minutes) meeting with the elders—all of the elders—not only those involved in that day's worship. In those few minutes, the pastor shared several items, such as those who were sick or some good happenings in the lives of members. The elders also shared items with the pastor—things he may not have known. I copied that concept and have used it ever since.[6] Those three minutes have been extremely productive in the churches I have pastored. In one church, the elders added a feature to the three-minute meeting. They suggested that at the end of the meeting we have a special prayer for the preacher of the day. Whenever I was the speaker, I felt that prayer was a blessing for me.

Worship

Sabbath worship can become such a routine event that it makes little impact on the congregation. On the other hand, if properly planned and coordinated, it will be a spiritual highlight for the members and a positive introduction to your visitors. In this section, we will focus on some actions pastors and elders can take in order to make worship a positive experience.

> *The time of welcoming and announcing—if done properly—is a congregation-building event.*

I have preached in hundreds of churches, and it is obvious that, in many churches, very little worship planning is done. It is not unusual to hear questions such as, What is the opening hymn? Do we have Scripture reading? Any prayer requests? and, my all-time favorite, "Do we have any announcements?" The last question is all too often followed by someone in the group saying, "I hope not—announcements just disturb worship." Disturb the worship? Really? How is it that welcoming a member who has been absent because of illness (or welcoming back a college student) is "disturbing" the worship? The time of welcoming and announcing—if done properly—is a congregation-building event. If, on the other hand, it is not planned, or if someone drones on with the announcements while the platform group is in the back and not hearing anything, it is a waste of time. Elders and pastors who plan the welcome and announcements create an experience of joyful togetherness in the congregation.

Most Seventh-day Adventist churches still have (though surprisingly some do not) Scripture reading. If done properly—coordinated with the sermon and not just a last-minute randomly chosen passage—it provides a blessing to the worshipers. I follow the practice of choosing passages from both of the Testaments and making certain that the reading includes a significant number of texts. Let the worshipers hear the Word of God. Bernhard Oestreich points out that Paul requested, on a number of occasions, that his epistles be read out loud.[7] At a time, when many—including our church members—do not read the Bible on a regular basis, let the Word be celebrated in our worship services. Just as we are generous with our dinner guests—offering to serve them more food—let us likewise be generous with the Word of God. Share it.

At a time, when many—including our church members—do not read the Bible on a regular basis, let the Word be celebrated in our worship services.

Prayer is a central part of Sabbath worship, yet in all too many congregations, it is not well planned. If not planned properly, it can be detrimental to worship; but if done well, it will be a highlight of the worship experience. Again, in churches where a few minutes before worship someone asks those leading in worship, "Who will do the main prayer?" this lack of planning is an invitation for potential problems. Advance planning helps the individual who will pray prepare and review prayer requests. In some congregations, prayer requests have become a long and rambling event and, unfortunately at times, embarrassing. In a congregation I was visiting, an elder took more than twenty minutes to ask the congregation if they had prayer requests. The entire congregation did not hear some of the prayer requests, and others crossed the line of what is appropriate. Some individuals gave very detailed information about the illness of a friend or family member. Others asked to remember—by name—some individuals who were having marital problems. The pastor and elders need to institute a system so that prayer requests are given to the one praying *before* worship begins and if the request is specific (illness, marriage, other personal issues), the person asking for the prayer should have permission to share the information. A similar policy needs to be followed for prayer requests listed in the bulletin.[8]

Church growth

All too often when evangelism or church growth is mentioned, we hear a chorus of what does not work. In this section, we will review two specific things that the pastor and elders can do for the congregation that have great potential for congregational growth.

Every profession and organization has its own language—a way of communicating. Have you ever listened to the communication between pilots and air controllers? It is important communication, but you have to spend some time listening to the conversations before you understand what is being said. Can you imagine the confusion first-time visitors encounter in some churches? It is tempting to assume that because we understand, everyone else understands. It is important that visitors understand the language we use in worship, Sabbath School, and all of our services.

Jesus is a good example of how to use language understood by all. His parables—as profound as they are—were told in a way that was easily understood. Even today—some two thousand years later—we understand His stories. Pastors and elders, as key leaders of the congregation, need to use easy-to-understand language. That in itself will go a long way to making our church events better appreciated. Visitors will feel comfortable. Pastors and elders also have the responsibility of working with other leaders so all visitors will understand us. Visitors who feel comfortable in our churches are more likely to return.

Church growth is vital for every congregation. Without growth, a congregation will dwindle and, sadly, someday disappear. All too often lack of finances is given as the reason why a church does not grow. I am suggesting that churches have potential for growth without major financial investment. Growth will happen if the leaders (I am thinking primarily of pastors and elders) become proactive in welcoming visitors.

Before discussing what can be done, churches need to avoid two extremes that are all too often practiced. In some churches, visitors are treated as if they do not exist; they come and leave without any personal contact with members—including a pastor or an elder. It is surprising how often that happens. The other extreme is asking every visitor to stand up and identify himself or herself—name, where are they from, the church they belong to, and so on. It is surprising how often that approach is used. It may be well intentioned, but the fact is that not every visitor wishes to give those details. Not every visitor is a member of another church. This approach scares some visitors, and they never come back.

I would like to suggest a way of welcoming visitors so that their privacy will be respected and yet meaningful contact will be made. Whether the pastor or elder does it, it is important to arrive early so that you can meet the very first visitor. I am not suggesting that you eliminate the greeters but that you become an additional person who will welcome the visitor. My pattern is to introduce myself and welcome them to the church. I then give them my card with my name on it, and I point out my phone numbers and e-mail, and invite them to feel free to contact me. By first sharing my information with the visitor, I find that they are willing to then share their information with me. During a one-year period, only one individual did not give me their contact information. The person kept coming back, though, and eventually did share their contact information. My suggestion is that initially the pastor and elders take on this special assignment and then train others. In multichurch districts, the pastor will need to depend on his or her elders, since the pastor will not always be present.

The idea of meeting visitors in the lobby of the church works well, but I have found something that is even more effective. I started meeting people on the sidewalk in front of the church (or in the parking lot). The members and visitors like this type of greeting, but I also started greeting community members who were just walking by the church. Over time, a number of the community members made it a point of greeting me and even stopping to talk with me. This, of course, works best in a city environment.

All too often predators look in churches for their next victim, and we must be proactive in protecting those in our care.

Protection and care for congregation

For several years, church leaders have been urged to focus on the protection of members, especially children, from predators. By now all churches should have adopted a policy and announced it to the congregation.[9] Some larger congregations have appointed specific individuals to care for these areas. Others have asked specific leaders to add this responsibility to their duties. Churches have also made their rooms safer, for example, by making certain that doors have glass inserts in them. Pastors and elders need to take an active interest in this important area so that our children and members are protected. All too often predators look in churches for their next victim, and we must be proactive in protecting those in our care.

Pastors and elders also need to protect the congregation from another source of ill will. Numerous individuals—many of them church members—are looking for churches to present their "special" programs or messages. Often these individuals will call someone in charge and try to convince that person that they want to come and help the congregation. Church leaders need to follow established policies of checking into prospective speakers and not only accepting the word of the one who wants to speak.[10] Similar caution should be exercised with materials sent to the church. Some dissident groups obtain mailing lists and send their material to specific church leaders. Just because the material is sent to the church does not mean it should be distributed. Recently, I came across a package of material in our church from an organization that is continually critical of the denomination. Such destructive material has no place in our churches. Pastors and elders need focus on the spiritual health of the members, by encouraging members to be faithful students of the Bible and not depend on individuals who prey on congregations.

> *Pastors and elders need focus on the spiritual health of the members, by encouraging members to be faithful students of the Bible and not depend on individuals who prey on congregations.*

Conclusion

From the first church I pastored to the last church I finished ministering to recently, I have been blessed with capable elders. They did not all possess the same talents, but they all were interested in the spiritual well-being of the congregation. Usually, our congregations choose responsible individuals to be elders, and pastors need to work closely with them. As pastors, we have the responsibility of not only working with the elders but also providing training and focusing on a team approach to ministry.

1. *Seventh-day Adventist Encyclopedia,* s.v. "Church Elders." This entry provides a helpful history of the church elder.

2. See *Seventh-day Adventist Church Manual,* 18th ed. (Silver Spring, MD: General Conference of Seventh-day Adventists, 2010) and *Seventh-day Adventist Elder's Handbook* (Silver Spring, MD, Ministerial Association of the General Conference of Seventh-day Adventists, 2013). Both of these books are helpful in describing the elder's responsibilities. Elders will also find helpful information in *Elders Digest,* published quarterly by the Ministerial Association, General Conference of Seventh-day Adventists, and distributed to elders by many conferences, http://www.EldersDigest.org.

3. More than 1,100 elders and 400 ministers responded to the survey—making it probably the most extensive survey of elders. This survey is instrumental in the development of resources the church in North America is preparing.

4. Except for very small churches, most churches usually have more than one elder. In this chapter, I will usually refer to "elders," except when referring to the head elder.

5. After a helpful discussion with the elders, we decided to have a similar discussion with the church board and other key members.

6. I have made it a point to observe what others are doing and then ask myself if I could do it in my church. Our effectiveness is often increased by observation and not by innovation.

7. Bernhard Oestreich, " 'This Letter Be Read to All': A Strategy for Christian Unity," *Ministry,* June 2007.

8. Just because a person tells a pastor, church leader, or office secretary (or whoever does the bulletin) that they have a particular health issue does not mean they are giving permission for the illness to be listed. I have had instances where a member shared rather private information and it was listed in a draft of the bulletin. When I asked the bulletin person if permission was given to list it, the response was, "But they told me." Upon checking with the member, we found out that the member was horrified at the thought of listing it. What people share with us and what they want shared with others is not necessarily the same.

9. If you need assistance, contact your conference insurance/risk management department or visit Adventist Risk Management at http://www.adventistrisk.org for guidelines.

10. For church policy and guidelines, see the *Seventh-day Adventist Church Manual.*

Mentoring Ministers

STEVE D. CASSIMY

Mentoring, advising or training someone, if done properly, can benefit both the mentor—the one doing the mentoring—and the mentee—the one being mentored. The outcome depends on how mentoring is done and the attitude of the individuals involved. In this chapter, I will focus on both the mentor and the mentee.

Mentoring is not a new concept. It comes from Mentor, a figure from Greek mythology. Mentor was believed to be the guardian, protector, teacher, and father figure to the young and impressionable apprentice Telemachus while his father was away. Since that time, mentoring has continued to develop and expand. Linda Phillips-Jones states that "although mentoring happened through the centuries, the modern variety began in the 1970s and 1980s. Today, mentors are experienced people who go out of their way to (1) help you clarify your vision and personal goals and (2) build skills to reach them. They have power—through whom and what they know—to help you succeed."[1]

Mentoring can be effective in various professions, but in this chapter we are focusing on mentoring in ministry. We will explore various aspects of mentoring and show how it can be a blessing to the mentee, as well as the mentor.

Seventh-day Adventists and mentoring

Mentoring was not practiced in the early years of the Seventh-day Adventist Church. At first, the church did not have a formal ministerial training program; that was true of many denominations. Some individuals who wanted to be ministers started preaching and holding meetings without training or supervision. Others attached themselves to experienced ministers and learned from them.[2] This voluntary system was formalized by the introduction of training programs (early on it was often limited to short-term courses) and by assigning the inexperienced to work under the supervision of an experienced pastor. Even the current formal internship program the church has in North America still leaves room for mentoring, and many individuals benefit from such relationships.

Biblical examples of mentoring

The Bible, especially the New Testament, has examples of mentoring. During the New Testament period, those who wanted to become teachers, pastors, or evangelists often attached themselves to those more experienced. The New Testament examples give us helpful scriptural reasons for mentoring.

> *The Bible, especially the New Testament, has examples of mentoring.*

- Growth through mentoring: Mark writes, "And he [Jesus] ordained twelve, that they should be with him, and that he might send them forth to preach" (Mark 3:14).[3] The individuals chosen by Jesus were not religious leaders or teachers—most of them were fishermen. When they responded to the call from Jesus, they did not enter into a formal training; rather, they chose to be mentored by Jesus. Their attachment to Him was voluntary, and yet the outcome of the relationship had universal implications.
- Role-modeling: "But thou hast fully known my doctrine, manner of life, purpose, faith, longsuffering, charity, patience" (2 Timothy 3:10). Timothy was a witness to Paul's spiritual life and benefited from this experience. This passage shows that Timothy had the opportunity to mentor Paul's teachings, but it does not stop there. Timothy also had the opportunity to learn from Paul's manner of life, purpose, faith, longsuffering, love, and patience.
- Building relationships: Paul, probably the best-known gospel proclaimer, was open to learning from others. Luke tells us Aquila and Priscilla were not only fellow tentmakers but they took Paul "and expounded unto him the way of God more perfectly" (Acts 18:26). The relationship developed to the point that they invited Paul to their home. It was in that informal setting that this couple mentored Paul. If mentoring is to be effective, there has to be a relationship of trust between the parties. Paul's relationship with

Timothy shows the personal nature of the mentor and mentee. Paul writes, "Thou therefore, my son, be strong in the grace that is in Christ Jesus. And the things that thou hast heard of me among many witnesses, the same commit thou to faithful men, who shall be able to teach others also" (2 Timothy 2:1, 2). To Paul, Timothy was more than just a junior member of the team—Paul considered him to be a son.

- The transparency of the mentor: A mentor is not someone who is above others. Paul writes, "Now if I do that I would not, it is no more I that do it, but sin that dwelleth in me. I find then a law, that, when I would do good, evil is present with me" (Romans 7:20, 21). The mentor—just as much as the mentee—is a person who needs the Savior. The mentor, according to Paul, is not an absolute example to the one being mentored due to struggles in this life. Admitting sin in his life made Paul a more effective mentor.

- The mentor exhibits trust: According to Matthew 10:1ff, Jesus trusted the disciples and even gave them authority. The mentor will not always be with their mentees; therefore, there has to be a relationship of trust between those involved in this special relationship.

The New Testament does not mandate mentoring, but it gives us examples of the benefits of mentoring. One writer points out the benefits experienced by being a mentee: "A mentor brings out the best in you in three areas: your roles, your goals and your soul. Mentors give us perspective. They help us look at our ministry and ourselves from the outside. We don't always see what we are doing outside of our own perspective. We see from our own limited focus."[4] Certainly the relationship between Paul and Timothy is an example of Paul bringing out the best in Timothy's life. Yet, the purpose of mentoring is not only to make someone more productive—although that will probably occur—rather, it is to help the mentee develop in all areas of life.

> *Yet, the purpose of mentoring is not only to make someone more productive—although that will probably occur—rather, it is to help the mentee develop in all areas of life.*

There is one more important outcome of mentoring. Ministers know from firsthand experience that ministry "is a lonely profession. Pastors need a mentor/companion to view the situation from the outside, to note what good things are happening, and to offer perspective and prayer support."[5] In the mentoring partnership, both individuals benefit and both are strengthened.

Identifying an effective mentor

It is one thing to recognize the benefits of mentoring, but it is another to find someone who is an effective mentor. How do you find an effective mentor?

How do you find an effective mentor?

Finding an effective mentor is a challenge and cannot be done on the basis of whether you like or do not like someone. Based on my reading, listening to lectures, and reflecting, I am sharing what I believe are important characteristics of a mentor.

- Someone you admire: The mentor must not necessarily be popular. Yet, he or she must have winsome characteristics and accomplishments in ministry that appeal to the one looking for a mentor. This admiration must focus on the mentor's character and not the position the individual has obtained. Certain individuals may never achieve a "high" position, as defined by some, but the person has been faithful to God's calling. Such an individual is worthy of consideration to be your mentor.
- Someone who is trustworthy: Does the prospective mentor have the reputation of being trustworthy? What will the individual do if you share personal fears and doubts? Will he or she pray with you, listen to you, and help you work through fears and doubts? Or will the individual broadcast those fears and doubts?
- Someone whose experience you value: Experience is an essential quality in the mentoring process. The mentor should not only be experienced, but that experience should have significant value to the one looking for a mentor.
- Someone who listens actively: Active listening is a critical characteristic of mentors. An active listener will help you probe the issue under discussion. When the conversation is over, the mentee should have a sense that the mentor really heard what was being said.
- Someone with good communication skills: A good mentor must

have the ability to ask tactful, intelligent, open-ended questions. The questions, at times, must also be probing so that the mentee is challenged to think through the issues. A good communicator will also be able to guide the conversation into productive directions.

- Someone who can guide without directing: One of the key differences between mentoring and coaching comes from a statement made by one of the founders of the Coaching Movement. John Whitmore writes, "When I am mentoring, I'm teaching a person, letting him draw from me or learn from my experience. When I'm coaching, I'm pushing a person to draw from his/her own resources and experiences. Coaching is helping people learn instead of teaching them."[6] A coach or supervisor will often direct. A mentor, on the other hand, provides guidance.
- Someone skilled in searching for meaningful answers: In the process of mentoring, the mentor needs to create an environment where answers to questions are developed and eventually gained by the mentee. The mentor should provide guidance so that the answer will emerge in a natural way.
- Someone who will facilitate a growth partnership: This is a partnership in which both individuals benefit. Though the mentor is the person with more experience, both individuals should learn from each other.

Does the prospective mentor have the reputation of being trustworthy?

- Someone who will provide valuable input: The one looking for a mentor often has specific needs. Will the prospective mentor be able to address those needs? If your supervisors are suggesting a mentor, they also need to assess the strengths of the potential mentor in order to determine if the suggested relationship will be beneficial.
- Someone who cares and has good social skills: A mentor must exhibit good social skills and a deep level of care for the mentee.
- Someone who focuses on the needs of the other: If you are looking for a mentor, what goals do you have in mind? Does the individual whom you are considering understand those goals, and more importantly, will this individual help you achieve the goals?

Thomas W. Dortch Jr. provides a helpful summary: "All that is required is the commitment to make a difference, the willingness to listen and hear, and the discipline to balance your heart and your mind. Mentors are advocates, advisers, and role models."[7] These characteristics seem to be basic, yet are crucial and necessary in the life of a perspective mentor.

Harold E. Johnson gives a helpful description of an effective mentor: "To be an effective mentor take a look at your communication and relationship-building skills. The mentor, has to listen even to the unspoken message. For the mentor listening becomes an art. They listen dramatically. Certainly, listening-preparedness should be the first skill evaluated before a potential mentor is allowed to take on such a sensitive role."[8]

My mentor

A number of individuals have served as my mentors. I will focus briefly on my first mentor and some of the benefits I received from the relationship. R. O. A. Samms was a well-prepared and gifted minister who showed interest in my ministerial growth and development. I benefited in many ways from the relationship, but perhaps the greatest benefit to me was his willingness to invest his time and experience into my ministry. This willingness on his part was crucial for me in the early years of my ministry and was a statement of faith on his part. When he invested his time and experience, he had no guarantee of the outcome. I benefited greatly, and I believe I am a better minister for it. Because I benefited, those to whom I ministered also benefited. The impact of an effective mentor is far-reaching.

> *The impact of an effective mentor is far-reaching.*

If you are just starting in your ministry, look around you for a mentor. If you have been in ministry for some time, you will still benefit from a mentor's input. Dortch reminds us that a mentor "is someone whose achievements we admire and who inspires us to greatness. A role model is someone who we admire as a person and whose behavior, attitudes, and beliefs we emulate."[9] A mentor is not a hero whom we admire—a mentor is a role model.

Conclusion

The relationship between the mentor and the mentee is a special one. If properly done, it can be a blessing to both. If implemented haphazardly or if the wrong parties enter into the relationship, it may be harmful to both.

"Mentoring is a journey, a road you and the mentee travel together as you prepare the mentee for what lies ahead. And when the time comes for your paths to diverge, you will carry with you the profound satisfaction of knowing that you have earned a mentee's unconditional regard."[10] Though the relationship will change over the years, the benefits of the relationship will remain with both forever.

1. Linda Phillips-Jones, *The New Mentors and Protégés* (Grass Valley, CA: Coalition of Counseling Centers/ The Mentoring Group, 2001), 21.

2. See the chapter by Michael W. Campbell in this book for a review of ministerial training in the Seventh-day Adventist Church.

3. All biblical citations are from the King James Version.

4. Rick Warren, "Every Pastor Needs a Mentor," pastors.com, July 30, 2012, http://pastors.com/you -need-a-mentor-by-rick-warren/.

5. Daniel L. Wong, "Why Pastors Need Mentoring," academia.edu, accessed December 3, 2014, http:// www.academia.edu/5820059/WHY_PASTORS_NEED_MENTORING.

6. Tony Stoltzfus, *Leadership Coaching* (Wheaton, IL: Tyndale House Pub., Inc., 2005), 8, 10.

7. Thomas W. Dortch Jr., *The Miracles of Mentoring* (New York: Doubleday, 2000), 7.

8. Harold E. Johnson, *Mentoring For Exceptional Performance* (Glendale, CA: Griffin Publishing, 1997), 258–260.

9. Dortch Jr., The Miracles of Mentoring, 94.

10. Ibid., 129.

☑ WORSHIP

Pastors facilitate an enriched corporate worship experience that brings people into the presence of God.

Descriptors of Worship include:
• passionate preaching
• Christ-centered sermons are interesting, instructive, and inspire spiritual growth
• well-prepared creative programming
• ensures the creation of entry points (phone, Web, etc.) for an inviting church
• sensitive to the needs of a diverse audience

Bringing the Biblical Text to Life

C. WESLEY KNIGHT

People are tired of hearing sermons. I am a preacher, and even I am often tired of hearing sermons. I think one of the reasons why preaching is called "foolishness" is because we have been using an ancient text as the basis for our teaching, instruction, and encouragement. We have been preaching the same stories, poems, and letters, and we have to continue until Christ returns. How do you keep reading the same book and stay interested?

There are those who view the biblical text as irrelevant, at best, or a fable, at worst. For the preacher, this poses a challenge to the preacher's vocational calling to preach the gospel, and it also creates an existential challenge for the church. Yet the church is called to preach the good news, and that is why content *and* presentation are critical. But the challenge lies in our method of sharing that gospel. The question is, How can we make our preaching come alive? How do we make the biblical message relevant in the marketplace of ideas? I suggest that we begin by clarifying our definition of preaching.

Defining preaching

Your definition of preaching will determine your preaching method. If you define preaching as the sharing of theological information, then your approach to the biblical text will be informational. This methodology includes a major focus on historical context and biblical literacy. The idea behind this method is that hearers will change if they have the right information. If you define preaching as sharing truth, then your approach to the biblical text will be propositional. This methodology includes a focus on exegesis, interpretation, and linear reasoning. The idea behind this method is that hearers will accept change, if the presentation is rational and convincing. Our evangelists and missionaries have historically used the propositional approach.

If you, however, define preaching as sharing "the story of salvation," then your approach will be *inspirational*. We can all agree that good biblical preaching must include theological information and truthful propositions, but people need more than information—they need inspiration. Inspiration is the most important step in making sustainable life decisions demanded by the Scripture.

In his book *Start With Why*, Simon Sinek argues, "For those who are inspired, the motivation to act is deeply personal. They are less likely to be swayed by incentives. Those who are inspired are willing to pay a premium or endure inconvenience, even personal suffering."[1] To inspire is to breathe life into the lives of the sermon hearers. Inspiration is the filling of and moving upon one's spirit. Our preaching is too often "head" focused and not sufficiently "heart" focused. Effective preaching must appeal to the human spirit so that hearers are inspired to act differently, and thus the actions are sustained by a deep sense of spiritual conviction.

> *Inspiration is the most important step in making sustainable life decisions demanded by the Scripture.*

Inspirational preaching versus motivational speaking

Motivational speaking identifies reasons for acting in a certain way in order to help the hearer act differently. Motivators identify your obstacles and help you circumnavigate them so that you can move forward in life. Motivational speaking has its place; however, motivation focuses on reasons for acting while inspiration speaks to the will or strength to act. To inspire literally means "to breathe life into." When we preach the gospel, we are co-laboring with God to breathe faith, hope, and love into the lives of the people who hear us. Motivation, on the other hand, has a temporary effect because it is an external stimulus. However, when the Word of God inspires someone, it works from the inside out. The biblical text becomes an internal driving force that moves them in a different direction. For the purposes of this chapter, I want us to focus on the characteristics of inspirational preaching. Let us look at principles that will help the biblical text come alive in the lives of those who hear the sermon.

Biblical text comes alive

When we present the biblical text, we must inspire people to experience God as the people of the Bible experienced Him. For example, if you are preaching on David and Goliath, it is not enough to inform people about David's lineage, his vocation as a shepherd, and how small he was in comparison to the colossal Goliath. While it may be interesting to note that David had great faith, the goal is to not simply inform them about David's faith in God. The goal is to inspire them to exercise the faith that David had. The goal is to inspire them to slay their own giants. The subtle difference between informing and inspiring is that the former *tells* them what David did and the latter *inspires* them to do what David did. When we inspire people, we tap into the place where the Holy Spirit does His best work. Preachers are not called to convict people with their preaching. Our job is to inspire. The Spirit's job is to convict and change the hearts of people.

Preaching is not only prescriptive but also descriptive

The reason why many people have moved away from referring to the preached Word as the "sermon" is because there is a prevailing connotation that sermons are simply prescriptions on how people should live. Few like to be told what to do all of the time. But the Bible is more than a collection of prescriptions for people to live morally and ethically. It is the written record of the story of salvation on earth. If we are to inspire, we cannot simply prescribe; we have to *describe*

> *The more senses that are accessed, the better the memories.*

how God works in the lives of people and how they responded and interacted with Him. The goal is not to simply have people hear the preached Word but to *experience* the Word of God. This means we must use descriptive language that helps people enter into the biblical message.

I am not simply making a case here for intentional word crafting for the sake of sounding clever. I am suggesting that we use words that engage as many of the human senses as possible. The preacher needs to help the congregation feel the dust on the feet of Jesus walking from town to town. The people need to vividly imagine the contorted look on the face of the demoniac in Mark 5, who ran out of the tombs toward Jesus. The congregation needs to smell the perfume as the woman pours it on the head of Jesus in Matthew 26:7. Thomas Long, speaking about the skilled preacher and theologian Will Ormond, illustrates what every preacher must do to make the text come alive. "Before he speaks, he sees. He can see humor in the drab landscapes of daily routine; he can see wisdom in neglected crannies of biblical texts; he can see imaginative and innovative sermon possibilities where others find only the prosaic and the predictable."[2] The careful description of these experiences in the Bible opens the minds of the people hearing the gospel, and they will have a greater opportunity to remember and recall the message given. The more senses that are accessed, the better the memories.

Humanize the biblical characters

One of the challenges people have with our preaching is that the people of the Bible seem to be so far beyond their reach. The heroes and heroines of the Bible seem to be so much closer to God than we could ever be. The stories are so grand in scale that people do not know how to relate to the biblical characters. Samson was like Superman. Esther was a beauty queen. Joseph was the consummate moral giant. Abraham's name is synonymous with faithfulness. Who could ever be as great as these people of the Bible? The role of the preacher is to bridge the two worlds by helping people see who these biblical characters really were. I believe people read the Bible with "religious eyes" instead of human eyes. Simply put, we forget that these people were human just like us and struggled in every way just like we do.

Effective preaching takes off the veneer of religious piety and places the biblical characters within reach of our own human existence.

In Genesis 22, we read the story of Abraham being told by God to sacrifice his beloved Isaac. We need to help people identify with the struggle that Abraham had in obeying God. While we must be careful to not add to the Scriptures, we can only imagine that the decision to obey God was not easy. When we preach the story, do we make it seem as if Abraham just got up and left the next morning without shedding a tear? Do we preach this story as if Abraham was not afraid for his son's life? If so, we take out the human element that people can relate to. Murray Frick says, "Those of us who have been charged with communicating the Word of God can learn a great lesson from the contemporary media scene—to turn the sermon into a total learning experience."[3]

People identify with complex and interesting characters. They need to see tears on Abraham's face. The people need to sense a bit of fear in Esther's voice when she goes before the king, so that they can know that before every act of courage, it is all right to have some level of fear. The people need to feel the hurt in Moses' eyes as the very people he seeks to deliver from slavery blame him, so that they will know that it is not easy to help others come out of their difficult circumstances. Effective preaching takes off the veneer of religious piety and places the biblical characters within reach of our own human existence. A shared experience in the human struggle can lead to a shared experience in human triumph. If God could work with Moses despite his anger, then God can work with us. If God could work with Peter's impetuous and self-centered nature, then God can work with us. We see ourselves in their lives, and that gives us hope.

The divine-human dialogue

When we preach, we not only speak for God *to the people*, but we must also speak to God *for the people*. Preaching is not a monologue; it is a divine-human dialogue. The congregation is hearing from God, and they are responding internally, emotionally, intellectually, and physically. Even when we do not see visible signs of their responses, they are being affected by hearing the Word of God. Sometimes they agree with what God is saying in the sermon, while at other times they disagree or doubt silently in their minds. They are fearful of what God is requiring. They are disappointed that God does not always answer their prayer as they want. They may even be angry with God about something. Part of the secret to effective preaching is to anticipate these responses and reactions from the people and give voice to the congregation's frustration with God.

In a real sense, the preacher needs to speak to God about the questions, frustrations, and concerns of the congregation while delivering the message from God. Fred Craddock suggests, "Sermons should speak *for* as well as *to* the congregation."[4] This creates a connection to the sermon because people can see their existential concerns being addressed in the sermon from a human perspective. For example, if you were preaching about the story of Jesus and the disciples in the boat during the storm, it would be helpful to point out the frustration and fear of the disciples. In Mark 4:38, the disciples asked Jesus, "Teacher, do You not care that we are perishing?" (NKJV). There is frustration in that question. Can you not sense the fear? This is a question that every person who struggles to believe in God asks Him. When you preach this text, you have to connect the disciples' question with the questions your congregation is asking God. Someone in your congregation is asking God, "Don't You care that I'm a single mother and I don't have enough money to pay rent?" Another member is asking God, "Don't You care that I obey the health laws and I am still dying of cancer?" Your job as the preacher is to give voice to the frustrations of Christ's modern-day disciples who follow Him into the storms of their own lives. When you give a voice to their pain and struggle, they will enter into the sermonic experience.

> *Your job as the preacher is to give voice to the frustrations of Christ's modern-day disciples who follow Him into the storms of their own lives.*

In order to give voice to the congregation during the sermon, we have to approach sermon preparation from a different angle. We have been taught to go into our studies and labor over the Word in order to bring a word for the people. However, I would posit that we also have to approach the sermon study from the pew's perspective. Leonora Tubbs Tisdale says, "Rather than looking at preaching from 'above'—from the pulpit or the scholar's study, we begin to consider it from 'below'—from its inception, birthing and hearing in the midst of congregational life."[5] We have to anticipate the possible questions and disagreement people will entertain mentally while we are preaching. This is important for two reasons. The congregation does not regularly have an opportunity to ask questions while we are preaching. Some people may dismiss the sermon over one point that they disagree with or misunderstood. When we ask the questions in the sermon for them, we have a greater change of connecting people to the text. Secondly, if we do not preach from the pew perspective, we may come across as dogmatic and not sympathetic. A non-sympathetic preacher will be ineffective in preaching in our post-Christian culture. While we cannot address every question that will arise from every person, if we approach the sermon with sensitivity to the possible reactions to the sermon, we increase our opportunity to make the text come alive to our hearers.

The need for prophetic preaching

When I use the word *prophetic*, I am not referring to the foretelling ministry of predicting future events. I am referring to the courageous proclamation of truth that critiques evil in all of its spiritual and social forms. As Adventist pastors, we have a high value of biblical prophecy, but we have often missed the call to be prophetic in our preaching after the pattern of Elijah, Amos, Joel, and John the Baptist. These biblical prophets not only predicted the future according to revelation they received from God, but they also spoke truth to the political and social powers of their day. They spoke about the evil of oppression, idolatry, injustice, greed, and discrimination both outside and even inside the church. According to Tisdale, "As prophets we are called to measure the adequacy of congregational local theologies in light of a bigger gospel, and to bring a word of judgment on all false theologies and idolatries our local communities of faith hold dear."[6]

The Adventist preacher cannot afford to keep talking about the future without talking about the present struggles people are facing in the church and the world. Every biblical text has a social context that has an element of social injustice, discrimination, or exploitation. In order to be faithful to the fullness of the text and be relevant to the twenty-first-century audience, we must expose these social contexts of the Bible and show people how it relates to their social context. Instances of racism, ageism, and sexism are all found throughout the Bible. If we do not preach about these biblical realities, the people we preach to will view our preaching as out of touch with reality.

The biblical text becomes meaningful when it speaks to the entire human experience, including our interactions with each other. The Bible talks about loving our enemies (Matthew 5:43). Who are our enemies in the present age? The Bible talks about looking after orphans and widows (James 1:27) and that God will exact justice on those who exploit the poor (Malachi 3:15). Jesus talked about preaching good news to the poor, blind, and incarcerated (Luke 4:18). The gospel that He intended for us to preach has both

> *The Adventist preacher cannot afford to keep talking about the future without talking about the present struggles people are facing in the church and the world.*

spiritual and social realities. The inability or unwillingness to preach the gospel from a social perspective is what hinders many of our sermons from being experienced by more people. When poor people are being exploited, we need to preach prophetically to hold accountable the systems that exploit people. For example, when Jesus turned over the tables in the temple, He was angry at how the priests were overtaxing the people and taking advantage of the weary travelers. He told them that the temple was a place of prayer for all people and not just those who could afford the best sacrifices (Mark 11:15–17). This was not just a lesson in prayer or reverence. Jesus made a statement against the economic exploitation of the poor. If there are groups of people who are being unfairly marginalized, we have to preach in a way that speaks up for their rights.

When the government oversteps its boundaries to take away the civil liberties of its own citizens, the preacher has to speak up about that injustice. For example, in August of 2014, the entire country was held captive by the news that an unarmed black teen was fatally shot by an armed police officer. The United States was divided on the guilt of the police officer. In October, when the grand jury decided to not indict the police officer, there were massive protests in the streets. Regardless of your opinion on the case, we as preachers are called to speak to the people when the country is divided. We are called to preach compassion for those communities who suffer disproportionate violence and police arrests. The preacher does not need to promote a particular political party's views. The Word of God is nonpartisan. The call of the preacher is to speak truth in and out of season. Could it be that one of the greatest obstacles to the church's preaching today is our lack of prophetic voice on these issues?

Perhaps our job is not to make the biblical text come alive, but to expose people to the life already residing in the text.

Howard Thurman remarked on the connection between the impotency of the Christian church and the lack of our application to the social conditions people live in. He said, "To those who need profound succor and strength to enable them to live in the present with dignity and creativity, Christianity often has been sterile and of little avail."[7] I believe we will be surprised how many new people will begin to accept the gospel, when we begin to take courage with us into the pulpit to expose the power of God in the social experience of all people.

Preaching will be relevant as long as people need hope. The preacher is needed more today than any other time in history. Perhaps our job is not to make the biblical text come alive, but to expose people to the life already residing in the text. Effective preaching helps people see their lives in the text. If we remember that the Bible really tells one great story, then we will approach the task of preaching with a renewed passion to tell the story of the

One who left all of heaven and gave His life for us. That is a great story. Better yet, it is a true story. Even better, it is our story. So, go tell the story.

1. Simon Sinek, *Start With Why* (New York: Penguin Group, 2009), 6.

2. J. Will Ormond, Lucy A. Rose, and Thomas G. Long, *Preaching Eyes for Listening Ears: Sermons and Commentary for Preachers and Students of Preaching* (Lima, OH: CSS Publishing, 1999), 7.

3. Murray Frick, *Reach the Back Row: Creative Approaches for High-Impact Preaching* (Loveland, CO: Vital Ministry, 1999), 17.

4. Fred Craddock, *Preaching* (Nashville, TN: Abingdon Press, 1985), 26.

5. Leonora Tubbs Tisdale, *Preaching as Local Theology and Folk Art* (Minneapolis, MN: Fortress Press, 1997), 40.

6. Ibid., 54.

7. Howard Thurman, *Jesus and the Disinherited* (Boston, MA: Beacon Press, 1976), 11.

Called to Proclaim

J. HAROLD ALOMIA

I n the beginning was the Word, and the Word was with God, and the Word was God" (John 1:1, NKJV). The opening phrase of the Gospel of John is cryptic, seemingly obvious, quite simple, and yet profound. The writer places the reader at the inception of time and space, at some point in eternity where the existence of the Word seems to be the only reality. John draws back the curtain on a setting that predates all that we know and places the unimaginable in the realm of our finite comprehension.

The Word breaks the continuum of space and time, interrupts its timeless-ness, and transcends all known barriers in order to achieve one goal—to dwell[1] with humanity. Spurred by a desire to be closer to the ones He has created, the Word dives into the realm of humanity in order to live with them and become "Emmanuel" (God is with us) in practice. The tragedy of the opening lines of John is that as the Word comes to the world He created, yet the world does not recognize Him. We are blind and cannot see that the Word is here. What is even more tragic is that those who belong to Him—His own kin—do not know or recognize Him. The creatures do not recognize their Creator.

Stepping beyond the exegetical interpretation, I ponder the significance of *word*, not as the eternal being, but as the simple face value meaning of *word*. At its basic sense, the combination of letters and sounds convey a state-ment and message, an oral or written clause of communication, the means by which we can mold and shape our abstract thoughts into a concrete lan-guage. The correct combination of twenty-six different singular characters from the English alphabet (or any alphabet for that matter) with their own particular sounds allows for an infinite combination of characters spawning endless possibilities and infinite ways to communicate. These words combine and generate concepts and convey messages.

The word on paper (or screen) becomes the impetus behind our communication; it remains as the creative source of language. A word carries weight, it has meaning, and it can have the power to build or destroy. Its capabilities are limitless. When tied to a particular context, with a certain intonation, words can become powerful instruments, even weapons. Be it verb, noun, adjective, or any part of the grammarian's lingo, word is the power of speech, the clarity of communicating, and the magnificence of intelligible language. Our ability to put our thoughts into words—into languages—is one of the main human characteristics. Words can build, words can destroy, words can spur into action, and words can stifle. It is no wonder that some maintain that the pen is mightier than the sword. A message, a discourse, or an idea will live or die depending on the use of the words. As part of our daily routine, we use (or sometimes abuse) words. As preachers, perhaps it is pertinent to ponder the use of our words in the seemingly common and constant practice of our preaching.

The proclamation

The word *preach* is ubiquitous in the New Testament.[2] According to Mark 1:38, it is what Jesus came to do. Preaching is at the heart not only of the Messiah's mission but at the proclamation when He tells His disciples to "go into all the world and preach the gospel to every creature" (Mark 16:15, NKJV).[3] The Gospel of Mark opens and closes[4] with preaching by Christ Himself, and ends with Christ commanding[5] His disciples to follow His lead and example of preaching.

The meaning of *kerusso* goes beyond that of a simple declaration of words or an elaborate speech delivered a certain way. In a more technical way, it conveys the meaning of the declaration of an event, the proclamation of an official matter or occurrence that is normally done by a herald.[6] It is a strange concept perhaps for us today—the notion of a designated announcer of official events, because we are not so prone to the formalities of royal declarations.[7] Perhaps the closest equivalent to this cultural staple of the Ancient Near East would be the press secretary speaking on behalf of the head of a country. The New Testament takes the concept of proclamation and paints it in a hue that goes beyond the royal

Paul emphasizes a couple of things in this text that explain what his mission and calling are, and thus by extension, our calling as preachers.

or official communiqués and gives it a tone that elevates our thoughts to go elsewhere with the same idea of a proclamation. In the sixty-one times that "preach" is used in the New Testament, the idea behind it is that of a verb that describes the actions of those that have a specific "proclamation" to make. This proclamation is that of the gospel. Acts uses the word to show us that the proclamation is the telling of the gospel of Jesus, His Messianic mission, and the disclosure of what the gospel or good news meant. Acts is an example of what *kerusso* looks like for the Christian community. The apostle Paul also uses the same idea of proclamation masterfully as he opens his epistle to the Corinthians. Paul takes the idea of the proclamation and ties it with a message in order to connect the "proclamation" with the "evangelization" (*euaggelizo*) as the center of what the apostle is called to do.

What do we proclaim?

Paul is arguably one of the main proclaimers of the young Christian community. Because of his role in the fledgling church, it is important to hear what he has to say about the use of words. "For Christ did not send me to baptize, but to preach the gospel—not with wisdom and eloquence, lest the cross of Christ be emptied of its power" (1 Corinthians 1:17, NIV). *Evangelization* is not a word that is commonly used in the English language, yet it captures the essence of what indeed it means to "preach sharing the good news."[8]

> *For Paul, there is only one principal element in the proclamation of the gospel, the proclamation of Jesus Christ.*

Paul emphasizes a couple of things in this text that explain what his mission and calling are, and thus by extension, our calling as preachers. The concept of evangelization is also central in Acts and usually tied to the concept of sharing the "good news."[9] In extrabiblical writing, the term carries a religious and civic connotation; ancient writers, for example, deemed the coronation of the emperor as a worthy cause for "evangelization."[10] However, it seems obvious that the New Testament authors take this civic-religious concept and redefine the word by tying it to the retelling of Christ's ministry. In Acts, "evangelize" is what the early church did when "declaring the good news." *Declaring* is what Paul deems as the ultimate and supreme task of apostleship, and it encompasses a broad concept of preaching.[11]

For Paul, there is only one principal element in the proclamation of the gospel, the proclamation of Jesus Christ. That is why he tells his readers that he "resolved to know nothing while I was with you except Jesus Christ and him crucified" (1 Corinthians 2:2, NIV). The entirety of the gospel annunciation is the narrative of Christ and His mission to save us. The good news was a revolutionary concept that was diametrically opposed to the common notion of religion in the Ancient Near East at the time. The penitent worshiper of that day had the options of coaxing, bribing, or appeasing angry gods.[12]

> *The proclaimer is a servant who faithfully delivers God's message.*

Religion was based on a quid-pro-quo ideology, a constant bartering in which humans followed a list of rituals and commands in order to guarantee the favor of a particular deity and thus ensure their well-being and satisfaction. It was also vital to pronounce the right formulas and bring the right offerings to the worship experience in order to secure the favor of the particular deity.[13] There was no other way to have a connection with the gods. The pattern of what religion meant for the mind of the non-Christian worshiper boils down to keeping gods at bay one way or another. That is the result of a theology that describes the deities, at best, as only interested in us for ulterior motives, if interested at all, or simply demonstrating a consistent contempt for humanity with only sparks of interest. All deities had some ulterior and dark motive of self-service at the cost of the humans involved. If a person was smitten with tragedy, disgrace, or disease, it must have been because the deity was angry. This idea is present even in the minds of the disciples of Jesus when they asked about the reason for the ailment of the blind man, "Who sinned . . . ?" (John 9:1, 2, NIV). In other words, who angered God enough to smite this man?

The coming of Christ changed the situation. The heart of the evangelistic proclamation is God's interest in humanity, with no ulterior motive and no strings attached. The "good news" then strips away the ideals of a religion that is based on preprogramed pious performance and places the burden of the "good" in the "news" on the One that delivers it. God is good; moreover, God is love (1 John 4:8), regardless of what we do or fail to do. Consequently, the concept of the proclaimer takes on a new significance. The proclaimer is a servant who faithfully delivers God's message. We are called to "proclaim the virtues of the one who called you out of darkness into his marvelous light" (1 Peter 2:9, NET).

This new proclamation is so radical that even Paul calls it "foolishness of our proclamation" (1 Corinthians 1:21, NRSV). And yet, it is God that chooses this "foolishness of preaching" as the center of the evangelistic proclamation. Not only is God interested in humanity, but He also removes the veil from our eyes so we can begin to understand the predicament we face as a fallen race. We discover that God is willing to pay the ultimate sacrifice by dying for us. A crucified Savior is both a foolish concept and a scandalous one, quite impossible to reconcile in the mind of the listeners. As John Stott writes, "This combination of death, crime and shame put him beyond the pale of respect, let alone of worship."[14]

Paul does not condemn eloquence; rather, proclaiming the good news is not to be centered solely on the effects of the speech or the speech giver but on the effects of the Cross.

Paul even tells us how the proclamation should be done: "To preach the gospel, not with wisdom of words, lest the cross of Christ should be made of no effect" (1 Corinthians 1:17, NKJV). The translation might give us the idea that the proclamation of the gospel should not be done in eloquence or intelligent words. Rather the translating suggestion to replace "wisdom of words" with "not by manipulative rhetoric"[15] is not at all lacking argumentation considering context and onus of the word used. Paul does not condemn eloquence; rather, proclaiming the good news is not to be centered solely on the effects of the speech or the speech giver but on the effects of the Cross. If the speech alone and its persuasiveness are to be the benchmarks of the gospel, then the gospel's power is limited solely to the ability of the herald, and thus emasculates the source of the proclamation, that is the sacrifice of Christ on the cross. Paul makes it clear that manipulative words or rhetoric alone nullify the message. As one writer states, "If everything rests on human cleverness, sophistication or achievement, the cross of Christ no longer functions as that which subverts and cuts across all human distinctions of race, class, gender, and status to make room for divine grace alone as sheer unconditional gift."[16]

So then, why preach?

If we are part of the body of Christ (Romans 12:15; 1 Corinthians 12:12), then we are also qualified and endowed with diverse talents and ministries. It is not farfetched to think of not just the hands, feet, or heart of Christ but also the voice of Christ. So the Word should be the central focus of the proclamation.

The world suffers from a loud dissonance due to a myriad of voices that speak a multiplicity of messages. In the era of the fact-checking, the doubt and skepticism of everything that is stated, standing at a pulpit week in and week out becomes as courageous and foolish today as it was for Paul.

The Word must be the center of our message; the Word must be what we uplift at all times. We wage a timeless and endless battle in being His voice in the confusing bedlam of noise that characterizes our world. That is our calling. When we are serious about Jesus being the central focus of our preaching, only then will our speech be a powerful life-changing proclamation.

It is not farfetched to think of not just the hands, feet, or heart of Christ but also the voice of Christ.

Revelation 14, central in Adventist proclamation, reveals that it is the "everlasting gospel" to be carried out in evangelic efficiency. The "everlastingness" of this gospel should compel us to proclaim it effectively. Maybe our methods will have to adapt and be re-evaluated.

God's message is the same benchmark that Noah used. It is the same as what Moses and Miriam sang out on the shores of the Red Sea. David declared it in poetic artistry, and it was eloquently foretold by Isaiah and emotionally retold by Jeremiah. God's message is proclaimed even as reluctantly as Jonah's day, or in the reassured fear of Elijah. The Word still declares through Daniel the everlasting nature of the gospel. This principle survived the corruption of its central keeper and was kept alive at times even as a small glimmer by the likes of Zwingli, Hus, and Luther. In its relentless desire to reach the world, the Word finds itself in the lips of farmers turned preachers like William Miller. It finds itself in the pen and lips of Ellen White, who preached it in power, conviction, and devotion. From H. M. S. Richards to E. E. Cleveland, C. D. Brooks to Mark Finley, and to you and me. It is today more than ever that the Word must be declared, even when

We wage a timeless and endless battle in being His voice in the confusing bedlam of noise that characterizes our world.

it seems that all other influences appear to drown out the voice of the gospel. It becomes imperative that the preacher draws his or her voice from the balancing grace of the Word. The preacher must center the proclamation to what was in the beginning and what will be at the end when we finally reach eternity's shore—the Word, His eternally sufficient grace, and everlasting love.

1. *Eskenosen* can be translated literally as "he pitched his tent," the sense of dwelling, moving in with humanity is the idea that conveys the text in John 1:14.

2. "Preach" and its derivatives show up 140 times in the New Testament (*Strong's Exhaustive Concordance of the Bible*).

3. Most popular English versions render the same translation of "preach the gospel" (NLT, NIV, NET, NASB, and NKJV).

4. The following essay has no intention of delving into the debate over the ending of the Gospel of Mark being past 16:8; we take the translation of the NKJV and follow it.

5. *Keruzate,* Verb 2 Person Plural Aorist Active Imperative of *kerusso.* (Accordance Bible Software, version 11.0.2, accessed November 2014, OakTree Software, Inc.) The aorist active imperative denotes a command made by the subject of the verb to the object, which, in this case, are the apostles. Their mission is a mission of proclamation and preaching.

6. Gerhard Kittel, ed., Gerhard Friedrich, *Theological Dictionary of the New Testament,* vol. III (Grand Rapids, MI: Wm. B. Eerdmans Pub. Co., 1995), 703, s.v. "keruz". Concept also repeated by R. T. France when analyzing the verse: "But here at the beginning of the mission it is Jesus himself who acts as herald." Quoted in I. Howard Marshall and Donald A. Hagnar, eds., "The Gospel of Mark," *New International Greek Testament Commentary* (Grand Rapids, MI: Wm. B. Eerdmans Pub. Co., 2002), 113.

7. Of the thirty-one times the root *kerusso* is used in the LXX, almost all of the instances have to do with royal or official use of a proclamation, a decree, or an official communiqué made to a group of people.

8. Evangelize: transitive verb, 1: to preach the gospel to; 2: to convert to Christianity. Intransitive verb: to preach the gospel. Merriam-Webster.com.

9. *Euaggelizo* appears fifteen times in the book of Acts. It is translated normally as "proclaim, preach, to address with good tidings, proclaim good tidings." Greek Dictionary, Robert Mounce, #G2294, Accordance Bible Software, s.v. "*euaggelizo.*"

10. Georg Strecker, *euaggelizo,* EDNT II:69.

11. Ibid., 70.

12. James S. Jeffers, *The Greco-Roman World of the New Testament Era* (Downers Grove, IL: IVP Academic, 1999), 90–92.

13. Everett Ferguson, *Backgrounds of Early Christianity,* 3rd ed. (Grand Rapids, MI: Wm. B. Eerdmans, 2003), 184–193.

14. John R. W. Stott, *The Cross of Christ* (Downers Grove, IL: IVP, 2006), 29. John Stott (pp. 24–50) relates in more detail the ignominious and insulting notion of death on the cross.

15. Anthony C. Thieselton makes a valid case for the translation of the phrase *ouk en sofia logou* as "not by manipulative rhetoric." He is aware however of the difficulty of imposing a certain translation to the reader and the complication of translation with no interpretation. For a more elaborate explanation as to why use the phrase "manipulative rhetoric," see Thiselton, "The First Epistle to the Corinthians," *New International Greek Testament Commentary* (Grand Rapids, MI: Wm. B. Eerdmans, 2000), 143–147.

16. Ibid., 145.

Preaching Resources

ROLLIN SHOEMAKER

Sermon preparation is a complex process, but an enriching experience, if time is taken to do it properly. Preparation involves a variety of tasks—selecting texts, studying texts, praying for guidance by the Holy Spirit, and outlining or writing the manuscript. The resources you, as the preacher, use in sermon preparation can be a real time saver as well as make the sermon more effective and relevant. In this chapter, I will suggest a variety of resources, how to evaluate them, and how to use them in sermon preparation.

Text selection and reading Scripture

The selection of texts is a multifaceted procedure and one that requires you to take into account various factors. The following are some factors you should consider:

- The season of the year. For example, it would be well to preach on the Resurrection during the Easter season.
- The occasion. Preparing sermons for funerals, for Communion, and so forth.
- The issues and problems the congregation or individuals are facing. That may include finances, building projects, and moral concerns.
- Where your congregation is located. Examples include inner city, suburbs, country, poverty-stricken area, middle-class or upper-class neighborhoods, and so on.
- The age range and education level of your audience.
- Social factors.

After taking into account these factors, you can choose the topic or, if appropriate, a theme-based series. If you decide on a series, choose the Bible texts for the sermon series before the first sermon is preached. Choosing the texts ahead of time makes it possible to be on the lookout for items that relate to the series. This also applies to an expository series.

Choosing the texts ahead of time makes it possible to be on the lookout for items that relate to the series.

After you have chosen the texts, read them within their contexts in various translations. There are a number of quality translations available.[1] You may choose to consider the New International Version (NIV),[2] the New Revised Standard Version (NRSV), the New King James Version (NKJV), the New American Standard Bible (NASB), or other modern languages. Those who have kept up with the biblical languages will greatly benefit by reading the passages in the original languages. This extensive reading will help you become familiar with the passages, various nuances.

There are two other things you can do to be immersed in the passages you are studying. Software programs such as BibleWorks, Logos, and Olive Tree can be helpful for reading texts from the various translations. Another method is to listen to recordings of the texts in various translations from sources such as Bible.is.

Sources for sermon preparation

After you have read the passage and found out its various nuances, turn to other literature to find out the meaning of words, terms, and phrases and other background material. This is an important phase of sermon preparation. Many resources exist, so you have to decide how much time to spend on the research. Also, consider the reliability and theological position of the resources. Just because a source has a particular viewpoint does not mean you have to accept it. Compare the sources and examine critically their theological perspective. Use your God-given ability to evaluate and determine the quality of what you are reading. If we look at the early years of the Seventh-day Adventist Church, we find that the ministers

Also, consider the reliability and theological position of the resources.

used a variety of resources—many of them written by authors who were not Seventh-day Adventists. Just as the early Adventists had to carefully evaluate sources, so we must do likewise.

Keep in mind that even though the theological position of an author may not be acceptable, the technical explanations—such as word studies—might still be helpful. It is important to learn how to use material without having to accept all conclusions of the author. Just make sure not to take anything out of context or twist the author's meaning to fit your views.

Selected Seventh-day Adventist resources

As a Seventh-day Adventist minister, you have access to quality sources published by the denomination. This chapter will list a number of them, but this section refers to several that should be accessed on a regular basis.

- *Andrews Study Bible*. Berrien Springs, MI: Andrews University Press, 2010. At the beginning of each book of the Bible and throughout this source, the editors include helpful study material.
- The Writings of Ellen G. White—books, articles, and other material—are a rich source of helpful material. These materials are available in print, or you may access them in many languages at http://egwwritings.org.
- Seventh-day Adventist Periodical Index (http://www.andrews.edu/library/car/sdaperiodicals.html) gives you access to numerous periodicals.

> *As a Seventh-day Adventist minister, you have access to quality sources published by the denomination.*

- *Ministry*, International Journal for Pastors, has been published since 1928 and its online index (http://www.ministrymagazine.org/archive) gives you access to articles containing helpful material for sermons.

Word studies

- Barclay, William. *New Testament Words*. Philadelphia, PA: The Westminster Press, 1964. This book explains the meaning of ninety-six Greek words. It was written primarily for the individuals who do not know Greek.

- Nichol, Francis D., ed. *The Seventh-day Adventist Bible Commentary.* 7 vols.; *The Seventh-day Adventist Bible Dictionary: Complete with Atlas,* vol. 8. Washington, DC: Review and Herald® Publishing Association, 1960. The commentary set contains valuable information on the terms, words, and biblical phrases, along with excellent maps.
- Robertson, A. T. *Word Pictures in the New Testament.* Vols. 1–5. Nashville, TN: Broadman Press, 1930. The writer gives introductory information about each book. It contains an English translation and the Greek transliteration of each term or phrase. The author explains what the terms or phrases mean and cites other New Testament verses and, if needed, other extrabiblical references.
- Kittel, Gerhard, Gerhard Friedrich, and Geoffrey W. Bromiley, eds. *Theological Dictionary of the New Testament. Abridged in One Volume.* Grand Rapids, MI: William B. Eerdmans Publishing Company, 1985. This is an abridgement of the nine-volume edition. It summarizes the meaning of key New Testament words. All words of theological significance are defined and transliterated.

Background and introductory information

- Brown, Raymond E. *An Introduction to the New Testament.* ABRL, edited by David Noel Freedman. Garden City, NY: Doubleday & Company, Inc., 1996. For each document in the New Testament, Brown has a summary table outlining the basic information and divisions of the book. He also discusses other important information for understanding and comprehending the author's intent. You may disagree with some of his views, but it is a valuable resource.
- Bruce, F. F. *The New Testament Documents: Are They Reliable?* Grand Rapids, MI.: William B. Eerdmands Publishing Company, 2003. This 120-page book has gone through a number of editions. It is packed with useful information about the New Testament.
- Cousar, Charles B. *An Introduction to the New Testament: Witnesses to God's New Work.* Louisville, KY: Westminster John Knox Press, 2006. This book contains an excellent essay articulating eight basic principles for studying the New Testament.
- Kümmel, Werner Georg. *Introduction to the New Testament.*

Translated by A. J. Mattill. 14th ed. Nashville, TN: Abingdon Press, 1966. Kümmel has good summaries and analysis of each book.

- Young, Edward J. *An Introduction to the Old Testament.* Revised 3rd ed. Grand Rapids, MI: William B. Eerdmans Publishing Co., 1965. Young gives an analysis of each book, plus its authorship.

Handbooks

- Bratcher, Robert G. and Eugene A. Nida. *A Translator's Handbook on the Gospel of Mark: Helps for Translators.* Vol. 2. New York: United Bible Society. E. J. Brill, Leiden, 1961. This volume is representative of a number of volumes published by the United Bible Society to guide one in how to translate the Greek text of the New Testament. However, one does not need to know Greek in order to use this and other volumes in this series. All Greek words are transliterated. The authors first cite the verse in English and then make some comments on the Greek text. After that there are exegetical comments on the verse. There is a helpful discussion about various ways the passage may be used. The insights gathered from this process are enlightening and useful in sermon preparation.
- Halley, Henry Hampton. *Halley's Bible Handbook.* Grand Rapids, MI: Zondervan, 2000. The author deals with such issues as how the Bible is organized, its setting, the main thought of each Bible book, and what the Bible is all about. There are articles on the Holy Land and the Jewish people. There is supplemental materials on how we got the Bible; the House of Herod; rediscovering the biblical past; distance charts on Old and New Testament cities; the Jewish calendar. The edition has color photos scattered throughout the book.
- Reid, George W., ed. *Handbook of Seventh-day Adventist Theology.* Vol. 12, Commentary Reference Series. Hagerstown, MD: Review and Herald® Publishing Association, 2000. The articles written in this book explain the various doctrines of the Seventh-day Adventist Church.

Illustrations

- Cox, Harvey. *When Jesus Came to Harvard: Making Moral Choices Today.* New York: Houghton Mifflin Company, 2004. Cox was asked to teach a class on Jesus in the Moral Reasoning division of the undergraduate curriculum at Harvard because there was a growing embarrassment of questionable legal practices, doctors who had more interest in money than patients, scientists fudging the data, and insider trading by Harvard graduates. The content of the book is about what happened in this class. The book is full of powerful illustrations about moral choices.

- Graham, Ruth Bell. *Prodigals and Those Who Love Them: Words of Encouragement for Those Who Wait.* Colorado Springs, CO: Focus on the Family Publishing, 1991. Graham talks about Luke's story of the prodigal son, Aurelius Augustine, John Newton, Fyodor Dostoyevsky, and some others.
- Kerr, Hugh T. and John M. Mulder, eds. *Famous Conversions: The Christian Experience.* Grand Rapids, MI: William B. Eerdmans Publishing Company, 1994. The book describes the conversions of such people as the apostle Paul, Augustine, John Calvin, John Wesley, Sojourner Truth, Leo Tolstoy, and others.
- LaHaye, Tim. *Power of the Cross.* Sisters, OR: Multnomah Books, 1998. LaHaye records stories about people who have been transformed by the gospel in today's world.

Additional helpful works

- *Doctrinal Discussions.* Washington, DC: Review and Herald® Publishing Association, 1961. This book deals with the law in Adventist theology, the investigative judgment, Sabbath and the Lord's Day, life only in Christ, Ellen White's writings, the judgment hour, the nature of Man, and a few other topics.
- Hengel, Martin. *Crucifixion.* Translated by John Bowden. Philadelphia, PA: Fortress Press, 1977. The book explains the historical background and implementation of the punishment of crucifixion.

Models and ideas for biblical preaching

- Achtemeier, Elizabeth. *Preaching About Family Relationships.* Philadelphia, PA: The Westminster Press, 1987. The book deals with what the Bible has to say about human nature, marriage, sex, divorce, roles of men and women, children, and the elderly, among other issues, including truth in love.

- Perry, Lloyd M. *Biblical Preaching for Today's World*. Chicago, IL: Moody Press, 1973. This book explains how a preacher can use the author's method to consistently and quickly construct excellent sermons.
- Warner, Michael, ed. *American Sermons*. New York: The Library of America, 1999. Find sermons in this book by different American preachers in the seventeenth to twentieth centuries, including Jonathan Edwards's sermon "Sinners in the Hand of an Angry God," preached July 8, 1741, which impressed many of the hearers, using two texts: Amos 9:2, 3 and Deuteronomy 32:35.
- Streett, R. Alan. *The Effective Invitation: A Practical Guide for the Pastor*. Old Tappan, NJ: Fleming H. Revell Company. Streett deals with the gospel and what it is, the theological content of an invitation, public invitations, evangelists, music, critics, and methods or models of invitations.

Example

We have reviewed some of the resources available to the preacher. In this section we will see how these and other resources are used in the development of a sermon. I have chosen to use Galatians 6:14 as the text to be preached in a series of sermons.[3]

Context

Text: Galatians 6:14, "May I never boast except in the cross of our Lord Jesus Christ, through which the world has been crucified to me, and I to the world" (NIV).

After reading the text in at least five translations, I focus on the context of this passage.

Historical: Galatians was probably written from Antioch about 49–50 C.E. (before the Jewish rebellion and Roman destruction of Jerusalem in 70, while the nascent Christian movement was still a sect within Judaism) in response to some "Judaizers" who had entered Galatia. The Judaizers were trying to convince the Galatian believers to become full-fledged Jews by being circumcised because they believed that one needed to be circumcised in order to be saved (Acts 15:1).

Literary: The text is in the last part of Galatians, Galatians 6:11–16. The book could be outlined as follows: salutation, 1:1–5; part one (the validity of

Paul's apostleship), 1:6–2:21; part two (faith and law), 3:1–5:12; and part three (freedom only in Christ), 5:13–6:18.[4] The type of writing of Galatians is "deliberate rhetoric."[5] The text we are analyzing is embedded in Paul's summary of the primary issue in his letter.

Words or terms of interest

Boasting: For Paul, the term boasting discloses the Jewish attitude. It is one of self-confidence. It seeks glory before God. It relies on itself. The contrast to this term is "faith," which is not only demanded but also made possible by Christ. Remember, Abraham did not boast before God (Romans 4:2). Paul has noted that boasting in the Law/torah and in God, which Judaism required, was perverted to resting/trusting in the Law (Romans 2:17, 23). This is exactly the same thing the apostle talks about in Philippians 3:3ff. When an individual comes to faith, that person surrenders all self-glorying. I can boast or glory only in the Cross.[6]

Circumcision: Circumcision is the sign of the covenant between Israel and God. It has the idea of redemption.[7] To be a Jew and member of God's people, a male must be circumcised.

Cross: The cross was an instrument of torture reserved for violent criminals.[8] Paul notes that anyone who hangs on a tree (cross) is cursed (Deuteronomy 21:22, 23). Human sins are laid on Christ to set us free. Christ's lowest stage of humiliation was when He was crucified on the cross, which is the means of salvation for the world (Philippians 2:8; 1 Corinthians 1:18).[9]

Flesh: The fleshly desires are centered on the world and what it has to offer.[10]

Israel of God: "If Jesus is Christ, then history has come to its fulfillment and Israel is no longer God's people."[11] The people of God are those who are in Christ Jesus.

Law: In Rabbinic Judaism, first of all, the Law means the Pentateuch (the books of Moses: Genesis, Exodus, Leviticus, Numbers, and Deuteronomy). Secondly, it could mean the Pentateuch plus the Prophets and Writings, the entire Old Testament. And thirdly, the term Law could include the entire revelation to Moses at Sinai, the torah that was transmitted orally, plus the rest of the Bible.[12]

Law in its narrowest sense included the moral law of the Ten Commandments and what Christians call the ceremonial law plus the rest of the Pentateuch. The Law in Judaism was an indissoluble unit. It could not be separated between moral and ceremonial.[13]

A true understanding of the Law does not come into view until we meet Christ Jesus. Note what Paul writes in Philippians 3:6, "As to zeal, a persecutor of the church; as to righteousness under the law, [I was] blameless" (NRSV). After he met Christ on the road to Damascus and went into Arabia to contemplate what had happened to him, he began to comprehend the true significance of the Law.[14]

World: The world represents the unredeemed, the enemy of God, and the obstacle to the life of a Christian. The church may be in the world, but it is not of the world. It does not belong to the world. As such, the term represents humanity.[15]

Writing a paraphrased translation

The paraphrased translation that follows is based on the study done so far:

It is not for me to boast before God because of what I have accomplished. The only boast I have is in the cross of our Lord Jesus Christ because in the judgment that is the only boast that is meaningful before God. It is through or by means of the cross of our Lord Jesus Christ that I have come and continue to be crucified (with Christ) to the world and the world to me.

The paraphrase for the entire paragraph of verses 6:11–16 follows:

Look how large the letters are that I have written to you Galatians with my own hand. The only thing those Jewish Christian teachers desire is to look good in respect to worldly standards. That is why they are pressuring you to be circumcised (i.e., to become Jews). They only preach this way because they do not want to be persecuted on account of the cross of Christ. For neither do these teachers who have been circumcised (i.e., who are Jews because of their circumcision) observe the Law/torah. On the contrary, they only want all of you to be circumcised (to become Jews) so that they would have a boast before their compatriots in the fact that they were responsible for your circumcision (becoming Jews).

It is not for me to boast before God or human beings because of what I have accomplished. The only boast I have is in the cross of our Lord Jesus Christ because that is the only boast that is meaningful before God in the judgment and as far as that goes before other human beings as well. It is through or by means of the cross of our Lord Jesus Christ that I have come and continue to be crucified (I am crucified with Christ) to the world and the world to me.

For neither circumcision (being a Jew) nor uncircumcision (being a Gentile) is anything at all. On the contrary, it is the new creation that matters (the new creation where all are one in Christ Jesus and heirs according to the promise). And as many of you who walk (live) by this principle, rule; peace and mercy be upon them and on the Israel of God (i.e., the believers in Christ Jesus).

The subject, theme, and thesis of the passage

The cross of Christ is the subject and theme of the passage and the thesis is, "The cross of Christ is what separates the believer from the world."

Outline and development of the thesis

The believer is in the world but not of the world, therefore the believer is not only separated from the world but is separated for service and to love unconditionally.

1. The first result: Separation from
    a. By freeing an individual from the power of sin
    b. By freeing an individual from the mores of the world
    c. By freeing an individual from the god of this age
2. The second result: Stiff opposition
    a. By freeing an individual from fear of verbal abuse
    b. By freeing an individual from fear of punishment
    c. By freeing an individual from fear of physical danger
3. The third result: Separation for discipleship
    a. By freeing the individual for service
    b. By freeing the individual for generosity among other gifts
    c. By freeing the individual for living
4. The fourth result: Separation by freeing an individual to be transformed
    a. By freeing an individual to love unconditionally
    b. By freeing an individual to accept all peoples unconditionally
    c. By freeing an individual to receive the power of the Spirit unconditionally

Conclusion

Close with an illustration or statement that nails down the thesis and sums up what has been preached. An illustration: The House of Hope is a place where abandoned girls find their way to Christ and a transformed life. At fourteen years of age, Katrina ran away from home and became a drug addict and prostitute. She was arrested countless times and condemned as absolutely hopeless. At the House of Hope, Katrina felt the unconditional love of Sara Trollinger, the founder. Through Trollinger's ministry, Katrina found Christ and became a transformed person. At twenty-three, she was married, had a child, and lives the Christian life.

---

1. For a review of various translations, see Nikolaus Satelmajer, "The Joys and Challenges of Choosing a Bible Translation," *Journal of Adventist Education,* December 2011/January 2012.

2. The 2011 edition of the NIV has made some translation corrections from the earlier edition.

3. For the study of this passage, I have used some resources listed in this chapter plus the following: Ellen G. White, *Steps to Christ* (Mountain View, CA: Pacific Press®, 1956).

4. M. Eugene Boring and Fred B. Craddock, *The People's New Testament Commentary* (Louisville, KY: Westminster John Knox Press, 2004), 576; see also Craig Keener, *The IVP Bible Background Commentary: New Testament* (Downers Grove, IL: IVP Academic, 1993), 520–537; Werner Georg Kümmel, *Introduction to the New Testament,* trans., A. J. Mattill, 14th. ed. (Nashville, TN: Abingdon Press, 1966), 190, 191; Charles B. Cousar, *An Introduction to the New Testament: Witnesses to God's New Work* (Louisville, KY: Westminster John Knox Press, 2006), 47–56; Raymond E. Brown, *An Introduction to the New Testament,* ed. David Noel Freedman, ABRL (Garden City, NY: Doubleday & Company, Inc., 1996), 468.

5. Keener, *The IVP Bible Background Commentary,* 517.

6. Gerhard Kittel, Gerhard Friedrich, and Geoffrey W. Bromiley, eds., *Theological Dictionary of the New Testament (TDNT), Abridged in One Volume* (Grand Rapids, MI: William B. Eerdmans Publishing Company, 1985), 424.

7. Ibid., 831.

8. Martin Hengel, *Crucifixion,* trans., John Bowden (Philadelphia, PA: Fortress Press, 1977), passim.

9. Kittel, Friedrich, and Bromiley, *TDNT-Abridged,* 666, 1071.

10. Ibid., 1005.

11. Jacob Neusner, *Rabbinic Judaism: Structure and System* (Minneapolis, MN: Fortress Press, 1995), 156.

12. Siegfried H. Horn, *Seventh-day Adventist Bible Dictionary,* ed. Don F. Neufeld, Seventh-day Adventist Bible Commentary Reference (Washington, DC: Review and Herald, 1960), 641; Neusner, 25 n. 1.

13. Ernst Käsemann, *Commentary on Romans,* trans., Geoffrey W. Bromiley (Grand Rapids, MI: William B. Eerdmans Publishing Company, 1980), 215; James D. G. Dunn, *Romans 1–8,* ed. David A. Hubbard et al., Word Biblical Commentary, vol. 38A (Dallas, TX: Word Books, 1988), 419; see also Kittel, Friedrich, and Bromiley, *TDNT-Abridged,* 1005; David A. deSilva, *Galatians: A Handbook on the Greek Text,* ed. Martin M. Culy, Baylor Handbook on the Greek New Testament (Waco, TX: Baylor University Press, 2014), 115.

14. Ellen G. White, *Steps to Christ* (Mountain View, CA: Pacific Press®, 1956), 29, 30.

15. Kittel, Friedrich, and Bromiley, *TDNT-Abridged,* 462–464.

⚙ MANAGEMENT

Pastors execute responsibilities in a timely and well-organized fashion.

Descriptors of Management include:
- skilled in organizing special events
- responsible in financial oversight
- promotes risk management
- executes, gets things done
- monitors staff and church leaders
- evaluates church outcomes
- skilled in leading committees, boards
- manages time well
- practices/promotes stewardship
- articulates clearly in oral and written communication
- prompt in reporting
- accessible to members
- proficient in computing and social media
- prepared for crises, emergencies

Pastoring a Multichurch District

STEPHEN REASOR

I awoke with a startle to the unsettling reality of someone staring at me. My six-year-old daughter, three inches from my face, waited for the expression of terror to leave my face then said, "Which church are we going to today?" It was a valid first-thing-Sabbath-morning question.

Pastoring more than one church presents benefits and challenges. I am the pastor of three small churches, and that impacts my family and ministry in significant ways. In this chapter, I will consider ministry specific to multichurch pastorate, including the pastor's family, staying connected, the value of local leaders, community dynamics, how to move toward change, and small church morale.

One of the hardest things our family had to adjust to was the reality of being in a different church each week.

The pastor's family

One of the hardest things our family had to adjust to was the reality of being in a different church each week. In a multichurch district, you and your family may not have a "home church," and attend the same Sabbath School. Some Sabbaths we leave home before 8:30 A.M., other Sabbaths not until 9:30 A.M. One of our churches has several families with small children, while sometimes our kids are the only children at another of our churches. We have found a few ways to cope with this reality.

Guard family Sabbath time

We guard our family Sabbath time by focusing on what our kids like in each church and taking time for family friends. Friday evenings are closely guarded in our home. We make sure we are all home to welcome the Sabbath together, except when I am involved in evangelism. Starting Sabbath the same way each week helps mitigate the effects of adjusting to a different Sabbath routine each week.

Focus on the positive

There is something about each church that my kids enjoy. So when they ask which church we are attending, we mention those things. On the other hand, there are things about each church that are less enjoyable. Like the song says, "You've got to accentuate the positive."

Take time for friends

We are blessed to live near several families that are good friends who do not attend any of our churches. Meeting them Sabbath afternoon or evening gives us all something to look forward to after our Sabbath responsibilities are done. Even if your friends attend your churches, taking time for them, like family time Friday night, helps make Sabbath a delight.

Stay connected

Because a pastor of a multichurch district is usually not in each church every week, it is difficult to stay connected with the life of each church. I have two strategies that help in overcoming this barrier: clear communication with all the churches and a regular presence in each community.

Communication

With the array of communication tools available, it seems that communicating with my churches and church members should be a simple task; sometimes it is not simple at all. Some of my church members are social media savvy, communicate easily through texting, and respond promptly to e-mails but are nearly impossible to contact by phone or visit in person. Other church members are not connected to social media, or even the Internet. The only avenue of communication is through phone, letter, or in person. This means that I do not have one way to communicate to all of my church members at once. The solution, of course, is to make the effort to communicate through those tools that meet the needs of each congregant. This is part of having a presence in each church.

Presence

I am committed to being in each of my three communities at least once a week. There is no substitute for physical presence. Which means I have developed a schedule (for me it is easiest if the basic components of the schedule are the same week by week) that makes the most of my time in each community and keeps travel to a minimum. This allows me to maintain connection to church members, church activities and ministries (like community centers and food banks), and community entities (senior organizations, police/fire/emergency medical services, public schools, etc.). I have found that regularly scheduled visits to each community keep me better informed of the community needs.

A colleague of mine, Tyler Rosengren, pastors a district that spans more than two hundred miles (about 330 km). Some of his members live an hour and a half away from the church they attend. The distances make his visitation difficult. He writes: "Other than the personal visit, I find that phone calls actually go a long way, especially in a district that is spread out. I have found that members respond well just to see that the pastor was thinking about them enough to call. I would recommend setting apart a couple of hours one evening per week just to make phone calls. I consider it visitation because that's truly what it is."[1] Rosengren has also found it helpful to even do counseling over the phone when counseling young women without an available public space.

The solution, of course, is to make the effort to communicate through those tools that meet the needs of each congregant.

The value of local church members

Pastoring a multichurch district requires cooperation for one simple reason: each of your church members is at their local church more than you are. This means the church members are the primary ministers in their community and the church leaders are the primary leaders in their congregation.

Local ministry and the priesthood of all believers

We have adopted an ecclesiology that separates clergy and laity. While pastors have an important and legitimate role to play in the local church, we are not the only ones called to ministry. The New Testament makes a distinction between Jesus, our High Priest, and those who believe in Him.[2] But among the believers, there is no distinction between those designated as ministers and those who are not; all of us are members of the ministering priesthood![3] We have too closely guarded our designated role as only belonging to us. James Killen suggests: "It should be an important part of the work of the pastor to recruit, train, and enable lay members of the church for the work of caring. This should not be understood as the pastor recruiting laypeople to help with the pastor's work. Instead, it should be seen as the pastor enabling the whole church to do its work."[4]

> *As the pastor of a small church, one of my primary roles is to encourage a climate of love and caring in my churches.*

This is where small churches have an opportunity to develop a culture of caring and ministry that makes the most of their small size. As the pastor of a small church, one of my primary roles is to encourage a climate of love and caring in my churches. In fact, regardless of church size, this is ideal. David Smith notes, "Ironically, the large and mega church is trying to capture the small church feel."[5] There is an honest and loving fellowship in small churches. This, Killen argues, is one of the great benefits of a small congregation since they "have a unique ability to become intimate fellowships in which the members all know and care for one another and in which the network of caring relationships reaches out into the community beyond the congregation."[6] This faithful service and kingdom success is not measured numerically.

Local leaders

You are not the primary overseer of your churches; the local leaders are. This can be a source of endless frustration for a pastor, but as Glenn Daman points out, "The pastor who desires to work effectively in the small church will be more successful by working with, not against or apart from, its contextually rooted, traditional leaders."[7] The local church leaders have likely been the leaders of the church longer than you have been there and will continue to be the church's leaders after you are gone. Some church members (and even church leaders) will say they want you to set the vision for the church. During my first board meeting at one of my churches, a board member asked me what my plan was for their church. As long as my plan was broad, vague, and did not change how they did things, the members would have been pleased with it. But any vision I develop unilaterally (especially in a multichurch district) will only be my vision. Daman shares Doran McCarty's point: "Doran McCarty points out that 'power in the small church is accessible to someone, and most often it is not the pastor. Laypersons are the seats of power in the small church in most situations, not the pastor. The pastor has the title but not the power.' Most books on vision development wrongly assume that the pastor has the power and authority to set the vision for the church. Within the small church, this often is not the case."[8]

Your most effective leadership role may be the influence you have on the local leaders' vision for their church, rather than fine-tuning your own vision for each congregation.

Community dynamics in small churches

Before I began my duties in my current district, I had a former pastor from that district describe one of my churches as "one of the warmest, friendliest churches you'll ever pastor." My first week at that particular church, I was met by one of the church leaders who told me that he was very concerned since visitors had told him they found the church unfriendly. How was that possible? This church had a reputation for being a friendly church. They thought they were friendly. They were honestly surprised that anyone would think they were unfriendly. Killen describes it this way: "But it would be a mistake to assume that, just because a church is small, it is a warm, caring community. Some are not. Some can be quite selfish in their orientation, thinking only of serving the needs of their own people. Some can allow themselves to be dominated by a few snobbish, negative, or critical people. And even some of those churches that do have a warm, caring fellowship among their members may have unintentionally become quite exclusive because it is hard for new people to get into the tight little circle of old friends. Small membership churches must decide intentionally to become caring fellowships."[9]

So, how do you move a church from being perceived as unfriendly and clique-ish to being a warm, caring community? This is a question of climate—emotional, relational, and community climate. By climate I mean the overall feeling of safety, warmth, acceptance, and love that should pervade the fellowship in our churches.

Changing the church climate

I have based the following section on the work of Mark Devries.[10] He writes from decades of youth ministry, but his perspective applies to any group. He recommends a five-part process to move the small church to a warm and loving climate:

Impart joy into the process. I have not met many people who are actually excited about changing the way they do things. Many churches have been functioning in their current dynamic for years, perhaps decades. It will be stressful for them to consider adjusting that dynamic, and they may blame you for it. Steve Bierly notes, "Small communities are very suspicious of, if not hostile to, outsiders, particularly outside 'experts' who have the potential to change the cherished status quo."[11] The best way to initiate change is to maintain a playful detachment from the negative emotional triggers surrounding the church.

My wife shares cartoons and jokes with her science students on her Pinterest board. She very effectively imparts joy into her environment. If you want to lead a climate shift in your church, your members need to believe that you are leading them into an experience of joy. One of my elders recently told me that he felt an excitement in the church about where we are going. That is an indicator that I have been at least somewhat successful in imparting joy into the church's climate.

> *The best way to initiate change is to maintain a playful detachment from the negative emotional triggers surrounding the church.*

Deliver results. Members want to believe that their church is warm and caring. If I tell them they are not warm and caring, they will fulfill that description. Start looking for the small things that are going in the right direction. Acknowledge them, celebrate them, and keep building on them. There are good things happening in the climate of every church. Find them, build on them.

Instill stories and metaphors. I once heard an old Hopi proverb, "The one who tells the stories rules the world." In churches where the membership has been in a prolonged decline, the stories we tell can become self-fulfilling. The metaphors we use are formative for climate dynamics. Imagine how the following statements would affect the climate of your church: "Our church is on a downward spiral. I don't know what it will take to pull it back up, but it doesn't seem like anything is working." Or, "It's hard to stand by and watch things crash and burn without addressing them."

I once had an elder lash out at the other board members because he was "the only one doing anything" in the church. Not only was that not so, it made those present less inclined to invest themselves in the church. The stories and metaphors we use shape how we think, and feel, about our church.

The good news is that we can create an intentional mythology (in the sense of our origins, purpose, and destiny) in our ministries. My wife and I decided to finish our basement a few years after we moved into our home. If you visited my home two years ago, you would have found a maze of lumber, pipes, and wires crisscrossing our basement. You would not think it looked like much, but I would have given you an enthusiastic tour as I described the unique details of each room. We had a story of what was to come, and we told ourselves, and everyone else, that story constantly. This made the mess of construction bearable, even enjoyable. The stories told will either buoy or sink the climate of your church.

Trust that change will happen.

Embrace positive traditions and rituals. Come and visit the fifth-grade classroom at College Heights Christian School in Lacombe, Alberta, with me. The homeroom teacher, Steven Gabrys, incorporates rituals into the daily life of his students. My favorite is the carabiner (a metal clip often used by climbers) and the rope. The arriving student takes a carabiner with their name on it and clips it onto a climbing rope. The carabiner slides down to join the carabiners of all the other students who are in the classroom. When you "clip in," the ritual signifies that you are ready to join the class and begin learning.

Our small churches are rich in traditions and rituals: when we sing and pray; whether we stand, kneel, or sit; how we acknowledge visitors; from where does the pastor enter the pulpit; and fellowship meals. These traditions and rituals mean something. Even if no one in the church knows what they mean, they communicate. What are they communicating? When a pastor enters the pulpit from a pastor's study behind the rostrum, this signals something different than when a pastor rises from a front pew and ascends the rostrum. The former signals that the pastor is coming from a place of holiness, communion with God and His Word, from outside the community of faith. The latter signals that the pastor is coming from inside the community of faith, as a fellow petitioner, from a point of commonality. Embrace the positive traditions in your church and maybe start some new ones.

Trust the process. Change takes time. Do not give up if some of your members are unfriendly to visitors even months after a friendlier attitude was introduced. My kids have been taking violin lessons for four years now. They had to develop step-by-step to bring them to the place that they are learning their first Bach pieces now. Change in small churches takes that kind of time. This is where pastoral tenure in districts is crucial to church health. I had the privilege of being in my last district for eight years. Real growth and change did not become evident until the last half of my time there, but it was built on the investment made in those early years. Trust that change will happen.

Small church morale

I used to be on the pastoral staff of the largest church (over 1,300 members) in my conference. Now I pastor three of the smallest churches in the conference. If, in the future, I accept a call to minister in a larger church, some will congratulate me on the "move up." But, where did we get the idea that moving from a small church to a big church is a "move up"? Some will point out that Jesus tells us of growth from small to large. For example, Jesus said, "The kingdom of heaven is like a mustard seed, which a man took and sowed in his field,

> *But in the kingdom of heaven, excellence is measured by investment, not return, by faithfulness to duty, not result.*

which indeed is the least of all the seeds; but when it is grown it is greater than the herbs and becomes a tree, so that the birds of the air come and nest in its branches" (Matthew 13:31, 32, NKJV). So bigger must mean more blessed. Yet Jesus also cautioned against equating bigger with better.

- He said in the kingdom the least are the greatest (Matthew 18; Mark 9; Luke 9; 22).
- A widow puts two pennies in the offering plate. Jesus says they are worth more than the bag of gold the rich man donated (Mark 12).
- He described the kingdom of heaven like a wealthy landowner who paid the man hired at 5:00 P.M. the same as the man hired at 6:00 A.M. (Matthew 20).

A small amount of work is as valuable as a large amount.

The challenge is that we want to be applauded for our twelve-hour workdays. We want a bag of gold to drop in the offering plate. We want to be a mustard tree, not a mustard seed. But in the kingdom of heaven, excellence is measured by investment, not return, by faithfulness to duty, not result. But there is something even inside Christians that rebels at the thought of being small. Small seems unimportant and forgotten. David Smith argues that small churches can be the ideal for Christian life, but are often treated otherwise: "The small membership congregation is the normal and healthy expression of the body of Christ. Unfortunately, it is treated like a malnourished miniature of a large congregation."[12] Where better, than in a small, close-knit group of believers, to grow in Christ and minister with the gifts He has given us? But if my small congregation spends much of its time trying to be like a big church, we are missing the point. If you believe a small church is the best place to worship, your congregations will believe it too.

Conclusion

Whether you pastor two or three, or more, churches, your ministry can thrive if you focus on what small churches do best. There is always something positive each church offers you and your family. Though sometimes difficult, you will reap the benefits of staying connected with each church and investing in your best resources, the local members and leaders. This is essential when working towards creating a warm, more caring climate within each of your churches. Small churches are the normal expression of God's work of grace within the church and larger community.

1. Tyler Rosengren, personal correspondence, November 19, 2014.
2. See Hebrews 4:14–16.
3. See Revelation 1:4–6; 5:10.
4. James L. Killen, *Pastoral Care in the Small Membership Church* (Nashville, TN: Abingdon Press, 2005), 99.
5. David B. Smith, *Small Does Not Mean Struggling: And Other Stories of Small Church Propaganda* (Enumclaw, WA: WinePress Publishing, 2011), 3.
6. Killen, *Pastoral Care,* 99.
7. Glenn C. Daman, *Shepherding the Small Church: A Leadership Guide for the Majority of Today's Churches* (Grand Rapids, MI: Kregel Publications, 2008), 225.
8. Ibid.
9. Killen, *Pastoral Care,* 100.
10. Mark DeVries, *Sustainable Youth Ministry: Why Most Youth Ministry Doesn't Last and What Your Church Can Do About It* (Downers Grove, IL: Intervarsity Press, 2008).
11. Steve R. Bierly, *How to Thrive as a Small-Church Pastor: A Guide to Spiritual and Emotional Well-Being* (Grand Rapids, MI: Zondervan, 1998), 6.
12. Smith, *Small Does Not Mean Struggling,* xi.

How Can a Pastor Do It All?

JOHN BRUNT

Q uestion: How can a pastor do it all? There is so much work that needs to be done. How can one person possibly get it all done?

Short answer: *You can't.*

This chapter will attempt to give a longer and hopefully more helpful answer to this question, but we have to begin with the honest realization that no one can really get it all done.

I was fortunate to learn this from a senior pastor for whom I worked when I first started out in ministry almost fifty years ago. He gave this good advice: "If you're going to be a pastor, you have to learn to live with guilt. There will always be much more to do than you can possibly do. Every night you will go to bed wishing you could have done more, knowing that more needs to be done. If, by God's grace, you can't live with that, you probably can't be a pastor."

I have a friend who says he asks himself every morning, "Who will I disappoint today?" Part of keeping our sanity means coming to terms with a task that is always beyond us, and living with the assurance that God knows we only have twenty-four hours in a day and that God does not expect us to do the impossible. The impossible is God's exclusive domain.

> *The impossible is God's exclusive domain.*

What I have chosen to do in this chapter is offer some personal reflections on the tasks of pastoral ministry. This is not a research presentation, nor is it a scholarly presentation on the latest work in pastoral journals. I simply want to share from personal experience some of the ways I have learned to cope with the challenging work of pastoral ministry. How do I maximize efficiency and minimize those things that can easily waste a lot of time? I will focus on practices that save time in the long run.

First, a caveat. I want to be honest right up front and admit that my pastorate is not typical. Not many of my pastoral colleagues have had the privilege of six full-time associate pastors. I think, however, that the principles outlined here are applicable to the sole pastor and district pastor, as well as the senior pastor. Of course, we all have to work in our own armor, so feel free to take what is helpful and ignore what is not.

Creating a team

The first time-spending practice that ends up saving time in the long run is selecting the right team. Nothing wastes time faster than micromanaging the work of others. We have to rely on others joining us in the work of ministry.

In my situation, where I am blessed with a team of associate pastors, this means paying a lot of attention to the gifts of those pastors. I know I will not have most of them forever. They will grow and move on to other responsibilities. One of the most important tasks I have is working with the conference and the congregation in choosing associates who fit with the congregation and are dedicated to ministry. I have been truly blessed in this regard.

> Micromanaging is one of the biggest time wasters for any pastor.

I try to be available to the associates whenever they need me, but a big part of my ability to get my work done is having talented, hard-working, initiative takers around me and letting them work without needing a lot of supervision. *Micromanaging is one of the biggest time wasters for any pastor.* The more I can trust those who work with me and let them run with their work, the more we all can accomplish.

Of course, we do all need to be singing off the same page, so it is essential to spend time together in bonding and planning with each other and with God. We meet as a pastoral staff twice each week. One meeting is our regular staff meeting, which begins with worship and then deals with the business of our work. We all keep track of what each one is doing. Our second meeting each week is without agenda. It is time for us to study and pray together as we feed our souls. This way we stay together in purpose.

Most of us find we have incredibly talented people in our churches. Helping people find meaningful and rewarding work to do for the church is often a great gift to them. I am amazed at how much people are willing to give of themselves when the work they are given fits their talents and interests. Any pastor who tries to do it all, will fail. As we have already deduced, there is far more ministry to do than any one of us can possibly do. We maximize our ministry when we not only do ministry but also facilitate empowering others to do ministry.

But working with a volunteer staff is quite a bit trickier. Volunteers work out of the goodness of their hearts and require more care and feeding. Our church would come to a grinding halt in no time if we did not have dedicated volunteers. *The two most important elements in working with volunteers are putting the right person in the right slot, and making sure they feel appreciated.*

Since I work with a team of associates, my direct work is with them more than with lay leadership. Nevertheless, I spend a lot of time with lay leaders when nominating committee time comes so that we choose the right people for the right slots. Time spent making the right lay leadership choices will save lots of time later on.

Fortunately, it does not take a lot for most people to sense genuine appreciation. One of our former children's pastors used to give a little gift for each of her Sabbath School division leaders and teachers every week. She would have it waiting for them when they arrived on Sabbath morning. People loved it.

Do not be afraid to make adjustments if you have people in the wrong volunteer positions. Most people sense it when things are not going well and will welcome the opportunity to switch to something that they find more rewarding.

The same principle applies to volunteers as well as full-time associates. Try to pick people who, once trained, can work without micromanaging and close supervision. It is a whole let better to spend your time picking the right people who can carry out their ministry on their own, than trying to spend time constantly helping people get out of trouble. Of course, this does not mean that you leave people completely on their own. Make sure you are available to meet with them regularly so you know that all is going well. And it is very important to make sure that time spent with coworkers is not just business, but includes time together with God in prayer and study.

Keeping in contact with members

We have to spend time with our members. If we do not, then our sermons will soon be irrelevant. That used to mean going out and visiting all the members in their homes, but today that is much more difficult. People are busy, and some are perhaps not that anxious to have the pastor come and disrupt their already frantic lives. This is especially true in large churches and urban areas.

Even in a large church there is an expectation that the senior pastor will be in contact with the members. If a person is in the hospital and other church leaders visit but I do not, a person will say, "The pastor didn't come to see me." Therefore, with the recognition that I cannot possibly do regular visitation on over two thousand people, I concentrate my visiting on acute situations. When someone is in the hospital, someone is going to have surgery, or someone in the family dies, I try to be there. That often means being at the hospital early in the morning to pray before surgery. I also try to see every member that goes into an acute care hospital.

Pastoral presence at church activities is also an important aspect of contact with the congregation.

Visits do not have to be long to be meaningful, however. I try to group hospital visiting to make it as efficient as possible (members are often in different hospitals). I then spend a few minutes with each person. Often hospital visiting takes me about an hour and a half a day, but it is time well spent.

When someone dies, on the other hand, I drop everything and take as much time with the family as needed. I find that people are very understanding when I have to break an appointment because there has been a death in a family.

I do not do any routine visiting to try and contact every member, however. One of the associate pastors does regular visiting of people who are no longer able to come to church and local elders take Communion to these each quarter. By limiting my visitation time to acute situations, I save time and still have important contact at crucial times with members.

Pastoral presence at church activities is also an important aspect of contact with the congregation. In our congregation there are often multiple activities at the same time. The Adventurer Club may be having a function the same night the young adults are having a party and there is an anniversary reception for a couple in the church. There is no way I can attend everything that is going on. Sometimes I drive into the church parking lot and have no idea why all the cars are there. This is part of that admission that we cannot do everything.

It can be very helpful, however, to learn the art of making appearances so that people know you are interested without staying through an entire event. Of course, when you are present, you need to be 100 percent present and genuinely interested and involved in what is happening. But you do not have to stay for the whole party or social event. I find that people appreciate my presence but are understanding of the fact that there is a lot going on. I often have members say, "We don't know how you seem to be everywhere at once." Obviously, I am not. But I do try to let every ministry of the church know that I am interested and appreciate what they do.

For example, every year our Adventurer Club (200 four- to nine-year-olds) takes a camping trip for a full weekend on a beach 150 miles from our church. There is no way I can attend an entire weekend. But every year I pack a sack lunch in the morning, and when our second worship service is over, I eat it while driving to the campsite. I arrive about 4:00 P.M., in time to eat supper with them and worship with them in their sundown vespers, then enjoy roasting marshmallows after sundown. I leave about 8:00 P.M., drive home, and arrive at about 11:00 P.M. It makes for a long day, but I have to admit I love doing it and feel like I need to let the Adventurer leaders know how much I appreciate their hard work (and just plain bravery) for taking all those kids for a weekend.

I know I cannot get to everything, but by selective and partial presence at important activities, I can have a significant amount of contact with members and communicate my genuine interest in all that the members are doing for the church.

Even though it is impossible to visit everyone, I feel that I have to have some kind of contact with all church members. That contact is never as much as I wish it were. I try to be in the lobby of the church after the services and greet people, but there is so much activity that it is hard to have meaningful contact.

One way I make sure to have at least minimum contact with members is to call them on their birthdays. (I stole this idea from my friend, Gordon Bietz, who did it when he pastored the church at Southern Adventist University, where he now serves as president.) That makes for an average of seven phone calls a day. I can usually do that in less than half an hour. If the member is not home, I

But I do try to let every ministry of the church know that I am interested and appreciate what they do.

leave a message on their answering machine or voicemail. I think members have appreciated this as much as anything I do. Some purposely do not answer the phone so they can keep the message on the machine or voicemail—then call back and tell me what they have done. I have been surprised how many times someone who has not attended church in a while will return the next week after their birthday call. It is not time-consuming but keeps me in touch in at least a minimal way. It also often opens the door to problems that need follow-up with a visit in their home or my office.

Time spent with members is never wasted. Yet, I do have to concentrate on maximizing that time. By concentrating on acute situations; making sure I have some contact with everyone, at least by phone; and trying to be present for part, though not necessarily all major events, I attempt to maximize my time with members.

Preaching

For any pastor who preaches regularly, preaching takes a huge chunk of time. There is no such thing as instant sermon preparation where you just dump in the ingredients, mix, and bake. Good sermons take time. And they should. The Sabbath morning sermon is where our main contact with the congregation takes place. Even in a church of one hundred, a half-hour sermon means fifty person contact hours. No other aspect of ministry will give you that many hours of access to the congregation. The sermon, therefore, deserves a major portion of our time. I have, however, found ways to maximize my sermon preparation time. There are ways of spending time in the short run to save time in the long run in sermon preparation.

One of the biggest time wasters in preaching is trying to figure out what I am going to preach about this week. It can take hours just to decide on a text and topic.

One way to minimize this waste of time is to do series preaching. This avoids the weekly concern for what I will preach about this week. It also means that much of the background and exegetical work I do for the series as a whole will benefit more than one sermon.

Good sermons take time.

I find it extremely useful to get away for a day or two and focus on the section of Scripture that will serve as the basis for my series. During that intensive focus, I try to outline what the preaching passages will be. I then make a computer file for each of the sermons. As I go about life and ministry, when ideas and illustrations occur to me, I take time to add them to my file. This way when I begin the specific sermon preparation at the beginning of the week, I do not start with a blank piece of paper. I have already studied the passage, have a general outline, and have some possible stories or illustrations. If I had to start from scratch every Monday, I would waste a lot of time just deciding what to do for that given week.

I also maximize sermon preparation time by trying to let the outline of the sermon flow from the passage. That way the biblical author has already done a lot of the work for me.

Keeping stories and illustrative material filed in a form that is easily accessible for you can also maximize sermon time. Taking time to write down stories and ideas you might use in the future is a great way to save time in the long run. Never let a good story go by unsaved. This is especially true of personal experiences, which are always the best kind of stories.

I keep a computer file where I list stories, even if I have no idea how I would ever use it at the time. I know the time will come when it will be the perfect illustration for a sermon. I also make a file every time I read a book and jot down what I might use, where it is found, and how it might be used. After I have done the biblical work so that I have a clear idea of what my thesis will be, I go down through the files looking for what might work as illustrative material. When the biblical passage, a clear thesis, and good illustrative material all come together, the sermon is well on its way.

When I was writing my dissertation, my professor used to say, "If you get the proposal and the outline right, the dissertation writes itself." I did not find that to be true, but it did make it a lot easier. Sermons will *not* write themselves, but with a regular program of diligent Bible study and keeping track of all the interesting things that you do or read about, it can be much easier. A few minutes at the end of the day keeping track of what happened of interest that might at some time be used in a sermon will save hours of searching later on.

Here is another preaching time saver. I try to personalize every wedding and funeral sermon so that I never give what sounds like "standard funeral sermon number two." Each sermon is different and relevant for the individual. This means a lot of extra sermons, since I average a funeral sermon every two to three weeks, and it is largely the same people who hear all of these sermons. I have found, however, that for every minute I spend listening to the family I save far more minutes in preparation. I sit down and ask the family to share stories and anecdotes that represent who the person really was. Then I ask for favorite texts and hymns. In a similar way, when doing a wedding, I listen to the couple's story, spend several hours in pre-marital counseling with them, and I ask them to pick a passage of Scripture for me to use as the basis for my wedding homily. Therefore, I am not starting with a blank piece of paper; I begin with a good start and plenty of material. Again, spending time in the short run saves time in the long run.

Take time for yourself

When there is more work to do every day than we can possibly do, there is a great temptation to spend every working hour trying to get it all done. There is an old saying, however, that goes, "All work and no play makes Jack a dull boy." It also makes anyone a dull preacher, as well as an ineffective minister. I find that a day with my grandsons not only invigorates me but also always gives me sermon illustrations and material. The church will not disappear if you are gone every now and then. I find that there is no such thing as a day off when I am at home. I need to get away in order to leave the work behind and be refreshed.

> *Our time spent in personal devotion not only saves time in the long run but also keeps us focused on what our work is all about.*

Trusting God

Finally, the most important part of the struggle to get everything done is trusting our work to God. It is God's work, not our own. God knows how many hours we have each day. He does not expect more than we can do. Ask Him for guidance each day in leading you to what is most important. Our time spent in personal devotion not only saves time in the long run but also keeps us focused on what our work is all about. Commit your work to God, and then at the end of the day, go to sleep with the assurance that God is in control and you have done your best.

📄 SCHOLARSHIP

Pastors diligently and carefully study the Bible and professional resources for continual personal growth in Christ.

Descriptors of Scholarship include:
- excellent doctrinal knowledge and integrity
- well-read
- prepared academically
- proficient in basic biblical studies
- masters exegesis, hermeneutics, and relevant application
- preaching reflects deep, continual study
- current on best practices of ministry
- seeks member feedback for continual professional growth
- fulfills continuing education requirements
- develops church as a learning community

The Minister as Theological Communicator

ÁNGEL MANUEL RODRÍGUEZ

I n this chapter we will examine the task of ministers as communicators of theological truth. We begin by discussing how they should evaluate different theological options and then proceed to examine the different ways they communicate biblical theology. But first, there are two words in the title of this exposition that need brief attention. The first one is *theological*. Throughout their ministry, ministers communicate the content of biblical theology. Theology, briefly defined, is the study of the nature, character, and work of God. It also studies how we come to experientially know about Him and how this impacts the way we relate to others. The theological task is rigorous and requires analysis and careful thinking.

Communication, the other word, is what defines the primary task of ministers. In an Adventist biblical theology, this communication happens in the context of a cosmic struggle that has clouded the truth about God and His intentions for suffering humanity. Therefore, ministry takes place in a setting of conflict that challenges ministers to find an appealing and effective way to mediate biblical theological truth using simple and clear language aimed, under the influence of the Spirit, at touching the minds and hearts of the listeners.

When we refer to ministers as theological communicators, we intend to say that they are well-informed on theological issues, their sermons and instructions are the outflow of biblical theology, and that their messages are logically structured and clearly expressed. Jesus and the apostles were, above all, communicators of the love of God for sinful humanity (e.g., Luke 6:27–36; Romans 5:5–8; 1 John 4:7–21). They powerfully proclaimed, throughout the land of Israel and the Roman Empire, this most glorious message of salvation. Jesus taught us that profound theological truths can be communicated through very simple language: "I am the bread of life" (John 6:35, NKJV). "The kingdom of heaven is like a mustard seed" (Matthew 13:31, NKJV). True communication takes place when its content is embodied in the language and experience of the receptor addressing his or her needs. This is the type of communicator a minister should be.

Evaluating theological options

Ministerial training provides the basic tools needed to engage and evaluate the multiplicity of theological positions found in the Christian market of theological ideas. The multiplicity of communication tools available to us today is unique in human history, as is also the amount of information placed at our religious and intellectual fingertips. In most places around the world, this flow of theological data is also accessible to church members who, after being exposed to it, are often left in a state of inquiry or disorientation. They do not have the tools needed to navigate safely in the ocean of theological options. Ministers are expected to open a safe way for parishioners through what is often the dead sea of theological speculations. The tools at the minister's disposal are the Scriptures, their convictions as ministers of the Adventist Church, and their knowledge of theological traditions with their assumptions in the Christian world.

Ministers are expected to open a safe way for parishioners through what is often the dead sea of theological speculations.

Christian theology finds its source in God's self-revelation as preserved for us in the Scriptures (2 Timothy 3:16). True Christian theology is, by its very nature, a theology that is biblical. Ministers have constant access to this theology as they read and analyze the Word of God. There are others doing the same and offering to the church theological alternatives. It is at this point that the ministers' knowledge of the Bible becomes indispensable for their own safety and for that of the parish. An Adventist minister is a servant of the Word of God and, as such, is well informed about its theological content. Discernment is indeed a gift of the Spirit, but it is developed through the constant study of the Bible. The Bible provides for us objective information that is to be used in weighing the value and truthfulness of theological options. Consequently, one of the primary responsibilities of ministers is to develop a way of thinking that has been shaped by their constant study of the Bible.

Therefore, Adventist ministers belong to a community of faith that has a well-defined identity and message. Here the issue of ethical responsibility surfaces and enters the discussion of the minister as communicator of theological truth. In the evaluation of theological options, ministers should take into consideration the biblical message that their community of faith identified, through the study of the Bible and the guidance of the Spirit, as having a particular and yet a major significance at the close of the cosmic conflict. This biblical message, embraced by the world community of faith, is authoritative for the church and can and should be used in the evaluation of theological alternatives placed at the table of the minister or the parish (1 Timothy 6:3). This message, entrusted by the risen and glorified Lord to the church for its proclamation (see Matthew 28:18–20), is biblically reliable. In order to use this tool to evaluate theological alternatives, ministers need to know it well and be persuaded of its truthfulness (2 Timothy 1:13, 14). In other words, it requires conviction on the part of the minister in order to be effective as an evaluative tool.

> *Our acquaintance with that history, in conjunction with a deep knowledge of the Bible, provides the discernment needed to establish parishioners in their faith.*

Ministers also need a basic knowledge of the development of Christian theology in order to evaluate theological options. This is not indispensable, but knowing the pre-history of theological options enhances the process of evaluation. Very often the theological options we face as ministers are a recycling of ancient teachings. In such cases, we have at our disposal answers already given to these false theological views. The history of Christianity demonstrates that Christian theology has been, to a significant extent, shaped by philosophical ideas and social concerns. Our acquaintance with that history, in conjunction with a deep knowledge of the Bible, provides the discernment needed to establish parishioners in their faith.

The experience of ministers as theological communicators

The life of ministers is complex and multifaceted. They minister parishioners through a myriad of personal experiences and in collective activities. In every situation ministers remain what they are—ministers of the Word of God and servants of the church. Their role as theological communicators is never placed in a drawer—it is never inactive. They cannot leave home without it. In most cases, when the telephone rings, they are expected to share the teachings and principles of the Bible to guide the Christian life and the church. Here we will look at some of these important ministerial settings.

Theological communication and the pulpit

It is during the worship hour that ministers are able to address most of their church members as a group. It is at this time the rhetorical skills of the minister are to be displayed in the proclamation of biblical truth. Theological ideas have to be communicated in a persuasive way by revealing its beauty, depth, consistency, and relevance. In such occasions, there is hardly any place for the use of technical theological jargon. Here the minister mediates theology by becoming a humble servant of the Scriptures and the congregation in its particular setting. The worship setting is the place where we are expected to proclaim the deepest biblical, theological truth of all: the work of Christ (1 Corinthians 1:23–25; 2:2).

But the pulpit is not a forum for theological debates and neither is the church a university where contradictory ideas are offered to the students in order for them to decide by themselves what to conclude.

Christ unifies true theology as well as the community of believers. Occasionally, the pulpit is used to debate theological issues that divide the church and destroy the spirit of worship. The church is left in a state of turmoil, and people get hurt. But the pulpit is not a forum for theological debates and neither is the church a university where contradictory ideas are offered to the students in order for them to decide by themselves what to conclude. By nature, the church is the depository of biblical truth with a well-defined message entrusted to it by the Lord (1 Timothy 3:15). It is this message that ministers are to proclaim every Sabbath. The heart of that message is the gospel of salvation through faith in Christ Jesus. This is the most important theological truth that ministers are to communicate from their pulpits. In the exposition of this most wonderful truth, the mind of church members is to be challenged as much as possible because, in seeing its depth, the ties of love that unite them to their Lord will be strengthened. When we are drawn into the mystery of the love of God, we respond with love.

It is part of the theological task of ministers to make Christ the center of every sermon they proclaim. This is a very important theological and ministerial responsibility in that ministers are called to reflect on the significance of Christ in every aspect of their personal lives and in the lives of the parishioners and to proclaim it with power and conviction. The pulpit should become the place from which every aspect of the Adventist message, mission, and lifestyle is proclaimed from the perspective of the cross of Christ. In doing this, ministers reach their highest call as theological communicators within the community of believers.

Theological communication and evangelism

As communicators, ministers reach out to the world at large beyond the borders of the parish. The church is a part of society and has a role to play within that society. It must leaven it with the message of the saving Lord. Truthfully, this is the reason for the existence of the church (cf. Matthew 4:14–16). As theological communicators, ministers should keep in mind several things. First, they have to stay in touch with the world of theology. Theologians must provide sound theological arguments for ministers to be used in the formulation of their messages in mission outreach. This is the place where theology faces other world religions, secularism, postmodernism, and so on, in order to reveal the magnificent power of Jesus. This means that theology, in order to be meaningful and fruitful, should always be at the service of the church. Ministers should constantly search for new theological insights that will help them reinforce the persuasive power of their messages to nonbelievers. As already indicated, ministers who are theological communicators are well informed about theological matters and incorporate that knowledge into their evangelism.

Ministers should constantly search for new theological insights that will help them reinforce the persuasive power of their messages to nonbelievers.

Second, in the case of church members, the theological content of the ministers' sermons seeks to reaffirm believers in their commitment to Christ and His church and to expound its implications for their daily lives. In the case of nonbelievers, ministers seek to motivate individuals to commit themselves to the Lord. In this last case, it is particularly important that the content of the message be clear, persuasive, and truthful. Biblical theological truth is grounded in Christ and to be insightfully presented in a logical and consistent way. The truthfulness of the message is determined by its biblical content, and its significance should not be underestimated. Ministers call individuals to place their whole lives on the side of the biblical truth they proclaim. This is a most radical change, and we owe it to them to be clear and personally committed to what we proclaim. Third, the communication of theological truth in evangelism should deal with the needs of the audience, make sense to them, and challenge them to break away from spiritual and intellectual inertia. A superficial message could hardly achieve these objectives. Theological reflection is indispensable as ministers prepare the content of their messages, because it will be used by the Spirit to touch the hearts of the audience.

Theological communication and instruction

Ministers are also called to function as teachers (Ephesians 4:11). They fulfill this role not only from the pulpit but also in many other ways. I would suggest that the content of the teaching is fundamentally of a theological nature. It is grounded in the theological content of the Bible, in its specific ethical and moral instructions, as well as in the principles found there that define the nature of the Christian life and the life of the community of believers. In this section, I want to concentrate on instructing church members on theological issues. It would be useful for the minister to meet with the elders or church board and discuss with them theological issues that the church is facing. This could also be done by giving seminars in the church for those interested in the topics. I would suggest that this be done with several objectives in mind.

First, local church members, and more specifically church leaders, should know some of the challenges they could face if individuals were to come to their church proclaiming theological or doctrinal alternatives. In this case, ministers would be equipping the church to identify theological deviations even in their absence. Second, this type of instruction should include proper ways to deal with the situation if it ever arises in the parish. In other words, theological communication should be preventive and should preempt, if possible, potential conflicts. Third, theological education in the local congregation must try to strengthen the unity of the church by affirming church members in the biblical reliability of and in their commitment to the message of the church. Although there are different areas in which theological diversity is acceptable, this should not be the case with respect to the message of the church.

Theological communication in the life of the church

Biblical theology expresses itself in the social interaction of church members. The church is a community of believers gathered together by the Spirit from different ways of life and cultures. Diversity characterizes this community as it comes together to worship and share with each other. Here we enter the realm of ecclesiology and its foundation. Ministers need to have a clear understanding of the nature of the church in order to minister to its real needs by creating an environment within which it can flourish. This environment is the result of both the minister and the church working together and the demands from the minister sharing the biblical understanding of the nature and function of the church with church members. First, as part of their role as theological communicators, ministers should visualize their local congregations as part of a global community

Church members are to be constantly gaining a deeper understanding of the message of the church and its implication for their lives.

of faith—the universality (catholicity) of the church. This important theological insight should be shared with church members. They are part of a divine program of global proportions in which each member is expected to play a role at both the local and the global level. The church is a world family.

Second, ministers are expected to speak theologically to the church in terms of its unity in message and mission. These two elements are at the heart of the nature and the role of the church as the body of Christ and will contribute in a direct way to its unity. Church members are to be constantly gaining a deeper understanding of the message of the church and its implication for their lives. This is to take place primarily through the minister as a communicator of biblical theology. Third, the peaceful coexistence of church members—a difficult and

The love of God for us that was manifested on the cross (1 John 4:9, 10) should determine the way church members treat each other.

challenging task for ministers—is theologically grounded in their fellowship with God, Christ, and each other through the power of the Holy Spirit (1 John 1:3, 6, 7). The love of God for us that was manifested on the cross (1 John 4:9,

10) should determine the way church members treat each other. The deeper the ministers' understanding and proclamation of that love is, the deeper would be the experience of fellowship among church members. It is one of the minister's responsibilities to communicate the theology of the church to the parishioners in clear and winsome ways in order to assist them in becoming what they ought to be in Christ.

Theological communication in informal settings

The work of ministers does not end after the sermon; on the contrary, it begins there. They will be involved in the lives of church members in a multiplicity of settings, some of which are pleasant (e.g., birth of a child, a baptism, a birthday celebration) and others not (e.g., sickness, funerals, divorce). In those settings, the minister as a theological communicator is also active in a variety of ways. It is often in these situations that the theology of the ministers is tested with questions coming from the daily experience of the parishioner. For instance, there are those whose faith needs to be reaffirmed in the midst of doubts and even disorientation. They want to truly understand how the theological message of the church or the Bible could help them end the intellectual dissonance they are facing. Here theological arguments play an important role but cannot and should not be separated from a faith commitment to the Lord in the midst of some uncertainty.

This is theology in overalls; in fact, true theology is always theology in overalls.

For others life is going well, but they are slowly drifting away; their spiritual life is dying, and they are sincerely concerned about it. They need from the minister a vision for their lives. Theology should be able to provide for them guidance on how to live the Christian life in an opulent society in which the need for God is hardly felt. In this case, theology takes the form of both theological instruction and personal inspiration or motivation to continue the Christian pilgrimage on parched land. Still others want to know the will of the Lord for their lives. The challenge of making decisions tends to disturb many parishioners. How can they be certain that what they are about to do is God's will for them? In many cases, what is needed is counseling, but in others theological instruction is also needed. In fact, unpacking for church members how to know God's will for them in the variety of situations they meet in life is one of the most important theological topics to be addressed not only in private conversations but particularly from the pulpit. This requires clear and sensitive theological thinking from ministers that is both pragmatic and biblically solid.

Then there are those who are facing personal conflict and suffering. Through them ministers confront questions about suffering not in the abstract, as theologians and philosophers often do, but in the very being of the parishioner. Their hearts are bleeding, and the intensity of their fears and anxieties deeply afflicts them. The minister appropriates it and suffers together with them. Interestingly, in some occasions they are not necessarily seeking to understand but to feel accepted and loved by the minister and the church while struggling with their pain. It is important for ministers to distinguish between cases that require a clear theological exposition of biblical truth and guidance in the midst of suffering from cases that require for theology to take the shape of an embrace, a tear, or a touch. In some cases, it is necessary to say, "I understand what you are going through . . ."; but in others, it would be better to say, "I do not understand, but I am here for you and your family . . ." This is theology in overalls; in fact, true theology is always theology in overalls.

One of the most important gifts of the Spirit that ministers need is the gift of discernment.

Conclusion

Communication is an intrinsic part of the role of ministers; there is no ministry without communication. But what is truly important is the content or what is communicated. We have suggested that ministers communicate biblical theology. This means that they have studied and continue to study the theological content of the Scriptures and that it provides the content of their message. It also means that they express it in a logical and persuasive way, taking into consideration the needs of the parish. This deep theological knowledge, together with a commitment to the message and mission of the church they serve, and a basic knowledge of the history of Christian theology, are instrumental in the ministers' evaluation of different theological options. One of the most important gifts of the Spirit that ministers need is the gift of discernment.

The role of the minister as theological communicator is active in every aspect of their ministry. It is particularly visible from the pulpit and in evangelism when the exposition of biblical theological themes is couched in clear, logical, and persuasive ways. At the heart of this theology is the Person and work of Christ. In every message, word of encouragement, prayer, and doctrinal exposition, Christ should be constantly at the center. Christian theology is precisely about what God has done for us through the sacrifice of His Son. We proclaim the deepest truth in the cosmos: God was in Christ reconciling the world to Himself (see 2 Corinthians 5:19).

Current Theological and Intellectual Trends

JIŘÍ MOSKALA

I n order for their ministry to be relevant, pastors need to understand the contemporary world. Without such understanding, our service is in jeopardy and our preaching shallow and unresponsive to current society's intellectual struggles. This isolation may hinder or even silence God's commission in the world.

Christian thinkers are wrestling with similar issues as we do in our church, and we can learn from their experiences. For example, Carl Raschke urges evangelicals to embrace postmodernity and predicts, if accepted, it would produce the next Christian reformation.[1] Gregory Boyd warns Protestants to be cautious in their eagerness to be involved in politics.[2] Many are engaged in in-depth conversations regarding hermeneutics, the role and ordination of women, homosexuality, interfaith marriages, evolution and theistic evolution, the relationship between faith and science, leadership style, relevancy of evangelism, church authority and structure, Christianity and other world religions, salvation of non-Christians, religious secularism, how to effectively work for youth and big cities, environmental studies, nonviolent atonement, meaning of justification by faith, contextualization, culture relativism, violence, participation in war and military service, entertainment, health (e.g., Rick Warren's *The Daniel Plan*[3]), and so forth. We are not able to deal with the vastness of these problems in this brief overview. However, we will focus on this question: What are the principal theological and intellectual trends that form thinking and influence behavior in our present-day world? I will limit this study to seven crucial trends that are important to Seventh-day Adventist ministers.

Attacks on religion and the picture of God

A growing number of films, and some contemporary music texts, contain negative statements about God and glorify crime as well as the powers of darkness. However, the most explicit focus on ridiculing God and His character is voiced by protagonistic neo-atheism, and sadly, even some theologians and Bible scholars add to this mix. These Christian thinkers question the biblical portrayal of God.

The classical atheists usually did not paint a dark picture of God. They asserted God's nonexistence and the folly of believing in God and claimed that religion was a human invention and only for the weak. Karl Marx stated it eloquently: "Religion is the opium of the people!"[4] However, with the rise of neo-atheism comes a new phenomenon. The naturalistic origin of life is mixed with aggressive attacks on religion. They not only try to demonstrate that it is foolish and wrong to believe in God but also claim that religion is evil, dangerous, and harmful. They attack the God of the Bible as well as religion in general, yet they express their anger with charm, wit, and eloquence.

Richard Dawkins, emeritus professor of evolutionary biology at Oxford, challenges the Christian religion[5] and attacks the God of the Bible: "The God of the Old Testament is arguably the most unpleasant character in all fiction: jealous and proud of it; a petty, unjust, unforgiving control freak; a vindictive, bloodthirsty ethnic cleanser; a misogynistic, homophobic, racist, infanticidal, genocidal, filicidal, pestilential, megalomaniacal, sadomasochistic, capriciously malevolent bully."[6] Thus, Dawkins plays *forte fortissimo* with the atheistic melody and presents the God of the Hebrew Scriptures as a moral monster.

Sam Harris, another critic of religion, wrote three books on the topic—*The End of Faith, Letter to a Christian Nation,* and *The Moral Landscape: How Science Can Determine Human Values.*[7] In *The Moral Landscape,* he acknowledges that people think that science and evolution have nothing to say on morality and the formation of human values. He tries to answer this puzzle through science, because otherwise people's ethical behavior is a primary justification for the Christian faith.

Christopher Hitchens, a polemicist and journalist makes a case against religion in his book *God Is Not Great: How Religion Poisons Everything.*[8] He denies the relevancy of religion and defines it as a social poison. He states that religion is a man-made wish, a cause of dangerous sexual control, and a distortion of our understanding of origins. He argues for a secular life based on science and reason.

Daniel Dennett, a Tufts University scientist, in his book *Darwin's Danger-ous Idea: Evolution and the Meanings of Life*,[9] argues that the evolutionary hypothesis is like a powerful "universal solvent, capable of cutting right to the heart of everything in sight." At the end, he states that "the truly dangerous aspect of Darwin's idea is its seductiveness."[10] Dennett claims that Christians manufacture terror, psychological abuse, hell, and phobias.[11]

The views of these scientists are gaining ground especially among the young generation, even though they have built their argumentation on naïve views of determination, our human nature, and the denial of the power of sin. This positivistic understanding of our nature is doomed to fail as human history demonstrates. The selfishness of our human heart is naturally incurable and not going from bad to good, but from bad to worse. Corruption, unfortunately, is a notorious problem in any human system.[12]

Even some Christian thinkers paint a dark picture of God. Difficult biblical texts are elaborated upon; usually with the author's own spin. For example, Julia O'Brien wrestles with images of God as "an abusive husband," "authoritarian father," and "angry warrior."[13] David Penchansky entitles the six chapters of his book as follows: "The Insecure God," "The Irrational God," "The Vindictive God," "The Dangerous God," "The Malevolent God," and "The Abusive God."[14] One of the attacks on God's character is expressed by Bart D. Ehrman, an authority on the early church, New Testament textual criticism, and the life of Jesus, in the book *God's Problem: How the Bible Fails to Answer Our Most Important Question—Why We Suffer*.[15]

Portraying God as immoral is nothing new, but the recent attacks come with innovative twists and arguments; they are disturbing, shocking, humiliating, and puzzling. The answer has much to do with a close reading of the sacred text, an understanding of biblical metanarrative, and the great controversy in its context. There are outstanding biblical and theological studies that can help us better understand the issues. The reader needs to think critically and will not agree with every detail because different writers explain things from their own perspectives and presuppositions. Our knowledge is limited, but the material they present is helpful and stimulating, and it leads to serious reflection.[16]

Evangelicals underline the importance of early Christian tradition

For some Protestants, the patristic tradition of Scripture interpretation has taken on new importance. Daniel Williams underlines the importance of such tradition and reclaims the patristic roots of evangelical faith.[17] He writes about the prominence of "canonical tradition of the patristic church"[18] and argues that the fathers of the earliest centuries can be considered authors and exponents of a "founding" tradition. He maintains these views have been expounded in subsequent centuries and need to be taken seriously by the contemporary expositors. In this view, the patristic tradition is almost normative for biblical interpretation. Thomas Oden claims, "The church fathers offer us context and tradition that will help us establish the roots we need."[19]

Jason Radcliff describes how evangelicals and Catholics should approach patristic tradition and take seriously the Church Fathers.[20] Michael Graves has a revealing subtitle to his book *The Inspiration and Interpretation of Scripture,* namely *What the Early Church Can Teach Us.*[21] There are many evangelical studies on the importance of patristic studies and their interpretation of Scriptures.[22]

Attractiveness of conditionalism/annihilationism

One of the most heated theological debates is over the view of eternal punishment in hell. R. C. Sproul claims "there is no topic in Christian theology more difficult to deal with, particularly on an emotional level, than the doctrine of hell."[23] The recent literature on this subject and closely related issues is abundant.[24] Three major views are being advanced: the traditional view of a never-ending torturing hellfire, the conditional view that the lake of fire irreversibly and totally consumes the damned, and the universalist/restorationist position that hellfire purifies and ultimately enables everyone to be saved.

Many scholars recognize that the doctrine of eternal punishment in hell is problematic and unethical.

Many scholars recognize that the doctrine of eternal punishment in hell is problematic and unethical. Why would a loving God send anyone to hell forever and punish them with never-ending suffering? Clark Pinnock states, "Everlasting torture is intolerable from a moral point of view because it pictures God acting like a bloodthirsty monster who maintains an everlasting Auschwitz for his enemies, whom he does not even allow to die. How can one love a God like that?"[25] Randy Klassen states, according to the foreword by Robert K. Johnston, "The goal of God's justice is closure, not torture."[26] This reasoning leads some evangelicals to a new search for a more relevant and biblically sound interpretation, and thus the acceptance of conditionalism/annihilationism.

The conditionalist view is built on the biblical conviction that human beings are not inherently immortal and that they do not possess immortal souls. On the contrary, they are mortal because they are created beings and sinners (immortality comes as a gift from God by staying in relationship with Him). As sinners, they are doomed to eternal death, unless and until they accept Jesus Christ as their personal Savior. Immortality is conditioned on receiving God's grace and exercising faith in Jesus (John 3:16; 5:24; Romans 3:21–31; Ephesians 2:1–10). Hell is not a place where wicked souls or spirits go immediately after death but is understood as a "lake of fire" in which, at the end of human history, the wicked will be totally consumed (Malachi 4:1; Matthew 25:41; 2 Thessalonians 1:7–10; Revelation 20:9, 10, 14, 15). This fire prepared for the devil and the fallen angels will annihilate them together with the wicked at the last judgment. It is final, no one can quench it, has eternal results, and it will accomplish its purpose—the destruction of evil, sin, death, the wicked, rebellious angels, and Satan himself. In other words, annihilationism teaches that whoever refuses to be saved by God's ultimate love, after God's final judgment, ceases to exist.

The first known advocate of annihilationism was Arnobius of Sicca (d. ca. A.D. 330), who was followed by others throughout Christian history. LeRoy Froom demonstrates this view in his book *The Conditionalist Faith of Our Fathers*.[27] Recently, a plethora of writers with this view have emerged. Among them are F. F. Bruce, John Wenham, Edward Fudge (the best current defender), Clark Pinnock (the most eloquent), David Edwards, John Stott, Phillip Hughes, Joel Green, Robert Brow, Nigel Wright, David Powys, F. LaGard Smith, and John Zens.[28]

Roger Olson argues that annihilationism is "simply a reinterpretation of hell" within the acceptable "mosaic of Christian belief" and laments over "its harsh condemnation by a few fundamentalists" and proposes that it "should not deter Christians from accepting one another as equally believers in the gospel of Jesus Christ."[29] Gregory Boyd affirms: "The joy of heaven is only conceivable if the damned have been annihilated and are remembered no more. When all the biblical evidence is viewed together, it must be admitted that the case for annihilationism is quite compelling."[30]

Clark Pinnock explains: "How can Christians possibly project a deity of such cruelty and vindictiveness whose ways include inflicting everlasting torture upon his creatures, however sinful they may have been? Surely a God who would do such a thing is more nearly like Satan than like God, at least by any ordinary moral standards, and by the Gospel itself."[31] Michael Green writes, "What sort of God would be he who could rejoice eternally in heaven with the saved, while downstairs the cries of the lost make an agonizing cacophony? Such a God is not the person revealed in Scripture as utterly just and utterly loving."[32] Gregory MacDonald asserts that such a God would be a "cosmic torturer."[33] John Wenham emphasizes: "I cannot see that endless punishment is either loving or just. . . . It is a doctrine which I do not know how to preach without negating the loveliness and glory of God."[34] Stephen Travis concurs that endless torture in hell is "incompatible with the love of God in Christ."[35]

Growing voices that defend universalism

Restorationists or universalists claim that all will ultimately be saved, including the wicked, because hell fire will purify them. They claim that the wicked will grow in their understanding of God's unselfish love for them, accept it, and at the end be restored and receive eternal life. This understanding is built on the recognition that after death the immortal soul of the wicked cannot go immediately to heaven but will suffer in the fire of God's judgment. This fire will gradually cleanse them and then, at some future time, everyone will finally be saved. Those who defend this position speak about God's last judgment in terms of His restorative (rather than retributive) justice, which is understood as another side of God's love.

It needs to be stressed, however, that there are various opinions regarding restorationism.[36] Gregory MacDonald argues for three different groups of universalists.[37] Proponents of universalism claim that at the end all people will be saved, even though some adherents allow for the final destruction of those who resist God's loving work for them and, after their suffering in hell, will end up in the lake of fire.[38] Generally speaking, in this interpretation the devil and the fallen angels will also be ultimately saved.

Advocates of universalism first appeared in the third century A.D. Clement of Alexandria introduced hell as the place where the fire will actually purify, and Origen of Alexandria and Gregory of Nyssa stressed that the love of God is a process that continues after death and that the decisions of people in this life are not final. This position is built on the presupposition that each person has an immortal soul. Recently, there has been a revival of universalism with Rob Bell's *Love Wins*,[39] provoking more discussion in reaction to his position.[40] The conviction that, after death, God gives another chance for people to be saved is appealing and has gained great popularity.[41] Furthermore, some prominent theologians like Karl Barth, Emil Brunner, Hans Küng, and Karl Rahner have been sympathetic toward universalism.[42]

Rob Bell summarizes this view eloquently:

And so a universal hug fest where everybody eventually ends up around the heavenly campfire singing "Kumbaya," with Jesus playing guitar, sounds a lot like fantasy to some people. . . . There must be some kind of "second chance" for those who don't believe in Jesus in this life-time. . . . "Who would doubt God's ability to do that?". . . And then there are others who ask if you get another chance after you die, why limit that chance to a one-off immediately after death? And so they expand the possibilities, trusting that there will be endless opportunities in an endless amount of time for people to say yes to God. As long as it takes, in other words. At the heart of this perspective is the belief that, given enough time, everybody will turn to God and find themselves in the joy and peace of God's presence.[43]

R. C. Sproul sharply criticizes universalism: "A prevailing notion is that all we have to do to enter the kingdom of God is to die. God is viewed as so 'loving' that he really doesn't care too much if we don't keep his law. The law is there to guide us, but if we stumble and fall, our celestial grandfather will merely wink and say, 'Boys will be boys.' "[44]

The universalist view stands in opposition to both the traditional view of eternal torment in hell and the conditionalist position, stressing that immortality is received as a gift on the basis of faith in Christ Jesus.

Room for purgatory

Closely related to universalism is the understanding of a special sort of purgatory. F. L. Cross explains that purgatory "was openly rejected by the Reformers, who taught that souls are freed from sin by faith in Christ alone without any works, and therefore, if saved, go straight to heaven."[45] However, today's situation is different. More evangelicals are attracted to some kind of purgatory.

This teaching about purgatory is built on the belief that a person's immortal soul goes after death either to heaven or hell. Those in hell go through the process of purification, some form of purgatory that, in the end, closes with the admittance of everyone into heaven. Those in hell receive many chances to appreciate God's love for them, "repent," and be admitted into heaven. Thus God's love wins and everyone is saved for eternity. God's redemption will be accomplished, and the Lord will finally be all in all (Ephesians 1:10). Here evangelical universalists are close to the Catholic doctrine of purgatory. An engaging book written by Brett Salkeld, *Can Catholics and Evangelicals*

Agree About Purgatory and the Last Judgment? demonstrates this close affinity.[46] Jerry Walls defends an understanding of purgatory that is compatible with Protestant theology and the doctrine of eternal hell.[47] Theologian Miroslav Volf states: "Post-mortem change is an essential precondition for the resolution of the problem within the sphere of cultural productivity; without it past cannot be redeemed and history cannot be set right."[48] Volf underlines the necessity of postmortem change, and he speaks about the "eschatological transition."[49] James Wellman, Jr., comments: "Without stating it, Bell implies a form of purgatory, a Catholic dogma that has long been rejected by Protestants. The doctrine of purgatory, however, provides a solution to many Christian dilemmas."[50]

Attractiveness of the Roman Catholic Church— Evangelical conversions to Catholicism

Thomas Howard wrote in the postscript to *Evangelical Is Not Enough*[51] that after completing the book in 1984, he converted to Catholicism. For him, the question that matters most is "What is the church?" and he explains why he became a Roman Catholic. The attractiveness of Catholicism for evangelicals is explained in many books.[52]

The diplomatic role of Pope Francis in a renewal of political conciliar relations between the United States and Cuba is an example of the influence of the Roman Catholic Church in politics. The recent visits of Rick Warren and Joel Osteen, well-known Protestant speakers; James and Betty Robison, cohosts of the *Life Today* television program; and Kenneth Copeland, cohost of *Believer's Voice of Victory*, are illustrations of the attractiveness of the Roman Catholic Church.

The Orthodox and the Roman Catholic churches have sought a closer relationship. For example, in June 2014, Pope Francis and Ecumenical Patriarch Bartholomew met in Je-

> *The conversion of evangelicals to Catholicism is only the tip of the iceberg of this trend.*

rusalem, and in November 30, 2014, they signed a Christian Unity Declaration in Istanbul. They reaffirmed "their desire to overcome the obstacles dividing their two churches."[53] Additional steps have been taken to reunite these two divided churches.[54] For the rapprochement of the Roman Catholic Church with other Christians and how the papacy officially apologies for acts of the Inquisition in the past, see the summary articles in Wikipedia on Pope Paul VI and Ecumenism as well as the impressive List of Apologies made by Pope John Paul II.[55]

The conversion of evangelicals to Catholicism is only the tip of the iceberg of this trend. North Park University professor Scot McKnight documented some of the reasons behind the conversion of evangelicals to Catholicism in his 2002 essay, "From Wheaton to Rome: Why Evangelicals Become Roman Catholic."[56] The essay was also included in a collection of conversion stories he co-edited with Hauna Ondrey entitled *Finding Faith, Losing Faith: Stories of Conversion and Apostasy.*[57]

Scott Hahn, former Presbyterian pastor and author of *Rome Sweet Home,*[58] converted to Catholicism as well as Marcus Grodi, founder of the Coming Home Network International, an organization that provides "fellowship, encouragement and support for Protestant pastors and laymen who are somewhere along the journey or have already been received into the Catholic Church," according to their Web site. Other featured converts include singer-songwriter John Michael Talbot and Patrick Madrid, editor of the *Surprised by Truth* books that showcase conversion stories.[59]

> *This spirituality wants Christ but not the Scriptures; desires the Spirit but not God's Word.*

The former president of the Evangelical Theological Society and Baylor University professor Francis J. Beckwith made a "return to Rome."[60] In May 2007, Beckwith made public his conversion to the Roman Catholic Church, which took place in late April 2007, and resigned as both president and member of the Evangelical Theological Society.[61]

Ulf Ekman, the pastor of a prominent megachurch in Sweden, announced in 2014 his conversion to Catholicism.[62] Other prominent individuals, including Tony Blair and Andrea Bocelli also converted.[63] The December 2014 cover story of *Christianity Today* has R. R. Reno's article "Pope Francis: Why Everyone Loves the Pope," with the subtitle "From secular journalists to Charismatic Christians, millions are taken with the Jesuit from Argentina." Christian Smith describes in ninety-five steps how evangelicals can become Catholics.[64]

Catholicism is attractive to Evangelicals due to its rich history, emphasis on liturgy, authoritative teaching and teaching office of the church, placement of the origin of the Bible within church tradition, and early patristic tradition. Ian Hunter states: "The very first place every serious Protestant that I know turns today for guidance on Christian doctrine is the *Catechism* of the Roman Catholic Church; failing that, the Encyclicals of Pope John Paul II."[65] It is not by chance that Mark Knoll and Carolyn Nystrom put a provocative title to their book, *Is Reformation Over? An Evangelical Assessment of Contemporary Roman Catholicism.*[66]

Clifford Goldstein describes "how Catholics and Protestants are undoing the Reformation and fulfilling prophecy."[67] This trend toward rapprochement between Protestants and Catholics is creating abundant literature on the issue.[68] Thus, the apostolic succession as well as the teaching office of the church, the pope's supremacy, the role of Mary, prayers to the saints, the role of Christian tradition, the unity of the Christian church, and the authority of the church are discussed once again in Evangelical circles.

Spirituality as transcendent feelings

Spirituality is understood to be like mysticism or transcendental meditation, where thinking is neutralized and empty silence is introduced. Being spiritual, but not religious, means to not belong to an organized church or religion and to not be bound by doctrine. This spirituality wants Christ but not the Scriptures; desires the Spirit but not God's Word. Jesus is important but not so much His teaching or doctrine. Experience and emotions are crucial components of life, and whatever feels good must be good. In-depth biblical spirituality and thinking is replaced by deep breathing and silence, and one's own imagination and inspiration of the moment is most important. There is a rising demand and attraction to the New Age movement and Eastern religions underlying the naturalistic relationship to the cosmic powers, an impersonal transcendent god, and the Mother Earth. On the other hand, religious secularism and pragmatism is gaining influence in conservative churches.

We live in a dangerous and complicated world.

However, biblical spirituality stresses meditation on the Word of God (Psalms 1; 119), prayer (Matthew 6:5–15), fasting (Matthew 6:16–18), witnessing (Acts 1:8, 9), and demonstrating practical love and living unselfishly for others (John 13:34, 35; Galatians 5:6; James 1:27; 1 John 2:8–11). It is a life lived in God's presence according to the Holy Spirit's guidance (Romans 8:4–16; Galatians 5:16–18, 25), full of the fruit of the Spirit (Galatians 5:22–24), immersed in God's grace and love (1 Corinthians 13:1–14:1; Colossians 3:14), and under the guidance of God's Word (Colossians 3:1, 2, 10, 16, 17).

Conclusion

We live in a dangerous and complicated world. The Bible reveals that in the "last days" the world will be full of perils (Daniel 12:1; Matthew 24:6–12; Acts 20:28–30; 1 Timothy 4:1, 2; 2 Peter 3:3). Richard Neibuhr expressed the situation of our time well when he criticized theological liberalism as being a social gospel by pointing out that they believe in "a God without wrath [who] brought men without sin into a kingdom without judgment through the ministration of a Christ without a cross."[69] Such religion is an empty emotional experience.

In this relativistic world, the first task of the followers of Christ is to present a right picture of God and His character.

For many there is no certainty, and absolute Truth does not exist according to their opinion. In this relativistic world, the first task of the followers of Christ is to present a right picture of God and His character. This is the work needed to be accomplished before the second coming of Christ, because Satan has grossly distorted the character of God (see Genesis 3:1–6), and the postmodern attacks on God, His character, and the Scriptures are more sophisticated and stronger than ever. Our task is to be witnesses for God and to let His glory shine through our characters (Revelation 14:4, 7).

Revelation 18:1 states that at the end of world history, the glory of God will shine throughout the world. The last work of God's people will be to let God illuminate the world with His glory through His people (Ezekiel 36:23). This will be the most powerful argument in favor of God's existence and love, and His true character will be defended when His people demonstrate His love for others. We are a spectacle to the world and to the whole universe (1 Corinthians 4:9)! His people need to live to the glory of God, reflecting in their characters the loving character of God. According to 2 Thessalonians 1:3–5, the evidence that God is true and His judgments are just is the believers' living faith and love. Ellen White explains our role when she interprets the work of the wise virgins in the parable about the ten virgins:

It is the darkness of misapprehension of God that is enshrouding the world. Men are losing their knowledge of His character. It has been misunderstood and misinterpreted. At this time a message from God is to be proclaimed, a message illuminating in its influence and saving in its power. His character is to be made known. Into the darkness of the world is to be shed the light of His glory, the light of His goodness, mercy, and truth. . . .

. . . *The last rays of merciful light, the last message of mercy to be given to the world, is a revelation of His character of love.* The children of God are to manifest His glory. In their own life and character they are to reveal what the grace of God has done for them.[70]

The best proof of God's existence and His goodness is a converted Christlike Christian, living a practical manifestation of one's personal experience with Him. Loving Christians are the ultimate argument for the God of love, truth, and justice.

---

1. Carl Raschke, *The Next Reformation: Why Evangelicals Must Embrace Postmodernity* (Grand Rapids, MI: Baker Academics, 2004). See also Steward E. Kelly, *Truth Considered and Applied: Examining Postmodernism, History, and Christian Faith* (Nashville, TN: B & H Academic, 2011).

2. Gregory A. Boyd, *The Myth of a Christian Nation: How the Quest for Political Power Is Destroying the Church* (Grand Rapids, MI: Zondervan, 2006).

3. Rick Warren, Daniel Amen, and Mark Hyman, *The Daniel Plan: 40 Days to a Healthier Life* (Grand Rapids, MI: Zondervan, 2013).

4. Karl Marx, *Introduction to a Contribution to the Critique of Hegel's Philosophy of Right, Collected Works* (New York: 1976), 3:1. Originally published in *Deutsch-Französische Jahrbücher,* 7 & 10 February 1844 in Paris.

5. Richard Dawkins's main works include: *The Selfish Gene,* new ed. (Oxford: Oxford University Press, 1989); *The Blind Watchmaker: Why the Evidence of Evolution Reveals a Universe Without Design* (New York: W. W. Norton & Company, 1986); *A Devil's Chaplain: Reflections on Hope, Lies, Science, and Love* (Boston, MA: Houghton Mifflin, 2003); *The God Delusion* (New York: Bantam Books, 2006); *The Greatest Show on Earth: The Evidence for Evolution* (New York: Bantam Press, 2009); *The Magic of Reality* (New York: Free Press, 2011); and *An Appetite for Wonder: The Making of a Scientist* (New York: Bantam Press, 2013).

6. Dawkins, *The God Delusion,* 31. In the edition published in Boston, MA: Houghton Mifflin, 2008, with a new Introduction, it is page 51.

7. Sam Harris, *The End of Faith: Religion, Terror, and the Future of Reason* (New York: W. W. Norton & Company, 2004); idem, *Letter to a Christian Nation* (New York: Alfred A. Knopf, Inc., 2006); idem, *The Moral Landscape: How Science Can Determine Human Values* (New York: Free Press, 2010). Other books by Sam Harris are *Lying* (Springfield, NJ: Four Elephants Press, 2011) and *Free Will* (New York: Free Press, 2012).

8. Christopher Hitchens, *God Is Not Great: How Religion Poisons Everything* (New York: Atlantic Books, 2007). See also his two other books, *The Portable Atheist: Essential Readings for the Nonbeliever* (New York: Da Capo Press, 2007) and *Mortality* (New York: Twelve Books, 2012).

9. Daniel Dennett, *Darwin's Dangerous Idea: Evolution and the Meanings of Life* (New York: Simon & Schuster, 1995); see also his book *Breaking the Spell: Religion as a Natural Phenomenon* (New York: Viking, 2006).

10. Dennett, *Darwin's Dangerous Idea,* 521.

11. Ibid., 279–283.

12. It is true that there were many crimes committed and wars fought in the name of God or Allah. Violence in the name of God is a plague in the history of Christianity and brings great shame on Christians; but atrocities were also committed by atheistic dictators. Neo-atheists would like to deny that many wrongs

have been committed as a result of a denial of God, e.g., Hitler, Stalin, Pol Pot, or Máo Zédōng. One simple illustration from the French Revolution should suffice. It is documented that in 1793 (when religion was replaced by reason), Madame Roland was sent to the guillotine to face execution on trumped-up charges. On November 8, 1793, she was beheaded. A few weeks afterwards, Marie Antoinette met the same fate. As Marie was going to her execution, she bowed mockingly toward the statue of liberty in the Place de la Revolution and uttered the words for which she is now remembered: "Liberty, what crimes are committed in your name." See Kindle Books and More (November 8, 2014): n.p. Cited February 5, 2015. Online: http://www.thisdayinquotes.com/2009/11/o-liberty-what-crimes-are-committed-in.html.

The point is that we are dealing with a common element, sinful human nature. The sinful heart cannot be changed (maybe it can be improved) by education, better economy, or different circumstances. Only conversion performed by the power of God's grace, Spirit, and Word changes the human heart.

13. Julia M. O'Brien, *Challenging Prophetic Metaphor: Theology and Ideology in the Prophets* (Louisville, KY: Westminster John Knox, 2008).

14. David Penchansky, *What Rough Beast? Images of God in the Hebrew Bible* (Louisville, KY: Westminster John Knox, 1999).

15. Bart D. Ehrman, *God's Problem: How the Bible Fails to Answer Our Most Important Question—Why We Suffer* (New York: HarperOne, 2008). Ehrman is the James A. Gray Distinguished Professor of Religious Studies at the University of North Carolina.

The most popular arguments used for purposes of putting God down are the following: suffering of innocent Job as well as many other people in the world; demanding Abraham's sacrifice of his own son; child abuse—forty-two children were killed by two bears, because they were laughing at the prophet Elijah; Joshua's genocide in Canaan; wars performed in the name of God and under His command; God's punishment of the Egyptians with ten plagues including the killing of their firstborn sons; ethnocentrism and racism (choice of a specific nation to be the bearer of light; curse on Canaan); sex scandals and polygamy in the Bible; institution of Levirate marriage; Old Testament legislation is full of violence (eye for eye; capital punishments); incest of Lot with his two daughters; life of David—warrior, polygamist, revengeful murderer, adulterer, yet a man after the heart of God, etc.

16. Among the best recent literature are the following volumes: Paul Copan, *Is God a Moral Monster? Making Sense of Old Testament God* (Grand Rapids, MI: Baker Books, 2011); William L. Craig and Chad Meister, eds., *God Is Good, God Is Great: Why Believing in God Is Reasonable and Responsible* (Downers Grove, IL: IVP Books, 2009); John F. Haught, *God and the New Atheism: A Critical Response to Dawkins, Harris, and Hitchens* (Louisville, KY: Westminster John Knox, 2008); Alister McGrath and Joanna Collicutt McGrath, *The Dawkins Delusion: Atheist Fundamentalism and the Denial of the Divine* (Downers Grove, IL: IVP Books, 2007); R. Albert Mohler, Jr., *Atheism REMIX: A Christian Confronts the New Atheists* (Wheaton, IL: Crossway Books, 2008); Christopher J. H. Wright, *The God I Don't Understand: Reflections on Tough Questions of Faith* (Grand Rapids, MI: Zondervan, 2008); and N. T. Wright, *Evil and the Justice of God* (Downers Grove, IL: IVP Books, 2006).

17. Daniel H. Williams, *Evangelicals and Tradition: The Formative Influence of the Early Church* (Grand Rapids, MI: Baker Academic, 2005). See also Hubertus R. Drobner, *The Fathers of the Church: A Comprehensive Introduction,* trans. Siegfried S. Schatzmann (Peabody, MA: Hendrickson, 2007), especially 3–5; Christopher A. Hall, *Learning Theology With the Church Fathers* (Downers Grove, IL: InterVarsity, 2002), especially 19–21; Daniel H. Williams, *Retrieving the Tradition and Renewing Evangelicalism: A Primer for Suspicious Protestants* (Grand Rapids, MI: Eerdmans, 1999).

18. Williams, *Evangelicals and Tradition,* 62.

19. Thomas C. Oden and Cindy Crosby, eds., *Ancient Christian Devotional* (Downers Grove, IL: InterVarsity, 2007), 7.

20. Jason Robert Radcliff, *Thomas F. Torrance and the Church Fathers: A Reformed, Evangelical, and Ecumenical Reconstruction of the Patristic Tradition* (n.p.: Pickwick Publications, 2014).

21. Michael Graves, *The Inspiration and Interpretation of Scripture: What the Early Church Can Teach Us* (Grand Rapids, MI: Eerdmans, 2014).

22. For example, see Michael Allen and Scott R. Swain, *Reformed Catholicity: The Promise of Retrieval for Theology and Biblical Interpretation* (Grand Rapids, MI: Baker, 2015); George Hunsinger, *Evangelical, Catholic, and Reformed: Essays on Barth and Other Themes* (Grand Rapids, MI: Eerdmans, 2015). Devin Rose, *The Protestant's Dilemma: How the Reformation's Shocking Consequences Point to the Truth of Catholicism* (San Diego, CA: Catholic Answers, 2014); Kenneth J. Stewart, "Evangelicalism and Patristic Christianity: 1517 to the Present," *Evangelical Quarterly* 80, no. 4 (2008): 307–321.

23. R. C. Sproul, *Unseen Realities: Heaven, Hell, Angels and Demons* (Lake Mary, FL: Ligonier Ministries, 2011), 51.

24. See, for example, the following representative literature: Sharon L. Baker, *Razing Hell: Rethinking Everything You've Been Taught About God's Wrath and Judgment* (Louisville, KY: Westminster John Knox, 2010); Joel Buenting, *The Problem of Hell* (Burlington, VT: Ashgate, 2010); Nigel M. de S. Cameron, ed., *Universalism and the Doctrine of Hell* (Grand Rapids, MI: Baker, 1992); David Clotfelter, *Sinners in the Hands of a Good God: Reconciling Divine Judgment and Mercy* (Chicago: Moody, 2004); Edward W. Fudge, *The Fire that Consumes: A Biblical and Historical Study of the Doctrine of Final Punishment,* 3rd ed., fully updated, rev., and exp. (Eugene, OR: Cascade Books, 2011); Edward W. Fudge and Robert A. Peterson, *Two Views of Hell: A Biblical and Theological Dialogue* (Downers Grove, IL: InterVarsity, 2000); David Hilborn, et al., *The Nature of Hell: A Report by the Evangelical Alliance Commission on Unity and Truth Among Evangelicals* (London: Evangelical Alliance, 2000); Randy Klassen, *What Does the Bible Really Say About Hell: Wrestling With the Traditional View* (Telford, PA: Pandora, 2001); Daniel Knauft, *Search for the Immortal Soul* (Nampa, ID: Torchlight Intel, 2006); David George Moore, *The Battle for Hell*: *A Survey and Evaluation of Evangelicals' Growing Attraction to the Doctrine of Annihilationism* (Lanham, MD: University Press of America, 1995); Christopher W. Morgan and Robert A. Peterson, eds., *Hell Under Fire* (Grand Rapids, MI: Zondervan, 2007); idem, *Is Hell for Real or Does Everyone Go to Heaven?* (Grand Rapids, MI: Zondervan, 2004); Robert A. Peterson, *Hell on Trial: The Case for Eternal Punishment* (Phillipsburg, NJ: P&P, 1995); Richard D. Phillips, *What Happens After Death?* (Phillipsburg, NJ: P & R Publishing, 2013); Clark H. Pinnock, "The Destruction of the Finally Impenitent," *Criswell Theological Review* 4 (Spring 1990): 243–260; David Powys, *"Hell": A Hard Look at a Hard Question* (Carlisle, UK: Paternoster, 1997); John Walvoord, et al., *Four Views on Hell* (Grand Rapids, MI: Zondervan, 1996); John W. Wenham, *The Goodness of God* (Downers Grove, IL: InterVarsity, 1974); Michael E. Wittmer, *Christ Alone: An Evangelical Response to Rob Bell's Love Wins* (Grand Rapids, MI: Edenridge, 2011).

25. Clark H. Pinnock, "The Conditional View," in *Four Views on Hell,* ed. William Crockett (Grand Rapids, MI: Zondervan, 1992), 149.

26. In the foreword by Robert K. Johnston to Randy Klassen, *What Does the Bible Really Say About Hell?,* 12 (see also p. 91).

27. LeRoy Edwin Froom, *The Conditionalist Faith of Our Fathers,* 2 vols. (Washington, DC: Review and Herald®, 1965). For a response to Froom's careful reading of the early fathers, see Robert A. Morey, *Death and the Afterlife* (Minneapolis, MN: Bethany, 1984), 58–60, 273–279, who questions Froom's treatment of the church fathers.

28. F. F. Bruce, "Paul on Immortality," *Scottish Journal of Theology* 24 (1971): 457–472; David L. Edwards and John R. W. Stott, *Evangelical Essentials: A Liberal-Evangelical Dialogue* (Downers Grove, IL: InterVarsity, 1988), 312–320; Edward W. Fudge, "Putting Hell in Its Place," *Christianity Today* (August 6, 1976): 14–17; Joel B. Green, *Body, Soul, and Human Life: The Nature of Humanity in the Bible* (Grand Rapids, MI: Baker Academics, 2008), 177–180; idem, ed., *In Search of the Soul: Perspectives on the Mind-Body Problem—Four Views of the Mind-Body Problem,* 2nd ed. (Downers Grove, IL: InterVarsity, 2005); Phillip E. Hughes, *The True Image: The Destiny of Man in Christ* (Grand Rapids, MI: Eerdmans, 1989); Clark H. Pinnock, "Fire, Then Nothing," *Christianity Today* (March 20, 1987): 40, 41; idem, "Annihilationism," in *The Oxford Handbook of Eschatology,* ed. Jerry L. Walls (New York: Oxford University Press, 2008), 462–475; Clark H. Pinnock and Robert C. Brow, *Unbounded Love: A Good News Theology for the Twenty-First Century* (Downers Grove, IL: InterVarsity, 1994); Powys, *"Hell"* (see note 24); F. LaGard Smith, "The Tormenting Conundrum of Hell," in *AfterLife: A Glimpse of Eternity Beyond Death's Door* (Nashville, TN: Cotswold, 2003), 165–197; John R. S. Stott, "The Logic of Hell:

A Brief Rejoinder," *Evangelical Review of Theology* 18 (January 1994): 33, 34; John W. Wenham, *The Enigma of Evil* (Grand Rapids, MI: Zondervan, 1985); Nigel Wright, *The Radical Evangelical: Seeking a Place to Stand* (London: SPCK, 1996); and John Zens, *Christ Minimized? A Response to Rob Bell's LOVE WINS* (Omaha, NE: Ekklesia, 2011).

29. Roger E. Olson, *The Mosaic of Christian Belief: Twenty Centuries of Unity and Diversity* (Downers Grove, IL: InterVarsity, 2002), 329.

30. Gregory A. Boyd, *Satan and the Problem of Evil: Constructing a Trinitarian Warfare Theodicy* (Downers Grove, IL: InterVarsity, 2001), 336.

31. Pinnock, "The Destruction of the Finally Impenitent" (see note 24), 246, 247.

32. Michael Green, *Evangelism Through the Local Church* (Nashville, TN: Oliver-Nelson, 1992), 69, 72.

33. Gregory MacDonald, *The Evangelical Universalist,* 2nd ed. (Eugene, OR: Wipf & Stock, 2012), 136.

34. John W. Wenham, "The Case for Conditional Immortality," in *Universalism and the Doctrine of Hell: Papers Presented at the Fourth Edinburgh Conference on Christian Dogmatics, 1991,* ed. Nigel M. de S. Cameron (Grand Rapids, MI: Baker, 1992), 185–187.

35. Stephen H. Travis, *Christian Hope and the Future* (Downers Grove, IL: InterVarsity Press, 1980), 135.

36. Trever Hart, "Universalism: Two Distinct Types," in *Universalism and the Doctrine of Hell: Papers Presented at the Fourth Edinburgh Conference on Christian Dogmatics, 1991,* ed. Nigel M. de S. Cameron (Grand Rapids, MI: Baker, 1992); Fudge, *The Fire That Consumes*, 3rd ed. (see note 24), 279–286.

37. MacDonald, *The Evangelical Universalist* (see note 33), 134, 135.

38. See Baker, *Razing Hell* (see note 24), 106–124. Her view is unique, allowing for the possibility that not all people will be saved. Thus she seeks to combine annihilationism and universalism.

39. Rob Bell, *Love Wins: A Book About Heaven, Hell, and the Fate of Every Person Who Ever Lived* (New York: HarperOne; 2011). See also idem, *The Love Wins Companion: A Study Guide for Those Who Want to Go Deeper,* ed. David Vanderveen (New York: HarperOne, 2011).

40. See, for example, Francis Chan and Preston Sprinkle, *Erasing Hell: What God Said About Eternity, and the Things We Made Up* (Colorado Springs, CO: David C. Cook, 2011); Kevin DeYoung's blog, "God is Still Holy and What You Learned in Sunday School is Still True: A Review of 'Love Wins,' " September 5, 2014, http://thegospelcoalition.org/blogs/kevindeyoung/2011/03/14/rob-bell-love-wins-review/; Larry Dixon, *"Farewell, Rob Bell": A Biblical Response to Love Wins* (Columbia, SC: Theomedian Resources, 2011); Mark Galli, *God Wins: Heaven, Hell, and Why the Good News Is Better Than Love Wins* (Carol Stream, IL: Tyndale House, 2011); James K. Wellman, Jr., *Rob Bell and a New American Christianity* (Nashville, TN: Abingdon, 2012); Zens, *Christ Minimized?* (see note 28).

41. The principal evangelical defenders of this view are Sharon Baker (2010; see note 24) and Rob Bell (2011; see note 39); Jan Bonda, *The One Purpose of God: An Answer to the Doctrine of Eternal Punishment* (Grand Rapids, MI: Eerdmans, 1998), Randy Klassen, *What Does the Bible Really Say About Hell* (see note 24); Gregory MacDonald, *The Evangelical Universalist* (Gregory MacDonald is a pseudonym of Robin Parry; see note 33); idem, ed. *All Shall Be Well: Explorations in Universalism and Christian Theology, From Origen to Moltmann* (Eugene, OR: Cascade, 2011); Thomas Talbott, *The Inescapable Love of God* (Boca Raton, FL: Universal, 1999).

42. For details, see MacDonald, ed., *All Shall Be Well,* 23, 24; James I. Packer, "Universalism: Will Everyone Ultimately Be Saved?" in *Hell Under Fire,* ed. Christopher W. Morgan and Robert A. Peterson (Grand Rapids, MI: Zondervan, 2004), 172, 173. John MacQuarrie asserts: "A doctrine of conditional immortality is at least preferable to the barbarous doctrine of an eternal hell. . . . But perhaps the Christian hope can carry us further even than a belief in conditional immortality. . . . We prefer a doctrine of 'universalism' to one of 'conditional immortality' " (*Principles of Christian Theology,* 2nd ed. [New York: Scribner's, 1977], 361).

43. Bell, *Love Wins,* 105–107 (see note 39).

44. R. C. Sproul, *Reason to Believe* (Grand Rapids, MI: Zondervan, 1982), 99, 100.

45. F. L. Cross, ed., *The Oxford Dictionary of the Christian Church* (Oxford: Oxford University Press, 1983), 1145.

46. See Brett Salkeld, *Can Catholics and Evangelicals Agree About Purgatory and the Last Judgment?* (New

York/Mahwah, NJ: Paulist, 2011). It needs to be stressed that both the Catholic teaching on mortal sins and Miroslav Volf affirm that some people will be condemned to hell: "We should not, however, shy away from the unpleasant and deeply tragic *possibility* that there *might* be human beings, created to the image of God, who, through the practice of evil, have immunized themselves from all attempts at their redemption" (Miroslav Volf, *Exclusion and Embrace: A Theological Exploration of Identity, Otherness, and Reconciliation* [Nashville, TN: Abingdon, 1996], 297; italics in original).

47. See also Jerry L. Walls, *Heaven, Hell, and Purgatory: Rethinking the Things That Matter Most. A Protestant View of the Cosmic Drama* (Grand Rapids, MI: Baker, 2015).

48. Miroslav Volf, "Enter Into Joy! Sin, Death, and the Life of the World to Come," in *End of the World and the Ends of God: Science and Theology on Eschatology,* ed. John Polkinghorne and Michael Welker (Harrisburg, PA: Trinity, 2000), 276, 277. See also his "The Final Reconciliation: Reflections on a Social Dimension of the Eschatological Transition," *Modern Theology* 16, no. 1 (January 2000): 91–113.

49. Volf, "Enter Into Joy," 257.

50. Wellman, *Rob Bell and a New American Christianity,* 131 (see note 40).

51. Thomas Howard, *Evangelical Is Not Enough: Worship of God in Liturgy and Sacraments (San Francisco, CA: Ignatius Press, 1984).*

52. For example, Francis J. Beckwith, *Return to Rome: Confessions of an Evangelical Catholic* (Grand Rapids, MI: Brazos, 2008); Scott and Kimberly Hahn, *Rome Sweet Home: Our Journey to Catholicism* (San Francisco, CA: Ignatius Press, 1993); Hunsinger, *Evangelical, Catholic, and Reformed* (see note 22); Mark A. Noll, *Is the Reformation Over? An Evangelical Assessment of Contemporary Roman Catholicism* (Grand Rapids, MI: Baker, 2008); Rose, *The Protestant's Dilemma* (see note 22).

53. Read more at "Pope Francis and Ecumenical Patriarch Sign Christian Unity Declaration," *Ecumenical News,* November 30, 2014, http://www.ecumenicalnews.com/article/pope-francis-and-ecumenical-patriarch-sign-christian-unity-declaration-27367#ixzz3QHugmb82.

54. Patriarch Bartholomew has scheduled the first ever pan-Orthodox synod for 2016 in the Hagia Irene Church in Istanbul, with the aim of adopting a framework for unified Orthodox talks with Rome. As a next step, he has proposed an Ecumenical Council of all churches, East and West, to meet in 2025 on the Sea of Marmara, 110 miles (180 kilometers) from Istanbul, where the first such Ecumenical Council was held in A.D. 325.

55. See "Pope Paul VI and Ecumenism," *Wikipedia,* accessed February 5, 2015, http://en.wikipedia.org/wiki/Pope_Paul_VI_and_Ecumenism; and "List of apologies made by Pope John Paul II," *Wikipedia,* accessed February 5, 2015, http://en.wikipedia.org/wiki/List_of_apologies_made_by_Pope_John_Paul_II.

56. Scot McKnight, "From Wheaton to Rome: Why Evangelicals Become Roman Catholic," *Journal of the Evangelical Theological Society* 5, no. 3 (September 2002): 451–472.

57. Scot McKnight and Hauna Ondrey, *Finding Faith, Losing Faith: Stories of Conversion and Apostasy* (Waco, TX: Baylor University Press, 2008).

58. Hahn, *Rome Sweet Home* (see note 52).

59. See Marcus Grodi, ed., *Journeys Home: The Journeys of Protestant Clergy and Laity Coming Home to the Catholic Church With the Help of the Coming Home Network International, a Lay Apostolate Committed to Helping Them,* 3rd rev. ed. (Zanesville, OH: CH Resources, 2011); Patrick Madrid, *Surprised by Truth: 11 Converts Give the Biblical and Historical Reasons for Becoming Catholic,* vol. 1 (San Diego, CA: Basilica Press, 1994); idem, *Surprised by Truth 2: 15 Men and Women Give the Biblical and Historical Reasons for Becoming Catholic,* vol. 2 (Manchester, NH: Sophia Institute Press, 2000); and idem, *Surprised by Truth 3: 10 More Converts Explain the Biblical and Historical Reasons for Becoming Catholic,* vol. 3 (Manchester, NH: Sophia Institute Press, 2002).

60. Francis J. Beckwith, "My Return to the Catholic Church," *The Coming Home Network International,* accessed February 5, 2015, http://web.archive.org/web/20090805090513/http://chnetwork.org/Conversion stories/francisbeckwith.html, this Web page has been discontinued.

61. Ibid.

62. See Ruth Moon, "Conversion of Sweden's Most Influential Pastor Causes 'Pain and Disillusion,' " *Gleanings,* March 14, 2014, http://www.christianitytoday.com/gleanings/2014/march/sweden-pentecostal -converts-catholicism-ulf-ekman-word-life.html.

63. See "List of Converts to Catholicism," *Wikipedia*, accessed February 5, 2015, http://en.wikipedia.org /wiki/List of converts to Catholicism.

64. Christian Smith, *How to Go From Being a Good Evangelical to a Committed Catholic in Ninety-Five Difficult Steps* (Eugene, OR: Wipf & Stock Publishers, 2011). These ninety-five steps are an allusion to the ninety-five theses of Martin Luther.

65. Ian Hunter, "God's Grace Central on Solitary Path of Suffering," *Christian Week* (January 6, 2004): 14.

66. Mark Knoll and Carolyn Nystrom, *Is the Reformation Over? An Evangelical Assessment of Contemporary Roman Catholicism* (Grand Rapids, MI: Baker Academics, 2005).

67. Clifford Goldstein, *The Great Compromise: How Catholics and Protestants are Undoing the Reformation and Fulfilling Prophecy* (Nampa, ID: Pacific Press®, 2001).

68. See, for example, John Ankerberg and John Weldon, *Protestants and Catholics: Do They Now Agree?* (Eugene, OR: Harvest House Publishers, 1995); Charles Colson and Richard John Neuhaus, eds., *Evangelicals and Catholics Together: Toward a Common Mission* (Dallas, TX: Word Publishing, 1995); idem, *Your Word is Truth: A Project of Evangelicals and Catholics Together* (Grand Rapids, MI: Eerdmans, 2002); Norman L. Geisler and Ralph E. MacKenzie, *Roman Catholics and Evangelicals: Agreements and Differences* (Grand Rapids, MI: Baker Books, 1995); Michael Scott Horton, *Evangelicals, Catholics and Unity* (Wheaton, IL: Crossway Books, 1999); The Lutheran World Federation and the Roman Catholic Church, *Joint Declaration on the Doctrine of Justification* (Grand Rapids, MI: Eerdmans, 2000); Thomas P. Rausch, ed., *Catholics and Evangelicals: Do They Share a Common Future?* (Downers Grove, IL: InterVarsity Press, 2000); Robert L. Reymond, *The Reformation's Conflict With Rome: Why It Must Continue* (Fearn, Ross-shire, Great Britain: Mentor, 2001).

69. H. Richard Niebuhr, *The Kingdom of God in America* (New York: Harper and Row, 1959), 193.

70. Ellen G. White, *Christ's Object Lessons* (Washington, DC: Review and Herald®, 1941), 415, 416; emphasis added.

Before Evil Days Come: A Biblical and Practical Reflection of Suffering

KYOSHIN AHN

S uffering is part of our lives. It can make even mature Christians wonder about the goodness and love of God. With the increasing amount
of senseless violence against the innocent, the ugly reality of suffering
penetrates every fiber of our being and society, forcing us to ask "Why?" If
God is all-powerful and good, why does He let suffering happen to us?[1] This
question is repeated every day as deeply committed Christians try to make
sense of suffering. Their theological understanding of the immanence of God
diametrically collides with their real-life experience of God's perceived absence or silence in suffering, as exemplified by Job and Asaph (Psalm 73),
respectively.

Pastors also struggle, at one time or another, with situations they need to
explain of why suffering happens within their family, congregation, or community. While they recognize their responsibility to lead believers with a balanced biblical and theological viewpoint, they often find themselves offering
inadequate responses to suffering.[2] They are also tempted to make a hasty
call, rationalizing or editorializing suffering without theological and biblical
reflections, resulting in unintended consequences.

In this chapter I will deal with several responses to suffering often heard in
church settings, and discuss their strengths and weaknesses so as to provide
some practical help to ministers.

Common responses to suffering

Many different responses have been made to this issue over the years,
with varying conclusions. Behind these responses lie one's view of God and
theodicy.[3] How we respond to evil reflects our understanding of God and our
worldview. At least six different responses to suffering can be identified in

church life, all that draw their basis from the Bible. These responses usually mean well, intended to be pastoral consolation, and have elements of truth in them, if not entirely.

1. There must be a *purpose* in suffering. This response is an outcome of our natural, inherent tendency to make sense of things hard to comprehend. After all, life without meaning is nonsense. God created the world with His infinite wisdom and is in full and absolute control. Therefore, there must be a reason for suffering. We may not know its purpose for now. We will know the purpose (1 Corinthians 13:12) in God's appointed time.

> *After all, life without meaning is nonsense.*

Several so-called "purpose texts" in the Bible lend their support to this view: God's ways and thoughts are "higher" than our ways and thoughts (Isaiah 55:8, 9); "no one can fathom what God has done from beginning to end" (Ecclesiastes 3:11);[4] "My purpose shall stand, and I will fulfill my intention" (cf. Isaiah 46:10, NRSV). These texts seem to indicate that our proper attitude is to wait and see how His purpose is recognized or accomplished in our life. This approach is quite appealing and provides Christians a sense of relief and encouragement that an all-powerful God is still in control of this out-of-control world.

These texts need, however, to be understood in their context. The context of Isaiah 55:8, 9, deals with the issue of a genuine change of behavior, stating two reasons why humans should turn from their wickedness to a life of seeking God. Forgiveness is possible in God's thought, and He keeps His covenant promises. On the other hand, Ecclesiastes 3:1–14 is more about a general description of God's absolute power and infinite wisdom than a text addressing the specific situations of suffering in human life. Besides, these texts do not assist us very much in dealing with a situation of senseless violence upon the innocent.

Romans 8:28 is another example of such a "purpose text": "in all things God works for the good of those who love him, who have been called according to his purpose." This text has been extensively abused in the life of the Christian church. The inappropriate and trite use of this text inevitably creates a wrong impression that anything can be justifiable. This text in its best popular reading is understood along this line: God has a mysterious purpose for what is happening in our lives that makes sense to Him, but not necessarily to us for now; we are to accept it as it is, bear with it until we come to recognize that mysterious purpose of God in our suffering. The context of this passage does not allow us to see an easy way out of suffering. Instead, the text maintains that bad things are happening to God's people in this world and are part of the groaning of the universe (Romans 8:22ff.). God is at work for the "good of those who love Him" even in the midst of such misery. There might not be a purpose in suffering, but we are to be assured that God is with us, and for us.

In suffering we naturally cry out, "Why, oh Lord?" Quite a few people in the Bible did that in their quest for God and meaning of life. Instead of an attitude of resigned acceptance toward suffering, we actively seek God to understand and experience Him more, and eventually pursue the justice of God in situations such as systematic oppression or suffering caused by human cruelty.

2. Suffering is a *punishment*. This argument has both theological and biblical foundations to make this claim. Based on the theological doctrine of retribution, this view sees suffering as the result of our wrongdoing. Ample evidences in the Bible support this approach: the righteous will be rewarded while the wicked will be punished (Deuteronomy 28; Psalm 1:6; Isaiah 3:10, 11; Proverbs 12:21; Ecclesiastes 9:2); Miriam was afflicted with leprosy because she questioned Moses' role (Numbers 12:1–10); and, an innocent child was punished unknowingly due to his father David's sin (2 Samuel 12:14–18). Suffering is viewed as a direct result of human responsibility. After all, God is punishing our transgression. God ordered the world in a way that every human receives a reward or punishment based on conduct. And this is certainly true of many situations in human life.

This approach, however, cannot explain some situations where innocent people suffer without any reason or cause on their part. In fact, people in the Bible began to voice their difficulty in applying the simple principle of "blessing and curse" (Deuteronomy 28) to every situation, as early as Jeremiah (12:1, 2). Job and Proverbs stand in diametrical opposition to each other over this issue. Job does not agree with the idea that human suffering is *always* deserved, or that the righteous do not *always* get rewarded (Job 1:21; 13:15; 19:25, 26). Proverbs, however, primarily suggests that the righteous are rewarded and do not suffer (Proverbs 10:3–21; 11:18, 21, 31; 13:21; 16:31, 20:7). This should not be considered as contradictory but complementary in pointing out the complexity of life situations.

Retributive justice does not fit nicely into many situations such as terrorist attacks, airplane crashes, a transmission of HIV by a contaminated needle, natural disasters, and so on. These situations do not show any phenomenon of cause-and-effect. Jesus, too, dismisses the universal applicability of this response in John 9:3, " 'Neither this man nor his parents sinned,' said Jesus, 'but

BEFORE EVIL DAYS COME: A BIBLICAL AND PRACTICAL REFLECTION OF SUFFERING | 203

this happened so that the works of God might be displayed in him.' "

3. Suffering is a *lesson*. According to this view, suffering educates and trains us, and purifies our character. As insisted by Elihu (Job 33:29, 30; 37:13), it helps us to be molded into the likeness of His image. We grow because of suffering. It refines us (Romans 5:3, 4; 1 Peter 4:12–16, 19). God is disciplining us to be a better Christian and His follower. No doubt suffering does build character. It matures and improves us. We become purified through suffering in life. The Bible carries several stories of people whose faith and characters were developed through suffering. This educational aspect of suffering began with Christ, who "learned . . . from what he suffered" (Hebrews 5:8). Hebrew 12:11 also reinforces this idea: "For the moment all discipline seems painful rather than pleasant; later it yields the peaceful fruit of righteousness to those who have been trained by it" (RSV).

This approach is applicable to certain situations, playing a teaching role in the life of those suffering. Universal application of this approach without considering various situations of suffering is, however, problematic, if not destructive. Why? For some people suffering becomes the main source of disconsolation and near despair, often shattering their faith in God. In addition, this view could also imply a wrong impression that evil is necessary for people to mature.

4. Suffering is a *test*. In this approach, God allows suffering to those whom He knows will pass the test. Suffering is seen not as a tragedy, but a spiritual test. The Bible renders its support for this approach too: Abraham was "tested" by God to offer his only son Isaac (Genesis 22:1, 2); the book of Job is a story of testing for a purpose; and, the New Testament Christians were told, "Count it all joy, my brothers, when you meet trials of various kinds, for you know that the testing of your faith produces steadfastness" (James 1:2, 3, ESV).

God may give us a test for a purpose. Abraham and Job were, however, unique cases. The situation for Job was especially an extreme case

For some people suffering becomes the main source of disconsolation and near despair, often shattering their faith in God.

that is not applicable to most believers. Truncating its historical and cultural context and unilaterally applying those stories to modern-day believers will certainly not create a healthy dynamic in the lives of those suffering. One implication in this approach is a heroic model of faith to seek instead of addressing the issues of many forms of suffering in an individual's life. In addition, who decides whether suffering is a test or not? It is certainly not a job of the preacher to do that.

5. Suffering points to an *eternal glory* we will experience in the future. In this approach, the present affliction, pain, or hardship is something that should be endured, because its rewards are far beyond description. Romans 8:18, "our present sufferings are not worth comparing with the glory that will be revealed in us," and 2 Corinthians 4:17, "For this slight momentary affliction is preparing for us an eternal weight of glory beyond all comparison" (RSV), are often used to support this approach.

> *The future glory we will have does not exonerate us from the present responsibility to make the created world a better place.*

The suffering in 2 Corinthians 4:17 must be seen in its literary context too. Paul experienced some unspecified afflictions so severe that it forced him to renounce all hope of survival in his evangelistic campaign (1:4, 8). He may have experienced an extreme form of persecution. And so were the Corinthians (1:6, 7), who may have been excluded and victimized because of their faith. Against this backdrop, Paul makes a contrast between this age, temporary and visible, and the age to come, forever and invisible (4:18). It is in this context that Paul makes a statement about suffering.

Universal application of this approach to a Christian's life with suffering is also problematic. First, it could encourage hiding or enduring the emotional pain, which could lead to deeper, long-lasting psychological illnesses. Secondly, this approach is less likely to pay attention to identifying the cause of suffering. The tragic consequence of that position weakens our stance in removing some causes of suffering from the world. The future glory we will have does not exonerate us from the present responsibility to make the created world a better place.

6. *The devil* is the source of all suffering. In this view, all of our affliction, pain, tragedy, and misery are attributed to the devil. After all, the Bible describes a cosmic conflict between the superhuman figure of God's enemy, the devil, and God (Revelation 12:7, 8; 19:1, 2; 20:2; 1 Peter 5:8; Ephesians 3:10; 6:12, 13). A recent article in *Ministry* magazine summarized it well.

This view is quite dramatic and persuasive, especially with cosmic conflict serving as the worldview. The primordial story of cosmic conflict provides us a framework through which we examine our existence that is exposed to suffering and evil in this world.[5]

This story line may be surprisingly appealing to modern readers too, if properly expressed. Yet the sweeping focus on this meta-discourse has an unintended consequence: individual life situations may be sidelined in the cosmic scale struggle. Furthermore, it tends to regard the suffering of the innocent as a casualty in this cosmic conflict to the point of being justified. Can the suffering of the innocent be considered a casualty or justifiable?

Further reflections

To be sure, some find consolation and strength in these responses, because they have some elements of truth as it pertains to the problem of suffering in the individual's life. These responses, however, often come up short, especially when applied universally, in addressing the complexity of suffering in a complicated life situation. When used universally, and without a reflection of their theological ramifications, they often becomes a reason of deep alienation and resentment in the life of the afflicted rather than providing comfort and hope. A balanced biblical understanding of suffering is needed in our attempt to minister to those who are suffering.

First and foremost, one has to recognize that not every evil is the same in terms of origin or intention. These evils have to be distinguished from one another in ministry settings: (1) natural evil that human decision is not particularly involved in (e.g., floods, tornadoes, tsunamis, droughts, etc.); (2) accidental evil with unintentional consequence impacts the life of another person (e.g., a building collapse, HIV transmission by contaminated blood transfusion, etc.); (3) moral evil resulting from human being's sinful nature (e.g., the Holocaust, child abuse, murder, sexual assault, slavery). These evils, however, are not uniquely Christian challenges. Everyone experiences these evils regardless of where they are in their journey of faith. Suffering can come to us through different evils, not necessarily with a particular action on our part. Our responses to suffering should begin by recognizing these differences.

First and foremost, one has to recognize that not every evil is the same in terms of origin or intention.

Suffering never makes perfect sense. There is simply no perfectly satisfying solution to the problem of suffering. Yet it is real and, to a certain extent, strange and mysterious. While the Bible considers it a reality in life, it does not provide us the complete picture about suffering and evil in this world. It also does not explore a philosophical inquiry into it. Therefore, there is not much data available to construct our understanding of it. We do not know much about evil, yet we see its consequences every day.

Second, there is no single perfect approach that answers the question of suffering. Each has its own strengths and weaknesses. In other words, no single approach to suffering perfectly accounts for it. Each situation is different and requires a different set of approaches. Consequently, any sweeping statement that implies a universal answer to suffering is always inappropriate and should be avoided.

Third, some of the approaches tend to seriously restrict a human's quest of God in the face of suffering. Human beings are created to ask questions. Any approach that denies such ability on our part is not rendering the best service for the life of a Christian seeking God in his or her own suffering.

Fourth, there are many situations where no direct relationship exists between sin and suffering. Suffering quite often comes to us randomly and incidentally (cf. Luke 13:1–5). The disciples of Jesus presumed that there was a direct correspondence between the blind man's sin and his suffering. Jesus was clear in his stance that logical fallacy should not be committed and that there was an alternative (John 9:1–3). We may experience suffering not necessarily as the judgment of God but because we are all under the sentence of death. Fifth, the suffering of the innocent is not God's will. It is the result of the stark fact that we are all under the sentence of death. God will abolish suffering of the innocent, but they must learn to wait in hope.

Practical implications

From these discussions we can deduce some practical wisdom in addressing the problem of suffering in the ministry setting.

First, refrain from making speculative linking of suffering with sin and spirituality. We often hear statements such as, "This must be happening because you have committed some grave sin"; "Your lack of faith in God has been one of the main reasons for your suffering"; and "This suffering is to help you mature in your spirituality." As discussed, these responses usually lack biblical basis in light of many unexplainable afflictions, and they distort the reality and variety of causes. Furthermore, it is up to God to decide whether there is any connection. There may even be situations where pastors want to remove speculative reasoning on the part of their members by saying that there is no connection between their current suffering and a specific sin they committed in the past.

Second, avoid rationalization. We often hear, "All things work together for good"; "There must be a good reason that you had to go through this"; or "This suffering will prevent you from getting into a more problematic situation." Instead of providing consolation and encouragement in dark times, this rationalization may become a source of deep alienation and resentment.

Third, stay away from editorializing. Pastors at times feel the urge to explain away suffering, persuade sufferers with philosophical theories, or say, "We will all die one day." This mistake is often made when pastors are not adequately equipped to deal with situations of suffering. Silence serves us better in many crisis situations.

The best response comes from pastors' deep reflections of the biblical passages, ministering to those who are suffering, standing by those who are oppressed, the avoidance of easy (and/or instantaneous) answers, openness to the multidimensional nature of suffering, proper use of language, and a Christian character of humility. This takes study and reflection, but it will reward them immensely.

The theology of the Cross

The Bible may never give us the full answers to the questions of sin and suffering. But there is one approach to this issue that comforts us and provides courage and strength, even without a sufficient theoretical solution to it. It is not theodicy.

While humans respond to suffering and evil with the question "Oh God, why?" God responds in the most powerful way. He comes to us in Jesus Christ (John 1:14) as a "man of sorrows" and "acquainted with grief" (Isaiah 53:3, RSV). He experiences our suffering in the Person of Jesus, who made that unimaginable, darkest cry of suffering, "Why have You forsaken Me?" He, Himself, not just the Incarnate Son of God, suffers. For God suffering does not imply "deficiency of being, weakness, subjection, instability,"[6] but in identifying with those who suffer—whether innocently or guiltily. A pathway to reconciliation and ultimate freedom was opened up through the suffering of Jesus Christ.

Instead of providing a theoretical or philosophical response, our God chooses to bear our suffering and pain because He knows that "only the suffering God can help" us.

God created the world and allowed His creatures to make their own choices, including departure from Him. God, because He is love, did not have a choice but to suffer with His creatures. Before there was a cross on the hill of Calvary, there was a cross in the heart of God.[7] The Cross reveals the divine nature, the love of God, in its most extreme form: that God willingly suffers with and for those He loves. Jesus Christ was nailed on the cross for us, suffers with us and for us until the regeneration of all things takes place (Romans 8). By the way, the resurrection of Jesus is "not merely consolation in suffering; it is also the sign of God's protest against suffering."[8]

Instead of providing a theoretical or philosophical response, our God chooses to bear our suffering and pain because He knows that "only the *suffering* God can help" us.[9] Because God chose the way of love on the cross and because Jesus is risen, we can now place our hope in God's sovereign control over the future, not because we can figure out the future but because we believe His kingdom will renew all things and wipe away every tear. We anticipate that our worst sufferings, full of misery and ugliness, may look beautiful in the light of God's redemption that we will enjoy permanently.

1. David Hume, *Dialogues Concerning Natural Religion,* edited by Martin Bell (London: Penguin, 1991), 108, 109.

2. For a concise survey of this issue, see Stephen T. Davis, "The Problem of Pain in Recent Philosophy," *Review and Expositors* 82 (1985): 535–48. Though not aimed at the Adventist audience, Richard Rice's book also provides a concise summary of various theodicies. Richard Rice, *Suffering and the Search for Meaning: Contemporary Responses to the Problem of Pain* (Downers Grove, IL; InterVarsity Press, 2014). For a complicated philosophical discussion of the Christian faith in this regard, see Alvin J. Plantinga, *God, Freedom and Evil* (Grand Rapids, MI: Eerdmans, 1974). For additional reading, you may want to start with the following: Timothy Keller, *Walking With God Through Pain and Suffering* (New York, NY: Dutton, 2013); Don Carson, *How Long, O Lord? Reflections on Suffering and Evil,* 2nd ed. (Grand Rapids, MI: Baker Academic, 2006); Thomas G. Long, *What Shall We Say? Evil, Suffering, and the Crisis of Faith* (W. B. Eerdmans Publishing Co., Grand Rapids, MI, 2011).

3. It was an eighteenth century philosopher, Leibniz, who first coined this word to denote theological and philosophical attempts to defend God's providence in light of evil and innocent suffering.

4. Unless otherwise indicated, all Scripture is from the New International Version.

5. Richard Rice extensively dealt with this response in his recent article "An Enemy Hath Done This: Cosmic Conflict Theodicy," *Ministry* (March 2015), 6–9.

6. Richard Bauckham, "Only the Suffering God Can Help," Divine Passibility in Modern Theology. *Themelios* 9.3 (April 1984), 6–12.

7. Horace Bushnell, *Vicarious Sacrifice* (London: Alexander Strahan, 1866), 31.

8. Jürgen Moltmann, *Experience of God,* trans. Margaret Kohl (Philadelphia: Fortress Press, 1980), 12.

9. Dietrich Bonhoeffer, *Letters and Papers From Prison* (London: SCM Press, 1967), 361.

Fostering a Ministry of Excellence: Continuing Education for Lifelong Learning

ESTHER R. KNOTT

At a recent convention in San Diego, California, I was browsing through a book at one of the many displays in the exhibit hall. Having been a church pastor for twenty-eight years, one sentence caught my attention. I purchased the paperback that was part of a series on foundations for learning.

In his book *Exploring the Life and Calling*, author Gary Black Jr.[1] shares a statement that he used in his *first* lecture, in his *first* class, on his *first* day as a professor of theology in a Christian seminary: "I am of the firm opinion that as professional ministers of the gospel of Jesus Christ, those of you sitting in this room represent the most important profession in the world today. And therefore, that makes you, by association, some of the most important people in the world today."[2] While not wanting to diminish the vital importance of other professions, Black wanted to drill home to his students the significance of becoming qualified to guide those whom they would be called to serve and lead.

We know that ministry well done has connections to matters of ultimate concern to society—both present and eternal. If our profession as ministers is indeed so important, then we must be intentional in modeling a life dependent on the Holy Spirit in order to transform us into the image of God. We must also be intentional to receive the proper education to be equipped for this calling. This equipping includes two phases: first, theological education in preparation for serving as a pastor and, second, continuing education for our ongoing professional development. When foundational formal education is combined with focused and enduring professional development, we will realize the ideal of lifelong learning discussed in the Bible and Ellen White.

Necessity for theological education

Years ago, Ellen White wrote about the need for equipping those who are called. These passages are still relevant today.

> The times demand an intelligent, educated ministry, not novices. False doctrines are being multiplied. The world is becoming educated to a high standard of literary attainment; and sin, unbelief, and infidelity are becoming more bold and defiant, as intellectual knowledge and acuteness are acquired. This state of things calls for the use of every power of the intellect; for it is keen minds, under the control of Satan, that the minister will have to meet. He should be well balanced by religious principles, growing in grace and in the knowledge of our Lord Jesus Christ. Too much haphazard work has been done, and minds have not been exercised to their fullest capacity.[3]

Whatever the case, the called must also seek to be equipped with the best education available to them.

Surely this statement continues to reflect the nature of our current society. She also wrote about being prepared for opportunities that God will open for you:

> Do men think that they will be able, under pressure of circumstances, to step into an important position, when they have neglected to train and discipline themselves for the work? Do they imagine that they can be polished instruments in the hands of God for the salvation of souls, if they have not used the opportunities placed at their command for obtaining a fitness for the work? The cause of God calls for all-round men, who can devise, plan, build up, and organize. And those who appreciate the probabilities and possibilities of the work for this time, will seek by earnest study to obtain all the knowledge they can from the Word, to use in ministering to needy, sin-sick souls.[4]

When God calls men and women to serve Him, He uses different routes. Some know from early childhood that ministry will be their lifework. Others enter the ministry after serving for years in another profession. Whatever the case, the called must also seek to be equipped with the best education available to them.

The standard education program for Seventh-day Adventist ministers in the North American Division (NAD) is first a bachelor's degree and then, the master of divinity (MDiv) degree from the Seventh-day Adventist Theological Seminary at Andrews University.[5] If you have been serving as a pastor for several years and have not had the opportunity to get an MDiv, keep reading to the end of this chapter to explore ways for you to earn a master in pastoral ministry (MAPMin). The seminary MDiv program provides a thorough understanding of the Bible and deepens the knowledge of Adventist theology and identity. It also provides the opportunity to deepen your walk with Jesus, receive tools to continue to dig deeply into God's Word, expand your cultural sensitivity as you attend classes with people from all around the world, and develop the skills of discipleship/evangelism, leadership, worship, management, and scholarship.

After you have your degree

Once you have your degree, you soon realize the enormous challenges of serving in an ever-changing world. Perhaps at no time in history has the profession of ministry been more complex. This is where professional development comes in. Professional development is all about being the absolute best you can be at your calling. It helps you maintain your expert status throughout your career, even decades after formal training.

My friends who are physicians, electricians, teachers, bankers, attorneys, and nurses all have professional development requirements. These occupations require continuing education because times change, technology improves, culture shifts, expectations vary, and unexpected challenges constantly emerge.[6] Professional development, in these and other professions, is key to maintaining specialized relevance and effectiveness in our ever-changing landscape. It is also customizable, because learning how to enhance skills can take many forms including reading a book, attending a seminar, or taking a college course.[7] Likewise, professional development and continuing education (CE) are critical to our ongoing ability to share the good news in this critical time of earth's history. Our church is taking steps to support pastors to receive this ongoing education. The rest of this chapter will discuss research about the need for continuing education, define continuing education, and describe how to receive and track it.

The need for continued professional development

If you are a minister who desires to keep growing, read the following quotes from Ellen White and be affirmed in your thirst for more. If you are one who has settled down and lost your desire to grow, read these inspired quotes about the need for continued development. Let the Holy Spirit breathe new life into you, your ministry, and thereby your church members as you disciple them and acquire fresh skills to serve the kingdom of God.

> A minister should never think that he has learned enough, and may now relax his efforts. His education should continue throughout his lifetime; every day he should be learning, and putting to use the knowledge gained.[8]

> The true minister of Christ should make continual improvement. The afternoon sun of his life may be more mellow and productive of fruit than the morning sun. It may continue to increase in size and brightness until it drops behind the western hills. My brethren in the ministry, it is better, far better, to die of hard work in some home or foreign mission field, than to rust out with inaction. Be not dismayed at difficulties; be not content to settle down without studying and without making improvement.[9]

> Our ministers will have to render to God an account for the rusting of the talents He has given to improve by exercise. They might have done tenfold more work intelligently had they cared to become intellectual giants. Their whole experience in their high calling is cheapened because they are content to remain where they are. Their efforts to acquire knowledge will not in the least hinder their spiritual growth if they will study with right motives and proper aims.[10]

As pastors move from one church to another, some use the same sermons in district after district. Other pastors, like Dwight K. Nelson, have been with the same congregation for many years. Out of the depth of his devotional time with God, commitment to scholarship, and faithful leadership, Nelson has served his congregation at Pioneer Memorial Church, Berrien Springs, Michigan, with new and relevant sermons week after week for more than thirty years.

Ellen White points out what happens if our presentations do not vary and if we use the same illustrations and even the same words:

Some of our ministers have a runway of discourses which they use without variation year after year. The same illustrations, the same figures, and almost the same words. They have ceased to be students. There is an end to improvement, and they stagger under the load of a few set discourses to prevent mental decrepitude. But by the ever-learning student new light, new ideas, new gems of truth will be found and eagerly grasped. . . . The gospel is not properly taught and represented before unbelievers by men who have ceased to be students, who have, as it were, graduated as far as searching the Scriptures is concerned, and they bring a reproach upon the truth by the manner in which they handle it.[11]

At the same time, Ellen White is very balanced in her approach about the need *to* study and also *leave* the study:

The ministers of the word are God's chosen agency to spread the knowledge of his will; but there is too little of a missionary spirit, even among our ministers. After preaching the word, some confine themselves almost wholly to reading and study, to the neglect of other and vitally important duties. While it is right to devote some time to study, every minister should feel a deep interest to do all that it is possible for him to do for the salvation of souls for whom Christ died. He should visit the people, and with care and wisdom seek to interest them in spiritual things.[12]

Continuing education

Church policy states that pastors should earn two continuing education units (CEU) per year. By making provision for the fulfillment of this policy, we demonstrate the value we place on our ministers. I well remember the first time my employer sent me off to a seminar for CE. I was so happy because I saw that they were investing in me and believed in my future.

Even though there is a policy to provide for CE, we have not always been diligent at making sure it was available, documented, and affirmed. I would often receive a CE certificate and it would end up in my own file folder, and no one knew I had invested time to grow.

Research from administrators

In 2014, the NAD conference presidents and other church administrators were surveyed about church structure and the need for strategic planning.[13] Answers to two of the survey questions are especially relevant to our topic.

1. Eighty-seven (87) percent said they agree or strongly agree with the statement "Pastors within the NAD **NEED** a system by which they can be professionally developed just as do other professions."
2. Only 13 percent said they agree or strongly agree with the statement "Most conferences within the NAD **HAVE** a strong system of pastoral growth and development."

The gap

This indicates a seventy-four-point gap between what we have and what we need. The North American Ministerial team was tasked with directing the division's efforts to support local conferences in building a comprehensive, sustainable continuing education system for pastors. It is our church's responsibility to ensure that our pastors continue to be trained and equipped with the skills and resources needed to effectively deliver the gospel in the twenty-first century. As disciples of Jesus, we all want to be good at our jobs. Lifelong continuous learning can make us the absolute best we can be for Christ.

As disciples of Jesus, we all want to be good at our jobs. Lifelong continuous learning can make us the absolute best we can be for Christ.

Research on the core competencies/ qualities of a pastor

To help guide pastors with professional development, research was done to determine the core competencies/qualities of a pastor.[14] Those surveyed included conference presidents, ministerial directors, pastors, and elders. After more than two years of research and thousands of responses, North American Division Ministerial Association has identified seven core qualities/competencies of pastors who are truly making an impact. The director of the Adventist Learning Community, Adam Fenner, writes, "These seven core qualities are the foundation of the pastoral profession. Not only do they provide a framework of occupational expectations, but they also provide guidance and a structure for what we need to provide for our pastors as we seek to inspire them and to provide for their excellence in making disciples who follow after Christ."[15]

Below is a brief description of the seven core qualities of the effective pastor. As you review the list, it will be beneficial for you to set a goal to select CE in each of these seven areas over each five-year period.[16]

Seven core competencies/qualities

Character—the foundational quality, allowing the character of Christ to be formed in us and modeled through personal integrity that aligns with biblical ideals.

Evangelism—skilled and passionate about making disciples, helping people accept, internalize, and share in a vibrant relationship with Jesus Christ and the Seventh-day Adventist message.

Leadership—building a church vision and equipping members to learn, grow, and serve.

Worship—facilitating an enriching corporate worship experience that brings people into the presence of God.

Management—executing responsibilities in a timely, well-organized fashion. (You cannot be an excellent leader without management skills.)

Scholarship—diligently and carefully studying the Bible and professional resources for continuous personal growth in Christ.

Relationship—relating well to others regardless of faith, age, ethnicity, personality, or gender.

Talk with your ministerial director about the areas you are interested in studying. Together, you can work out your personal plan to cover the seven competencies.

Sharon Aka, associate director of the ALC, states:

Imagine a professional environment where pastors can annually demonstrate their eagerness to learn new ministry skills and strategies. Imagine too, a congregation who has the opportunity to be educated about the defining qualities of a pastor, and what they should and should not expect from their pastor. A church congregation will not define their pastor, the profession will; this creates safety for a pastor. Additionally, the success of a pastor will not be entirely determined by the perceptions of a congregation. Professional qualities will drive the development of both professional development content for CEU credit, and create a benchmark for determining success in the role of pastor.[17]

Definition of continuing education and CEU

NAD Working Policy states that pastors should earn two continuing education units (CEU) per year. The term *CEU* equals the value associated with professional activities used for the purpose of increasing professional learning and practice. If you are in an academic program, you are already fulfilling your CE requirement.

Working in tandem with the Adventist Learning Community, the Continuing Education ministerial team (composed of selected ministerial directors from across the division) has developed a table of values that will be used for assigning the number of CEUs per professional development activity. Using already established professional standards, the ALC and CE Ministerial Committee has determined that one CEU equals ten hours of professional engagement. The term *hours* reflects value and/or quality of activity or content, not necessarily literal time. Additionally, a table of standardized values will be used for assessing the number of CEUs per activity. These values will be consistent across the division and posted online where all pastors and ministerial directors will have access to the information.

The development of professional standards and continuing education opportunities is part of a larger church initiative to maximize our discipleship and effectiveness for furthering the Great Commission. The church is developing a structure to support the professional development of ministers and teachers, performing various roles in the church. By fostering lifelong learning throughout all church professions, our church will have a higher level of professional transparency, equity, and continuity and, most importantly, an enhanced ability to effectively strengthen Christ's kingdom.[18]

Options for completing your CEU

The list below provides you with ideas on where to go and how best to complete your CEUs.

Adventist Learning Community. There are a variety of ways to complete your CEU. One of the newest ways is through the Adventist Learning Community (ALC) of the North American Division. "Its mission is to empower people with the passion and skills necessary to further the kingdom of Christ in the 21st Century. Because of technology, ALC can put training, education, and resources into the palms of people's hands anywhere, any time. On the ALC site[19] you can find free courses for continuing education, certification, or just for fun. Their ministerial education library puts Adventist resources from around the world at your fingertips."[20]

Reading, writing, attending conferences. Other ways to complete your CEU include attending a professional conference, reading a book, writing a book, writing an article, creating a new seminar, developing a course for the ALC, writing course content for the professional development of pastors or the training of church members. Your conference may decide that every pastor needs to be updated on some legal issues affecting pastors and can work with the ALC to provide that resource online. At times you may receive CEU credit at your local ministers meeting when the conference brings in a speaker for a specialized topic, not just reports.

The seminary. The seminary at Andrews University has numerous opportunities for ongoing professional development both on and off campus, for credit and not for credit. Those who wish to receive academic credit toward a degree must apply for admission to the university either to enroll in one of the seminary degree programs or to take classes as a guest student. Some courses are available for a nominal fee.

Master of arts in pastoral ministry intensives. Weeklong intensives for the master of arts (MA) in pastoral ministry are offered in all union conferences twice a year. Because the program is subsidized, pastors can attend any of these classes free for both academic and continuing education credit.

Doctor of ministry. Graduates of the Andrews doctor of ministry program are able to attend intensives in any of the multiple concentration areas of the program for the rest of their lives without charge. This opportunity provides a lifelong learning community and interaction with current thinking in the essential ministry specialties the program addresses.[21]

Local university/college. Contact the Adventist university near you and see what they have to offer for continuing education. In some cases, even your local community college may have what you need. Attending the local public college provides a wonderful opportunity to have contact with people in your community and gives you the chance to be a contagious Adventist.

Tracking and reporting for CEU

Once you have participated in a CE event, you will want to keep track of it and let your conference administration know what you have been doing. There is a mechanism in place for you to track and report this. Simply create and thereafter log in to your account on the ALC Web site[22] and answer three questions: (1) What was the activity? (2) What did you learn? (3) How will this knowledge/experience make a difference with those you serve? This reflective piece is one of the most important aspects of professional development because it is a precursor to thoughtful application and transformation.[23]

Once you submit your electronic report, your ministerial director will be notified to approve the CEU. The record of your CE will move with you wherever you go within North America. Much fulfillment will come as you track all the ways you have grown professionally.

The masters in pastoral ministry comes to you

Earlier in this chapter, we referred to the master of divinity as the standard training for the Adventist ministry. Perhaps you are one who has pastored for many years without completing a master's degree and it would be nearly impossible for you to now attend the seminary. Realizing that not everyone follows the same path to ministry, almost thirty years ago the union conferences made provision for this. They asked the seminary to develop the MA in pastoral ministry degree. This is a forty-eight-credit professional degree that is delivered through two one-week intensives, twice a year, in all nine unions. The denomination subsidizes the program, so the only cost to the conference is to help the pastor with travel and lodging expenses. Since these classes are taught as intensives, usually Sunday through Thursday, there is work to complete before the class (pre-intensive assignments) and work to complete after the class (post-intensive assignments). The program, consisting of sixteen three-credit classes, can be completed in three and a half years.[24] You can learn more about the program at http://www.andrews.edu/inministry.

Therefore, foster a ministry of excellence as you go and make disciples who make disciples.

Seasoned pastors who have been in the MA in pastoral ministry program (MAP-Min) have found it to be a very workable option for them to earn their master's degree. These men and women enjoy the interaction with their colleagues and seminary professors. Things that they may have done intuitively now have purpose and organization. They find out why some things worked and some things did not. Our seminary professors especially enjoy the interaction that comes with teaching pastors who are actively working and immediately applying the lessons that have been shared in the classroom.

Lifelong learning

In keeping with Gary Black's attempt to prod his students toward excellence, I repeat his statement here: I am of the firm opinion that as professional ministers of the gospel of Jesus Christ, those of you reading this represent "the most important profession in the world today. And therefore, that makes you, by association, some of the most important people in the world today."[25] Therefore, foster a ministry of excellence as you go and make disciples who make disciples.

---

1. Gary Black Jr. is chair of Azusa Pacific University's department of Advanced Studies and director of the Doctor of Ministry program.

2. Gary Black, *Exploring the Life and Calling* (Minneapolis, MN: Fortress Press, 2014), 3.

3. Ellen G. White, *Testimonies for the Church* (Mountain View, CA: Pacific Press®, 1948), 5:528.

4. Ellen G. White, *Gospel Workers* (Washington, DC: Review and Herald®, 1948), 93, 94.

5. *Working Policy: North American Division of the General Conference of Seventh-day Adventists* (2012–2013 ed.,), section L.

6. These concepts are contributed by Adam Fenner, director of the Adventist Learning Community (ALC) and adjunct professor of Andrews University History and Honors Departments.

7. These concepts are contributed by Sharon Aka, associate director of the Adventist Learning Community and former professor and professional development specialist, Humber College, Toronto, Ontario.

8. White, *Gospel Workers,* 94.

9. Ellen G. White, "Diligence a Necessary Qualification in the Minister," *The Review and Herald,* April 6, 1886, par. 5.

10. Ellen G. White, *Testimonies to Ministers and Gospel Workers* (Mountain View, CA: Pacific Press®, 1962), 194.

11. Ellen G. White, *The Voice in Speech and Song* (Boise, ID: Pacific Press®, 1988), 323, 324.

12. Ellen G. White, "The True Missionary Spirit," *The Review and Herald,* July 10, 1883, par. 10.

13. For more information on this survey, contact Paul Brantley, vice president for Strategic Planning and Assessment, North American Division of Seventh-day Adventists. The information was obtained from a slide presentation by Paul Brantley.

14. For more information on this survey, contact Dave Gemmell, associate director, North American Division Ministerial Department.

15. Concepts and wording contributed by Adam Fenner.

16. For a copy of the descriptors and indicators of each quality, go to http://www.nadministerial.org.

17. Contributed by Sharon Aka.

18. Concepts and wording contributed by Sharon Aka and Adam Fenner.

19. http://www.adventistlearningcommunity.com.

20. Contributed by the Adventist Learning Community.

21. Contributed by Skip Bell, professor of Christian Leadership and director of the doctor of ministry program (2001–2015) at the Seventh-day Adventist Theological Seminary at Andrews University.

22. http://www.adventistlearningcommunity.com.

23. Contributed by the Adventist Learning Community.

24. Class completion in three and one half years includes spending two weeks (taking two classes) in residence during the first year in the program. Course completion for Lake Union and Canadian Union students is four years. Canadian students complete all of their classes in Canada.

25. Black, *Exploring the Life and Calling,* 3.

 RELATIONSHIP

Pastors relate well to others regardless of faith, age, ethnicity, personality, or gender.

Descriptors of Relationship include:
• participates actively in church life dynamics
• loves people
• adapts well to new situations
• respects boundaries, confidentiality
• models and ensures member visitation
• avoids compromising situations
• effective spiritual counselor
• compassionate
• hospitable
• supportive team player
• able to screen/refer for mental health
• senses the feelings of others

Married to a Minister

DIANE THURBER

I did not marry a pastor but knew this could be in my future. My husband Gary's education prepared him to teach or pastor. However, he accepted a teaching ministry position across the country from our families. At twenty-one, I was relieved not to add "pastor's wife" to my list of titles. He would teach, and I would be office manager. *Plenty of opportunities to minister in those roles,* we thought, and soon it was true.

Before the first school year ended, however, Gary received a call to pastoral ministry. After much prayer, neither of us could shake the strong impression that God was calling us to new roles: pastor and pastor's wife, though neither of us fully understood the scope of this invitation.

Gary was prepared to move whenever God called because his parents did so frequently in their ministry journey. Though very mission-focused in their workplace, church, and community, my parents were not called to the transient lifestyle many ministry families experience. Because of this, I found it challenging and stressful to move. However, lyrics to "Whither Thou Goest,"[1] performed at our wedding, echoed in my mind. With renewed commitment, I packed for our first pastoral district.

> *We did not think "No, thank you," was an option, but that is what I wanted to say.*

I recalled what other ministers' wives experienced (I do not recall any female pastors in those days). Doubt crept in, and I did not see how I could measure up to what these ladies had been or done, nor was I sure I wanted a life like theirs—busy, scrutinized, demanding, and more! I began to think, *What does God want of me?*

Reality set in when Gary phoned church leaders to let them know our arrival date. One leader said, "By the way, the nominating committee is placing

Diane in the Kindergarten class as a leader. Will you let her know?" Gary hesitantly relayed the message. After learning the church's plans for me, I wanted to turn around and go back.

I pummeled my husband with questions as we drove: "Why did they decide that without talking to me? Why do they think I have the gifts to lead a children's division? When do I have to start?" Gary tried, but did not have all the answers.

We did not think "No, thank you," was an option, but that is what I wanted to say. The knot twisted tighter in my stomach. We continued a journey I no longer was excited about. My prayer life took on a new dimension that day, as did my faith walk.

Four years later, shortly before Gary's ordination, we attended the service for our friend, Gaylen Herr. I asked his wife, "Laurie, are you ready to be a pastor's wife for the rest of your life?"[2]

Her response is what I needed to hear, and her words have echoed often in my mind: "Diane, another pastor's wife shared with me that what I need to do first is decide what kind of Christian I want to be and how I would serve God if I was just another member in the pew." That made a lot of sense and lessened my anxiety. I desired to serve God and would wait for Him to reveal His will for my life.

A ministry journey is much like a tapestry, and each side tells unique stories.

God strengthened me and continues to equip me, although I have learned it is OK to say "No" when others' expectations do not align with God's priorities for my life. He has used His timid, skeptical-at-times daughter in surprising ways. I am reminded, "But we have this treasure in jars of clay to show that this all-surpassing power is from God and not from us" (2 Corinthians 4:7, NIV).

The devil is resolute and cunning with his plans to distract, destroy, and rob pastors' families of joy in service. A ministry journey is much like a tapestry, and each side tells unique stories. On the front are colorful strands of yarn woven to form beautiful images. On the reverse are redirected threads and knots. Some threads, like communication, time, friendships, health, personal growth, and shared mission, bring understanding and add joy on the journey. Let us consider these threads that your spouse and you use to weave a ministry tapestry.

Communication

Brenda Aufderhar and her pastoral husband, Mike, have a passion for families, and their focus on communication has blessed many ministry couples. They highly recommend *Talking and Listening Together: Couple Communication I*,[3] a practical curriculum to help couples acquire a set of talking and listening skills. Brenda says,

> Communication that flows easily, creates understanding, and supports finding solutions is essential and necessary for the minister's home to survive and thrive. It helps each person better manage the stresses of the outside world while preventing a volcano from forming inside the glass house. Good communication decreases the blame game, formation of bitterness, and the emotional chaos that follows. An open heart with the skills to listen, talk and problem solve increases self-responsibility by strengthening self-awareness, which is foundational for relational stewardship—the work of owning and being responsible for one's part of the interactions with others. At its best, the flow of words and ease of attentive ears is authentic, godly love in action.

Learning *and* living better communication skills have been part of the Aufderhars' experience. Brenda says, "Each time we prepared to present together at various parenting junctures, and dealt with 'attacks of friendly fire,' in various places we have served, we were stretched to grow the most. While our learning times often have been messy, hard, and tedious, we have noted with gratitude, like finishing a marathon, a sense of accomplishment and satisfaction that our hearts were more knit together and a greater sense of God's love rested in and between us."

Couples who acquire and practice these skills also offer a gift to the churches they serve.

Time

In a 2014 study of Adventist pastors and families, "Over two-thirds of pastors and spouses felt that the time demands of their roles prevented sufficient leisure time with their families."[4] Absence of time together results in stressed, fractured relationships. Couples who dialogue about workloads and are intentional about guarding family time are more content. There is less tug-of-war between the demands of their respective responsibilities with a commitment to support and build stronger relationships.

Kim Kennedy and her pastoral husband, Dave, highly value strong relationships in their home. For them, this comes through quality time. Kim says,

> Family meal times around the kitchen table and a scheduled weekly family night are essential to making relationship-building a priority. Thursday nights are off-limits to anyone who wants to do something that does not include the whole family. In the beginning, church members tried to schedule appointments on this night, but the beauty of family night is being able to say "no" for a great reason. Our boys appreciate that work is not the priority that evening, and Dave and I gain respect with our church and friends for making time for family. We still experience family night together even though our family dynamics have changed with older children. Lucas, a junior in college, has this constant rhythm to depend on when he visits, and our youngest, Logan, soon a senior in high school, asks every week, "What are we doing for family night?"

Absence of time together results in stressed, fractured relationships.

Jed Dart and his pastoral wife, Lee Lee, are proactive in making date nights and time "to keep us connected, so our marriage stays strong!" Jed finds that "time together can be challenging because Lee Lee's evenings are more full now, and that is when I am off work," he says.

Ronald Knott and his pastoral wife, Esther, have been in ministry together since 1990. They have another approach to family function. "I don't believe we have ever ordered our marriage and family life on the basis of 'quality time.' By accident or design, we operate more on the basis of 'continuous engagement.' We share everything of interest, and have been blessed to find many opportunities for creative synergy between our jobs, which makes it all the more fun," Ronald says. The Knotts also determined to implement the continuous engagement principle when their daughter, Livvy, joined the family. This commitment resulted in realigned personal and professional priorities for Ronald and Esther.

Thoughtfully devise a plan with your spouse to nurture family relationships. Try the plan for a period of time and evaluate the benefits. Adjust if necessary.

Friendships

Laurie Snyman and her pastor husband, Royce, have learned the value of forming friendships for support. Laurie says, "Personal friendships are a wonderful blessing, but not always possible for the ministry spouse. We sometimes have to keep boundaries to be able to maintain objectivity since our role is to serve and avoid conflicting dual relationships. These boundaries can make one feel isolated."

Laurie felt this isolation when raising a toddler.

> My daughter had been acting up, and I tried to think of someone to call with more experience in parenting than myself. I could not think of one person I could fully trust.
>
> Not long after that, my husband initiated inviting pastoral families and couples to our home on Saturday nights. We found new friends (who had always been there) and, by spending time together, formed intimate connections. We prayed, discussed, and problem-solved. What a benefit we had missed throughout all those early years in ministry!

José Hernandez's wife, Ann Roda, is a pastor. He says a unique challenge male ministry spouses face is "that there are so few male ministry spouses. It is very difficult to get to know one another and establish a network of support. It can be isolating, especially during pastors' meetings or retreats when the entire family is invited and all the male pastors have established friendships with one another, and the pastors' wives have their own meetings." While well intended, José also finds that "publications, letters, cards, and gifts sent to the home are geared specifically for the pastor's wife rather than a pastor's husband."

If you do not serve where close fellowship with other Adventist pastoral couples is possible, connect with the minister and ministerial spouse community groups on Facebook where fellowship and support are plentiful.[5]

Health

There are numerous reasons to support one another on your pathway to health. The stresses of life and ministry are detrimental if not guarded. In addition to healthy eating and other counseled lifestyle habits,[6] consider supporting each other's exercise goals. Better yet, find time to exercise together.

In her blog *Meet, Catch, and Keep,* Theresa DiDonata shares "5 Reasons

Why Couples Who Sweat Together, Stay Together." The benefits include (1) increasing happiness with your relationship; (2) improving efficiency of your workouts; (3) making your partner fall in love with you; (4) helping you achieve your fitness goals; and (5) increasing your emotional bond.[7]

Why not involve the whole family? It is never too early to model a healthy lifestyle. This can be part of your plan to build family relationships too.

Personal growth

Charles H. Spurgeon said, "Man's wonder grows with his knowledge,"[8] and Jesus "kept increasing in wisdom and stature, and in favor with God and men" (Luke 2:52, NASB). Learning new skills or advancing education goals can open new doors professionally, provide opportunities in ministry for your spouse, and may bring a greater fulfillment in service. Continued spiritual growth brings a deepening awe, trust, and faith in our Savior too.

Sandi Case, a retired pastor's wife, recently reflected on her spiritual journey: " 'She's a pastor's wife; devotional life is easy for her.' We all know it is not true, but we do not explain how we struggle daily to maintain that life! . . . It was important to discover why I was a Seventh-day Adventist believer. My beliefs and personal walk first had to be *mine.* With that perspective, it was more difficult for hurts, disappointments, and frustrations to 'derail' me. Owning my beliefs, I was able to encourage my husband's faithfulness and exhort him in his ministry."

Shared mission

Jed Dart states that he and his wife, Lee Lee, "have always made a good team. Our strengths complement each other, and we love serving together. I also love having a front row seat to watch my wife tell people about Jesus firsthand with her words and actions. This blesses me so much. My prayer life has become richer and deeper, too, as we pray for those to whom she ministers."

José Hernandez enjoys being a part of the process as Ann Roda, his wife, prepares her sermons. He says, "We discuss the biblical passage, and she shares how God's Word has spoken to her. She invites me to take the same journey in the passage, then together we share what God has put in our hearts. Our different thoughts and perspectives are spiritually enriching. On Sabbath morning, I try to listen with fresh ears. God enables me to hear and see something different from His Word. I praise God for this experience. It's been a wonderful journey that strengthens our spiritual connection with one another."

Scripture reveals the supportive roles of husband and wife within a family unit. Yet, it does not clearly outline God's expectations of a pastor's spouse. However, we learn that all believers are called to serve in a royal priesthood that we "may proclaim the excellencies of Him who has called you out of darkness into His marvelous light" (1 Peter 2:9, NASB).

> *It took a while to accept that Gary and I are* together *in ministry for a purpose.*

It took a while to accept that Gary and I are *together* in ministry for a purpose.[9] I am not just the spouse along for the ride (though I have been to unimagined destinations). I am not just the spouse to hold up the preacher (though I now realize how much he values that support). I am not just the mother who endeavors to produce perfect role models for the congregation (though if the wife and mother "works for the best interests of her family, seeking to fashion their characters after the divine Model, the recording angel writes her name as one of the greatest missionaries in the world").[10] I have been called to serve, and there is much variety in what He asks me to do.

God has a significant ministry calling for your spouse too. He wants you *and* your spouse to influence for Christ, faithfully serve, and share God's grace in its various forms (1 Peter 4:10). The question I continue to ask myself is, "Will I develop the gifts God has entrusted to me for mission, or will I waste those talents?" It is a question each ministry spouse faces.

God partners with ministry spouses in many ways. They teach, greet visitors, host hospitality lunches, prepare newsletters, minister to the sick and aging, preach sermons or evangelistic series, lead small groups or Bible studies, present family-strengthening classes, operate audio-visual equipment, write songs or lead music groups, coordinate community outreach events, and so on. We are encouraged to "individually consider the many branches of the work. . . . Consider prayerfully what would best tell for the cause of God. If there is a humble, unselfish heart, and a contrite spirit, in seeking to know the Lord's will, he will lead each of us in the path where he would have us walk."[11] All of us are stewards trusted by God to do a work appointed by Him.[12]

Not all pastors' spouses embrace or realize God's desire, and some have been discouraged when they have served. In his blog post "Is There an Office for Pastors' Wives?" John Leeman states that a pastor should help his wife "not compare herself to other women, but to seek to be faithful with the gifts and opportunities God has given her."[13] If this is happening, one might expect to find an exuberant, engaged pastor's spouse in every district. However, Flourish, a Baptist equipping ministry for ministry wives, suggests that in relationship to her or his calling, a pastor's spouse's response falls into one of four categories: (1) uncertain, (2) solid, (3) struggling, or (4) robust.[14] The category in which pastors' spouses find themselves could vary at different points in the ministry journey. Flourish identifies situations or variables that impact a ministry spouse in her or his lifetime: (1) stages of life; (2) field in which the couple serves; (3) challenges of personality; (4) spiritual issues encountered; and (5) ministry issues that arise.[15]

Most pastoral couples acknowledge that the home is their first mission field and that each should labor for the salvation of the family.[16] They also accept that "love for that which is human is to be secondary to [their] love for God."[17] It is the variables and challenges in life that can cause a spouse to struggle for life balance and impede, at least temporarily, their response to or fulfillment of God's calling to serve. I encourage each pastor to seek a better understanding of your spouse's journey.

As God inspires a pastor's spouse to serve, some church members may express disapproval or make unrealistic demands or expectations. Some believe every pastor and pastor's spouse should function in a prescribed way. "Our duty is not decided by what others may plan for us,"[18] Ellen White counsels.

We may blend our strengths, but God does not ask the pastor's spouse to lose her or his individuality. "Of Him you are to ask: What is right? What is wrong? How may I best fulfill the purpose of my creation?"[19]

God has a significant ministry calling for your spouse too.

As the number of female pastors increases, men married to these ministers enter uncharted waters. Michael Nixon serves alongside his pastoral wife, Tacyana. He did not know what to expect from their first congregation. "At first, it wasn't clear where my place was or if it was even necessary for me to have one," Michael says. He later realized "the church did not have any true expectations." He believes that was, in part, because "the role and function of a pastor's wife is more natural and familiar to churches." In another congregation, Michael realizes the members' willingness to allow him to "function and contribute in ways that are more natural and comfortable." He and Tacyana seek God "on a regular basis to discern His plan" for their church, and Michael strives "to be ready, willing, and available to do whatever is necessary to support the ministry of my wife."

It is not just ministry role expectations male spouses face. For Jed Dart, preparing potluck food was an unexpected necessity "because Fridays are super busy" for Lee Lee. He says, "I now make a mean *vegan* cottage cheese roast, thank you very much!"

In his article "I'm Ted and I'm Married to Your Minister," a husband tells how time fixed the problem faced by some parishioners who, at first, did not know how to treat him. Deeper concerns include his natural defense for his pastoral wife to be treated fairly, those who undercut her pastoral authority for lack of comfort with her assignment, and unsubstantiated judgments about the couple's child-rearing outcomes. His greatest concern is knowing he is "married to a gifted pastor, but wondering whether [she] will get a real chance to maximize her God-given potential."[20]

Closing

Pastors' spouses receive joy and love from members but also may experience persecution and sacrifice in their duty for God. Ellen White offers some encouraging words: "In former years the wives of ministers endured want and persecution. When their husbands suffered imprisonment, and sometimes death, those noble, self-sacrificing women suffered with them, and their reward will be equal to that bestowed on the husband."[21]

> *Pastors' spouses receive joy and love from members but also may experience persecution and sacrifice in their duty for God.*

The spouse shares many pastoral burdens, because we are one flesh (Mark 10:8). However, "Nothing in all creation is hidden from God's sight" (Hebrews 4:13, NIV). "The eyes of the Lord search the whole earth in order to strengthen those whose hearts are fully committed to him" (2 Chronicles 16:9, NLT). May this knowledge comfort and embolden you as *together* you continue your ministry journey. Let your deep love for Jesus enable you both to hold on by faith.

1. Music and lyrics by Guy Singer, "Whither Thou Goest," Warner/Chappell Music, Inc., Karin Music, 1954.

2. For this chapter, I interviewed a number of individuals.

3. See Couple Communication, http://www.couplecommunication.com.

4. Duane McBride, David Sedlacek, and René Drumm, "Seminary Training, Role Demands, Family Stressors and Strategies for Alleviation of Stressors in Pastors' Families: Final Report to the North American Division Ministerial and Family Ministries Departments in conjunction with the General Conference of Seventh-day Adventists", presented September 8, 2014.

5. See https://www.facebook.com/groups/adventist.pastors/, http://www.facebook.com/Ministerial SpousesAssociation, or https://www.facebok.com/groups/ministerialspouses/.

6. Learn the CREATION Health principles at http://creationhealth.com/CREATION-Health.

7. Theresa E. DiDonata, "5 Reasons Why Couples Who Sweat Together, Stay Together" in Meet, Catch, and Keep (blog), January 10, 2014, http://www.psychologytoday.com/blog/meet-catch-and-keep/201401/5-reasons-why-couples-who-sweat-together-stay-together.

8. Charles Spurgeon, http://www.goodreads.com/quotes/76910-man-s-wonder-grows-with-his-knowledge, retrieved December 17, 2014.

9. Ellen G. White, *Manuscript Releases,* vol. 12 (Silver Spring, MD: Ellen G. White Estate, 1909), 165–167.

10. Ellen G. White, "The Appearance of Evil" in *Testimonies for the Church* (Nampa, ID: Pacific Press®, 1948), 5:594.

11. Ellen G. White, "Adopting Infant Children" in *Spalding and Magan Collection* (Washington, DC: Ellen G. White Estate 1987), 116.2.

12. Ellen G. White, "Stewards of God" in *The Adventist Home* (Hagerstown, MD: Review and Herald®, 2001), 367.

13. Jonathan Leeman,"Is There an Office for Pastors' Wives?" 9Marks, August 22, 2014, http://9marks.org/article/is-there-an-office-for-pastors-wives/.

14. Flourish, accessed December 17, 2014, http://www.flourish.me/Tools/, this Web page has been discontinued.

15. Ibid.

16. Ellen G. White, "Missionaries in the Home" in *Testimonies for the Church*, 4:138.

17. Ellen G. White, "Marriage" in *Counsels for the Church* (Nampa, ID: Pacific Press®, 1991), 126.

18. Ellen G. White, "Adopting Infant Children" in *Spalding and Magan Collection,* 116.

19. Ellen G. White, "Responsibilities of Married Life," *Testimonies for the Church,* 7:45.

20. Anonymous "I'm Ted and I'm Married to Your Minister," Weslayan Holiness Women, Summer 1992, http://www.whwomenclergy.org/articles/article57.php.

21. Ellen G. White, "The Minister's Wife" in *Gospel Workers* (Hagerstown, MD: Review and Herald®, 1915), 201.

Ministering to Seniors: The Family of God

MACY MCVAY

A few days ago, I found myself perusing a display of devotional books in the church foyer. There were Bible storybooks for toddlers and daily devotionals for Primary kids, Juniors, several for youth, two for young adults, one specifically for moms, and a selection of three or more for "adults." I noted with interest that there were no devotional books designed for the family unit as a whole and none addressing the specific needs of seniors.

Seniors are a large and growing demographic within the countries comprising the North American Division of Seventh-day Adventists.[1] In the United States (U.S.), as baby boomers, who make up close to one-quarter of the population,[2] retire in increasing numbers, this group will become more numerous in congregations. The median age of the North American population? Thirty-six. The median age within the North American church? Fifty-one.[3] According to Monte Sahlin, the "graying of Adventism" is an increasing trend across North America.[4] A 2008 demographic survey of Adventism compares percentages of generations in churches to U.S. and Canadian census data. Their conclusions show that the number of seniors in our churches is 20 percent higher than that of the general population.[5] With "boomers" entering retirement, this statistic will likely increase in the foreseeable future. It is important that pastors anticipate the en masse retirement of baby boomers and have a plan for expanded ministry to them. What form should such ministry take?

Fragmented worship

In the 1930s and 1940s, with the birth of youth groups, a new phenomenon appeared: generation-specific worship.[6] Youth services began popping up. Today, in larger churches and on school campuses it is possible, on any given

Sabbath, for youth or young adults to interact exclusively with their own generational group. Churches have tended toward bright lights, worship leaders in blue jeans, and smartphone participation in a creative attempt to appeal to youth and young adults. Such strategies, though, can have costly collateral damage—widening the divide between the generations. If we customize worship for the young, how will we meet the needs of our seniors so they feel they are a part of the family of God?

Specialization focused on younger groups is true of Sabbath School programming and curricula as well. These are often customized for various age groups from infants up through primary, juniors, and youth. Maturity level, attention span, and mobility are taken into account in doing so. And then, just like that, it stops. Suddenly, you are an adult.

> *We gravitate toward circles of people with whom we share significant characteristics, people who look and sound and smell and see just like us.*

As we contemplate the needs of a growing senior population in our churches and the increasing specialization of worship and Bible study, how should pastors respond? Focus on specific groups within the congregation makes good sense. There is a natural draw to be with people our age, our peers and colleagues. We gravitate toward circles of people with whom we share significant characteristics, people who look and sound and smell and see just like us. And "adult" is not one size fits all. Ministering to retirees is very different from ministering to adults in mid-career, since retirees face a different set of life tasks and a dramatically different set of emotional needs.

> *Do we modify worship so completely that age becomes the defining characteristic of believers?*

Should we, though, resign ourselves to a segmented church in which small, generational groups are congregations unto themselves within the larger congregation? Do we modify worship so completely that age becomes the defining characteristic of believers? Are we destined to be a fragmented church? Paul often dealt with fragmented congregations and, in doing so, set forth the ideal. Time and time again, he points out that congregations should live out the unity for which Christ died.[7] Paul pays close attention to what was dividing congregations—often the distinction between Jews and Gentiles—and does his best to break down the barriers and encourage church families to come together. In the Epistle to the Ephesians, Paul casts the vision of a church which is "one family where all barriers of race, culture and social status are broken down."[8] Likewise, in 1 Corinthians 12, Paul uses the metaphor of the body to describe how a group of believers should function; each "member" is different, but ultimately they function together. If we take Paul's exhortations as informing ministry, then each part—each person—should feel valued, while all members work together as a functional whole.

Crossing generations

To tease out the implications of Paul's thought, allow me to share a story. As a freshman academy student, I traveled to Austria through a study abroad program. There, I lived and studied at Seminar Schloss Bogenhofen, a Seventh-day Adventist academy and undergraduate theology program. There were lots of youth groups at Bogenhofen; each with eight to fifteen members. These "youth groups" were unlike anything I had experienced. Each group consisted of academy students, undergraduate students, a faculty or staff family, and other church members from the campus church. It seemed a strange mix to bear the label "youth group." Friday nights and Sabbath mornings were spent with this varied group of people.

Bogenhofen's "youth groups" provided an inclusive experience that crossed boundaries of language, culture, and age.

As one of the academy students, the others could have seen me as an annoying kid, but they took me and two other language students under their wings. They encouraged our feeble attempts to communicate in German, translating when needed. Their insights and examples made me approach faith differently and enriched my view of what it meant to be a follower of Christ. They encouraged me (forced me, if truth be told) to take an active part in ministry—from stuffing bulletins to teaching Sabbath school lessons and participating in outreach activities. It was not exciting or flashy. There were no gimmicks or creative videography. It was just a simple group of believers gathering in an upstairs apartment or an empty basement to study the Word of God and our German adult lesson guides. Bogenhofen's "youth groups" provided an inclusive experience that crossed boundaries of language, culture, and age.

I was only at Bogenhofen for a short time, but the type of faith and community I experienced there has impacted the trajectory of my professional and spiritual life. The type of youth group that congregation had embraced created a cross-generational space for me within the context of faith. How do we build a faith community where the retired and retiring feel that type of cross-generational acceptance and support?

We should encourage this group, like their younger counterparts, to surround themselves with their peers. It may be a monthly retiree's breakfast or a Sabbath School lesson study group that caters to seniors. Maybe quarterly senior socials are in order or a weekly Bible study in the church library or a church-sponsored book club, knitting group, or car restoration work bee. In other words, *we encourage study and fellowship among seniors.*

However, to meet the full needs of seniors, we should not limit ourselves to generation-specific fellowship, study, and worship; to congregations segregated by age within the larger congregation. Solomon reminds us that "there is a time for everything, and a season for every activity under the heavens" (Ecclesiastes 3:1, NIV). There is a time to interact with peers, and there is a time to come together as a whole. *Plan cross-generational worship.* One of the Seventh-day Adventist fundamental beliefs is titled "Marriage and the family." In this statement of belief, it is pointed out that "increasing family closeness is one of the earmarks of the final gospel message."[9] Jesus applies similar language to the church family when He declares, "By this everyone will know that you are my disciples, if you have love for one another" (John 13:35, NRSV). There should be specific time set aside for cross-generational worship, when the church gathers as a whole. Generation-specific services can occur at other times on Sabbath or during the week. We should not be timid to champion cross-generational worship and help seniors find their place in the broad family of God.

> *We should not be timid to champion cross-generational worship and help seniors find their place in the broad family of God.*

Mentoring—ministry within ministries

While helping a group of academy students present a series of morning worships for a kindergarten class, I observed something peculiar. In this particular church school there had been some bullying and rivalry between grades. In searching for a solution, the administrators had decided there needed to be more community across the grades. To accomplish this, "family groups" had been formed; clusters of five or six children, all from different grades and classrooms. These "family groups" ate lunch together on a daily basis, and every few weeks they were given a half-hour of free time to do a fun activity. During school spirit days, "family groups" competed together to earn points and prizes. It was remarkable to see sixth and seventh graders herding their younger and adoring charges to lunch, answering a litany of questions, and teaching their young friends how to be "big kids." A commitment to cross-generational worship can have a similar, positive impact on congregations.

In addition to fostering generation-specific fellowship and cross-generational worship, *recruit seniors for cross-generational mentoring and ministry*. Our churches could not run without volunteers. Retirees often have more time than working adults or parents with children still in the home. They can be our most effective resource. To recruit seniors effectively to positions that will be meaningful and rewarding, we must know them well. Bulletin stuffing is a necessary task, but it might not be the best use of a retired engineer's skills. Go for a visit. Take them out to lunch. Listen to their stories.[10] It is only once you know their stories that you learn what their talents and gifts are and can ask them to use them. And do ask! One of our church elders is fond of reminding me that sometimes people need permission to participate. As you learn their stories, you will discover a hidden wealth of knowledge, skills, wisdom, and experience.

In our congregation, we have a gentleman who formerly worked as a milkman. His stories of getting stuck in snowstorms make him the center of attention at Pathfinder outings. A retired math teacher serves as a deacon and helps out weekly at the local church school. One member, an elegant lady who was once a fashion model, delights in arranging the foyer flowers and teaches Sabbath School classes. Retired hospital chaplains, truck drivers, housewives, builders, restaurant owners, and newspaper editors populate our congregation. Knowing their areas of expertise can help us utilize the God-given talents of seniors to the fullest as we create space in our congregations and in our hearts for them to minister.

While attending a pastors' conference, I participated in a workshop presented by Pastor Brenda Billingy.[11] Pastor Billingy spoke about the importance of hanging on to our youth; keeping our church from dying. And while she emphasized meeting young people where they are culturally, she also underscored the need for teams within ministries. According to Billingy, a team should not be made up of peers but of a senior, an adult, a young adult, and a teen all working together.[12] This mentorship structure creates an ever-renewing cycle. Joseph Kidder, author of *The Big Four*, also accents the importance of mentoring, seeing it as the "mandate of the New Testament to raise and equip the new generation of leaders. Every member should be seeking both to be discipled and to disciple." This system should be "everywhere in your church."[13]

In our congregation there is a teenager who has been helping with audio-visual needs for several years. Through the mentorship that has taken place in the sound booth, he has gained confidence and skill. This did not just happen. It represents an important investment by the leaders of our audio-visual ministry who have more in mind than just delivering quality sound. They strive to have at least one young person working with them whenever the sound booth is in action. Mentoring is as much a part of what they do as adjusting microphones.

Mentoring is an effective way for younger generations not to just see seniors but to interact with them and learn from them. Many tasks can be accomplished while mentoring; it might be administering the church library, coordinating the church service, pouring juice at potluck, or passing out bulletins. Essentially, any task presents an opportunity to nourish relationships across the generations. Mentoring relationships with seniors give young people spiritual mentors in addition to their parents. It gives seniors and retirees a chance to see the difference they are making, an opportunity to pass their expertise along, and an opportunity to better understand today's youth. Mentoring helps nurture the cross-generational church family by creating bonds that transcend biology and age. It creates an environment where age ceases to be the defining attribute. Prioritizing family worship, creating mentoring opportunities, and coming together for the church service as a church family make it hard to stay in your small, generational circle.

More than a card

With the appointment of seven deacons in Acts 6, we see the early church taking organizational steps toward the care of their less fortunate brothers and sisters. In preparing to minister to our graying congregations, *prepare for intensive ministry to seniors in need.* Fellowship and cross-generational worship along with mentoring and ministry are wonderful ways to engage retirees, but what do we do when members are in crisis?

Ellen White tells us that taking care of our aging brothers and sisters "is the very work God would have the church do, and they will obtain a blessing in doing it."[14] Intensive ministry to seniors in need is more than sending a card. Aging includes many aspects. Loss of friends or a spouse can lead to depression, and infirmities can lead to loss of independence. Many times, seniors need encouragement and a friend to spend time with them. On other occasions, professional counseling is in order.

Upon entering the retired years, money often becomes a concern. Individuals must live on their savings. Despite the best-laid plans, there are often unanticipated expenses. With unexpected complications come unforeseen costs. Financial support is one area the church should be ready to help seniors. The church can assist in costs associated with medication, counseling, care providers, and transportation. As pastors prepare for an influx of retirees in the coming years, it would be prudent to begin a fund that could be used especially for financial assistance to the aging.

> *Intensive ministry to seniors in need is more than sending a card.*

Perhaps the largest financial cost for seniors has to do with housing. Our church secretary recently opened her home to a church member who had been placed on hospice care. His family crowded into her living room while the sunny front bedroom was converted into a care facility for his last weeks of life. The cost of a care facility was avoided, and the familial setting put the family at ease.

Identity—God's family

According to authors James Houston and Michael Parker, identity is an important part of aging.[15] Let seniors know how much they mean to the church family. Tell their stories—help them know that they are not forgotten, nor will they be. Help members assert their identities by planning and decision-making prior to crisis. Encourage members to update their wills and talk with loved ones about their future wishes. If appropriate, suggest involving the church's trust services department.[16]

Identity in the church is important, but it fades in comparison to identity in Christ. As we prepare for intensive ministry to seniors in need, we cannot overlook the importance of the assurance of salvation; identity as a saved individual. Encouragement can be found in Paul's words, "If you declare with your mouth, 'Jesus is Lord,' and believe in your heart that God raised him from the dead, you will be saved" (Romans 10:9, NIV). In preparing for intensive ministry to seniors in need, pastors should look for ways to provide affirmation, encouragement, financial support, and identity confirmation.

In the book *Mudhouse Sabbath*, author Lauren Winner recounts how, during a trip to her boyfriend's hometown, she was miffed when seated next to his somewhat senile grandfather during a worship service. However, before the service's end, Lauren had learned an important lesson about prayer. She writes, "God Himself had a hand in arranging the seating. Because sitting next to him I could see (and hear) that Dr. Gatewood, who might not even remember how to count to ten, remembered how to pray."[17] From newly retired baby boomers to the most senior member of the congregation, those who have long walked the narrow road of Christianity have lessons to teach those of us who are younger. By creating space for generation-specific study and fellowship, expanding opportunities for cross-generational ministry, prioritizing cross-generational worship, and preparing for intensive ministry to seniors in need, the church affords the young the priceless privilege of learning from their elders. It also provides seniors with the satisfaction of being known and treasured members who find their identity in the family of God.

Identity in the church is important, but it fades in comparison to identity in Christ.

1. Jennifer Orman, Victoria Velkoff, and Howard Hogan, "An Aging Nation: The Older Population in the United States," *United States Census Bureau*, May 2014, http://www.census.gov/prod/2014pubs/p25-1140.pdf. While this is a report for the United States, the other countries are similar.

2. CNN, "Baby Boomer Generation Fast Facts," last modified September 1, 2014, http://www.cnn.com/2013/11/06/us/baby-boomer-generation-fast-facts.

3. David Beckworth and Joseph S. Kidder, "Reflections on the Future of the Seventh-day Adventist Church in North America; Trends and Challenges," *Ministry*, December 2010, http://www.ministrymagazine.org/archive/2010/12/reflections-on-the-future-of-north-american-seventh-day-adventism.html.

4. Monte Sahlin, *Adventist Congregations Today* (Lincoln, NE: Center for Creative Ministry, 2003), 35, 36.

5. Center for Creative Ministry, *Demographic Survey of Adventist Church in North America* (2008), http://www.cye.org/assets/resources/cor/documents/nad-demographic-survey-report.ppt

6. Thomas E. Bergler, "When Are We Going to Grow Up? The Juvenilization of American Christianity," *Christianity Today* (June 2012), 19.

7. Romans 3; Colossians 3:11; Ephesians 3:6; Ephesians 4; 1 Corinthians 12:27, to name just a few.

8. Ralph P. Martin, "Ephesians" in *The New Bible Commentary: Revised,* D. Guthrie and J. A. Motyer, ed. (Grand Rapids, MI: WM. B. Eerdmans Publishing Co., 1970), 1105.

9. Seventh-day Adventist Fundamental Belief #23 from *Seventh-day Adventists Believe* (Silver Spring, MD: Ministerial Association, General Conference of Seventh-day Adventists, 2005), 330.

10. I am not naturally a good listener. The book *Hearing Beyond the Words; How to Become a Listening*

Pastor (Nashville, TN: Abingdon Press, 2006) by Emma J. Justes has helped me learn to be better.

11. Currently ministering as the senior pastor of the Metropolitan church in Hyattsville, Maryland.

12. Pastor Brenda Langford-Billingy, "The Dynamics of Leading Change," presentation, Pastoral Evangelism Leadership Council, Huntsville, AL, December 7–11, 2013.

13. S. Joseph Kidder, *The Big Four: Secrets to a Thriving Church Family* (Hagerstown, MD: Review and Herald®, 2011), 51.

14. Ellen G. White, *Welfare Ministry* (Washington, DC: Review and Herald®, 1952), 238.

15. James M. Houston and Michael Parker, *A Vision for the Aging Church* (Downers Grove, IL: InterVarsity Press, 2011).

16. Visit http://www.willplan.org.

17. Lauren Winner, *Mudhouse Sabbath* (Brewster, MA: Paraclete Press, 2003), 63.

Additional reading: Donald Koepke, ed., *Ministering to Older Adults: The Building Blocks* (Binghamton, NY: The Haworth Pastoral Press, 2011).

Thom S. Rainer, "Five Implications for Churches as the Boomers Retire," accessed May 2014, http://thomrainer.com/2014/05/19/five-implications-churches-boomers-retire.

New Hope Digital, "A Hands on Approach to Ministering to Seniors," accessed February 11, 2015, http://www.newhopedigital.com/2012/10/a-hands-on-approach-to-ministering-to-seniors/?doing_wp_cron=1420653464.7881410121917724609375.

Know Your Members

DAN JACKSON

T hroughout my nearly twenty-five years of pastoral experience, God has taught me (or at least tried to teach me) many things. I responded by trying hard to be a good student. The ministry is a calling where intense learning is required. One must be teachable in order to succeed.

Each individual pastor adapts more readily to the aspects of ministry where he or she has aptitudes. Evangelism drew me like a magnet. I wanted to be an itinerant evangelist, and I believed from my earliest days that God would take me down that track. However, our perceptions of who we ought to be and where we ought to be and where we ought to serve often differ from the eternal perspectives of a God who says, "I know the thoughts that I think toward you . . . thoughts of peace and not of evil, to give you a future and a hope" (Jeremiah 29:11, NKJV). We think that we should be able to tell our future, but God actually does know the future and our individual place in it. For reasons known only to Him, my life was moving toward pastoral ministry.

Over time I developed a strong sense of ministry. I focused my energies on the work of leading people to Jesus in churches, schools, and the communities where I served. While settling into the pastoral role did take some time, through the years I gained a great appreciation for the pastorate and the work of the pastor.

It is wonderful to enter into the lives of individuals at the most vulnerable points in their lives; to be able to stand next to the person who has just become a parent, to share with someone who is walking through the deep valleys of life, and to look into the eyes of one who has just given their life to the God of the universe. These are the experiences that not only place the pastor at the crossroads of human experience but that the pastor will treasure forever.

To have the privilege and responsibility of standing behind a pulpit

Sabbath after Sabbath, proclaiming the truths of God's Word with passion and without fear, is an experience with very few comparables. To work through issues and struggles with wonderful people at your side brings you into close contact and communion—not only with one another but also with God. The work of a pastor is a great calling, and it is also a great blessing.

> *The work of a pastor is a great calling, and it is also a great blessing.*

So, what are the characteristics that identify the successful pastor? What traits set this person apart and make him or her an effective minister? Allow me to start at a very basic point.

Understanding members

The successful pastor must become a people specialist. Jesus, speaking of Himself, said: "I am the good shepherd; and I know My sheep, and am known by My own. As the Father knows Me, even so I know the Father; and I lay down My life for the sheep" (John 10:14, 15, NKJV). In the book *The Desire of Ages*, Ellen White describes the ministry of Jesus in the following way: "Jesus knows us individually, and is touched with the feeling of our infirmities. He knows us all by name. He knows the very house in which we live, the name of each occupant. . . .

"Every soul is as fully known to Jesus as if he were the only one for whom the Saviour died."[1] So the effective pastor, the genuine under-shepherd, must come to understand the nature and character of those he or she has come to serve.

Without keen insight into the individual lives of the members and the character of the congregation-at-large, the pastor walks through an ongoing and incessant "mine field" of human sensitivity and the nuances of "nations, kindreds, tongues and people." Failure to accrue this understanding leaves the pastor in a remote position from the members. It removes the pastor from the vital center—the life—of the congregation and sets the pastor up for failure.

The awareness of this truth grew over years and with experience for me. It did not come without some embarrassment or pain. Sensitivity to the individual members did not come naturally to me either.

In my first year in ministry I was filled with zeal to proclaim the messages of the Scriptures. That is still my belief, but it does not only consist of "crying aloud and sparing not and telling the house of Israel their sins" (see Isaiah

58:1). I was hard on my members and had high expectations that they would respond to all of my negativism with positivity. I was busy in the church and community, and I expected that they would be as well.

One day I heard a group of members complaining about others in the congregation. To be honest, I had just about had enough of it. I went to the members involved and told them: "Your attitude is leading you directly down the road to hell." Having given the prophetic injunction, I ceremoniously turned around and left. Later on those same members accused me of "telling them where to go." Rather than trying to understand their pain, I used my opportunity to pontificate on their weakness.

Several years later I was once again brought face to face with the need to understand. The lesson learned through a series of early morning conversations was one I have never forgotten.

Sunday was always my day off. I often worked throughout the other six days as though there would not be another six days. Sermon preparation, Bible studies, home and hospital visitation, devotionals at the school, as well as the never-ending round of boards and committee meetings seemed to fill every minute. There was time spent with my wife and our children. (The pastor, after all, is a family person.) By the time Saturday night rolled around, I was tired and needed rest. But even Sunday was a day for "lesson learning."

My awareness of the need to connect with, listen to, and understand people in order to effectively minister to them became very prominent in my mind the longer I spent time as a pastor. However, it all came into laser sharp focus one Sunday morning at approximately 5:30 A.M. I was sound asleep in my bed and no creature was stirring—not even my spouse. Suddenly, and to my great chagrin, the phone started ringing and would not stop. I pulled the covers over my head and tried to pretend that it would stop—but it did not. After a few moments, the guilt of failing to respond to family or church members in a time of need began to hit. In great exasperation I finally reached for the phone and pulled it angrily to my ear.

The voice on the other end of the phone seemed fragile and tentative. The words that came out were beyond my "early Sunday morning" comprehension. "Pastor," she queried, "will there be prayer meeting this week?" I was so stunned by the question that I thought that someone was joking. I thought of saying, "Does the sun shine?" and then hanging up. However, even at that early hour I tried to be careful, and I responded by simply saying, "Yes, sister, there will be prayer meeting this week." I shook my head—shook off the call—and returned to my sweet slumber.

Having discussed the event with my wife, I thought nothing more of it. The lady in question was a long-standing church member probably in her late seventies or early eighties. She was faithful in church and prayer-meeting attendance, and I just concluded that she had insomnia. I went through that Sunday and all the rest of the next week, and nothing about the call was brought to mind or even referenced. But then . . .

It was the next Sunday morning at approximately 5:30 A.M., and I was once again within the sweet embrace of sleep. The week had been a busy one, and Saturday evening had been played out at a local skating rink where a bunch of "older folks" like me had played a feverish game of hockey. I was enjoying my needed rest. It was the phone—*again*! It was the same lady—*again*! Her voice did not contain the least bit of reticence or apology: "Pastor," she queried, "will there be prayer meeting this week?" I could hardly believe my ears. How is it that a woman who had attended this church for probably thirty years and had become accustomed to the routine of church life could ask such a question? I quickly called myself to account and responded: "Yes, sister, there will be prayer meeting on Wednesday evening." With that she said goodbye. I, on the other hand, did not go back to sleep. I lay in my bed trying to figure out what these phone calls were all about. It would all come together in about seven days.

The very next Sunday morning—true to her pattern—she called again at 5:30 A.M. I picked up the phone and the same dear sister made the same query and I gave her the same answer. However, before she could say goodbye, I engaged her in a conversation.

"Sister," I said, "you must be lonely. Is this the reason that you call me so early in the morning?" There was a period of silence and then the confession through tears and quiet sobs. She told me that it was just at that time of the year when her husband had died. She recounted the excruciating pain of long nights and lonely days. She shared how she ached to hear a human voice and how even a brief affirmation from the pastor that there would be prayer meeting three days hence seemed to bring temporary relief. She told me how much she looked forward to prayer meeting each week because it meant be-ing around others.

My dear sister was hurting, and it took time for my little head to figure out the fact that I needed to help her in whatever way I could. I will never forget the change in her voice when, as we neared the end of our conversation that day. I said to her, "Would you like me to come and visit with you this week?" She responded with joy. My final words to her that morning were: "Now, sis-ter, you can call me next Sunday morning or any time you wish."

The Sunday morning phone calls only came a few more times, but they were always prefaced with the same precious question: "Will there be prayer meeting this week?" Of course, the words once translated really meant: "Pastor, I am so lonely. Will you please spend a few moments talking to me?" And each time the call came, I spent time talking and praying with a dear, lonely sister.

Lesson learned: A pastor must be able to decode the words spoken. The skill is developed as we observe the people who are speaking them. We need to develop the skills to understand how and why the people are thinking the way they do. Dietrich Bonhoeffer, the well-known German theologian, pastor, and ultimately martyr for his faith, wrote: "We must learn to regard people less in the light of what they do or omit to do, and more in the light of what they suffer."[2]

> *Lesson learned: A pastor must be able to decode the words spoken.*

I had a head elder once who often told me to take him out and put him on an ice floe when he got too old to serve. At first I thought that he was being proactive and forward thinking. As time progressed however, I came to understand that his words were a warning. They basically were the expression of his own personal anxiety: "Don't ever throw me aside just because you think that I am too old." He had a basic feeling of insecurity. I reached out to him as a friend and did a lot of visitation with him. Several years later when the nominating committee chose someone else as the head elder, the experience was not nearly as traumatic as he thought. You do not learn that on day one.

Understanding the congregation

Then there is the question of understanding the congregation as a whole. Having had the privilege of pastoring several "multicongregation" districts, I discovered that every congregation has its own nature and personality. Failure to understand the complexity of this concept is also fraught with danger. Recognizing that, as a pastor, you must relate in specific ways to specific congregations is significant.

The leadership of Moses has always intrigued me. He was a man who had been endowed by God with wonderful natural gifts. He was a great leader who learned from a variety of experiences and circumstances what it meant to be a true leader of God's people.

However, earlier in his life, while in the court of Pharaoh, he had thought that God had called him to liberate his people. He sensed God's plans for His people, and I believe that he understood God's long-term goal. The related events of his life clearly inform us that, while he had a basic understanding of the direction, he was not aware of the best way to get there. Furthermore, he did not comprehend the principles of really knowing his people or how it was that God was going to liberate them.

The story is familiar: one day Moses observed the terrible conditions his people were living under, and it was almost more than he could take. However, when he saw the cruelty that one of the people was suffering at the hands of an Egyptian master, he was moved not only with compassion, but also with anger. Thinking about himself, his pain, and the pain of his people, he swung into action.

> *Thinking about himself, his pain, and the pain of his people, he swung into action.*

Moses' mistaken thinking became obvious. He thought, for certain, that the Israelites would appreciate his actions and honor him as the people's leader. He concluded that eliminating the Egyptian would provide him with the status that he needed in order to deliver his people from bondage.

It was a complete misreading of his people, how they thought and felt. He killed the Egyptian, buried him in the desert sand, and waited for the accolades to come. They never came! There was no great revival among his people. There was no great appreciation for his "daring" feat. How wrong he was.

In witnessing his outburst of passion, the Israelites came to disdain him rather than to honor him. He had completely misunderstood them. Unfortunately, Moses learned the painful lesson that people do not respect outbursts of passion.

If you really want to know what is going on—go to where the people are. Find out their problems, anxieties, needs, and dreams. This does not, however, mean that you should act as they act or do what they do.

I was just about to go on to the platform as a guest speaker at a camp meeting, when the conference president approached me. I asked him how he was doing, and then in exasperation he said: "Some pastors just have no sense!" It is true that "fools rush in where angels fear to tread," and so I asked why he would make such a comment. He told me of a pastor in a nearby district had attended a business meeting where things got a "little heated," and the pastor concluded that the only way to bring things under control was to "slap the head elder in the face." The conference president now had to deal with a furious congregation and consider suspension, move, or termination of the pastor.

True ministry means that we go to where the people are and are with them in the midst of their experiences. A man was a struggling farmer, and sickness had held him up in terms of getting his fields plowed and crops sown. It was a very large predicament for a man of the land. On the other hand, I grew up in a city. The major work that I had been charged with as a child was that of taking out the garbage—which entailed a walk of fifty feet to the back of the yard. However, I called this brother up and let him know that I had driven a tractor and that if he would teach me I would come and give him a couple of days. He readily accepted my offer, so off to his farm I went.

After some instruction he let me loose, and I spent the first morning harrowing the soil with a rather large piece of machinery that, at first, was challenging to manipulate. At lunchtime he came out and took me to his house for the noon meal. There was only one problem; there was no food in the house. My brother looked through the refrigerator, through every nook and cranny of the house, but found nothing except a jar of peanut butter. So he brought out the china, silverware, and crystal, and the two of us sat and ate big piles of peanut butter—laughing about it the whole time; that is, until his wife came home. She brought the groceries with her and made us some delicious sandwiches. I came to understand that family that day. I knew very little about farming, but I did know about people. Honest, sincere, and godly—but nearly broke. Struggling for an existence, all the while true to God. They *were* and *are* a blessing to my ministry.

> *I knew very little about farming, but I did know about people.*

There are people in every congregation who show up at church, as regular as "clock-work," who are faithful to God and love the church. They give of their time, talents, and themselves, yet they have little to give. They live their lives attempting to survive, make their payments, feed their children, and pay for schooling. We must understand them in that context. We must just simply say: Not everyone is the same—everyone who enters our churches comes with a unique story. Every congregation is different and has different expectations of their pastor.

Jesus' life, ministry, and example create the standard for you and for me: "I am the good shepherd; and I know My sheep, and am known by My own . . . and I lay down My life for the sheep" (John 10:14, 15, NKJV).

1. Ellen G. White, *The Desire of Ages* (Mountain View, CA: Pacific Press®, 1940), 479, 480.
2. Dietrich Bonhoeffer, *Letters and Papers From Prison* (New York: Touchstone, 1997), 10.

Biographical Sketches

Kyoshin Ahn

Kyoshin Ahn, PhD, is associate secretary of the North American Division of Seventh-day Adventists. Ahn has served in the Adventist Church for a number of years, beginning with pastoral ministry in Virginia. Before assuming his present responsibility, he served as executive secretary of the Illinois Conference.

Ahn is married to You Mi and has two daughters who are currently studying at Andrews University. In his spare time, he enjoys hiking and traveling, especially to Bible lands.

J. Harold Alomia

J. Harold Alomia, MDiv, was born in Lima, Peru. In 2002, Alomia immigrated and worked as a Bible worker for the Pinion Hills Seventh-day Adventist Church in Farmington, NM. He then was hired as a part-time pastor for the Rocky Mountain Conference (RMC). In 2007, he started his studies at the seminary at Andrews University. Upon graduation Alomia and his wife, Rosie, returned to RMC and served nine churches in the Wyoming/Colorado district and then functioned as the Campion Academy senior pastor. As of August 2014, he and his wife reside in Lincoln, Nebraska, where he is the senior pastor for the College View Church at Union College.

BJ Boles

BJ Boles, MDiv, is currently pursuing a doctorate of ministry. Having ministered in Chile, he speaks fluent Spanish. Boles is a minister with more than twenty-four years of service as missionary, task force worker, teacher, evangelist, and pastor. Having previously pastored in Georgia and Tennessee, he is currently the senior pastor of the Mountain View Seventh-day Adventist Church in Las Vegas, Nevada. Boles is married to Mygdalia, and they have three children: Julia, Westin, and Eastin.

John Brunt

John Brunt, PhD, has been the senior pastor of the Azure Hills Seventh-day Adventist Church in Grand Terrace, California, for twelve and a half years. Previously, he worked at Walla Walla University for thirty-one years, nineteen years teaching in the School of Theology and twelve years as vice president for academic administration. Brunt has written twelve books and more than sixty articles.

His wife, Ione, is a retired certified nurse midwife. They have two grown children and three grandsons, ages seven, ten, and eleven.

Alex Bryan

Alex Bryan, DMin, is senior pastor of the Walla Walla University Church in College Place, Washington, where he also serves as an adjunct professor in the school of theology. Bryan has served the church for more than twenty years as pastor, teacher, and college administrator. His areas of interest include Christian apologetics, missiology in the Global West, and homiletics.

Michael W. Campbell

Michael W. Campbell, PhD, is assistant professor of historical/theological studies at the Adventist International Institute for Advanced Studies (AIIAS) in Silang, Cavite, Philippines. Prior to AIIAS he pastored in Colorado and Kansas for five years. Born in Texas to Canadian parents, Campbell has published numerous articles in scholarly and denominational periodicals, has worked as assistant editor of *The Ellen G. White Encyclopedia*, and actively blogs at AdventistHistory.org. He is married to Heidi Olson, and they have two children, Emma (age eight) and David (age six). He enjoys camping, gardening, and bird watching, along with helping with Adventurers and Pathfinders.

Steve D. Cassimy

Steve D. Cassimy, DMin, began his ministry in Canada in 1978. For the last thirty-seven years his ministry has taken him to five continents and most of the Caribbean islands. He has served as youth pastor, senior pastor, campus chaplain, television host, mentor, and departmental director. Presently he serves as the English Ministries Department director for the Greater New York Conference of Seventh-day Adventists. In 2010, Cassimy co-authored and edited, with Nikolaus Satelmajer and Abraham Jules, *A Guide to Effective Pastoral Ministry*. Cassimy resides in New York City with Marilyn, his wife. They are the proud parents of two young adult children, David and Lavona.

Roger Hernandez

Roger Hernandez, MDiv, is the Ministerial and Evangelism director of the Southern Union Conference of Seventh-day Adventists. He is currently in a DMin program. Hernandez is bilingual, has spoken to many youth and young adult groups, and has provided evangelism training for lay people. Hernandez was born in Cuba. He and his wife, Kathy, have four children. His hobbies are attending growing churches, sports, and reading.

Dan Jackson

Dan Jackson, MA, was elected president of the North American Division of Seventh-day Adventists, Silver Spring, Maryland, in 2010. Jackson is a native Canadian and, with the exception of five years of service in the Southern Asia, has lived and ministered in Canada. During his career, Jackson has served the church as a pastor, teacher, and administrator. He and his wife, Donna, enjoy their three children and four grandchildren.

Marquis D. Johns

Marquis D. Johns, BS, was born in Los Angeles, California. In 2002, after accepting Christ, Johns committed himself to literature evangelism and Bible work. He currently is associate pastor at the Metropolitan Seventh-day Adventist Church in Hyattsville, Maryland. He also has enjoyed work with Barna Group researching Adventist young adults.

Abraham J. Jules

Abraham J. Jules, DMin, was born in Trinidad, West Indies, and has served as a pastor in the New York City area for the past thirty-two years. He has enjoyed preaching in North America, Africa, Europe, the West Indies, and the South Pacific. His passion is for evangelism. Jules lectures occasionally at Andrews University on preaching and leadership. He currently serves as the senior pastor of the Community Worship Center in Queens, New York. He is married to Dr. Dominique Jules, formerly Juste, and is the father of two children.

C. Wesley Knight

C. Wesley Knight, DMin, is the pastor of the Mt. Olive Seventh-day Adventist Church in Metro Atlanta, Georgia, and enjoys speaking worldwide. He contributed to the book *Preaching With Power*. He is happily married to Stephanie, formerly Johnson, of Orlando, Florida. They have two children.

Esther R. Knott

Esther R. Knott, M.A, serves as associate director of the North American Division of Seventh-day Adventists Ministerial department, and Director of the InMinistry Center located at the Seventh-day Adventist Theological Seminary on the campus of Andrews University. She is also the division's ministerial department liaison with the seminary. Her responsibilities include (1) being a pastor to the pastors across the division, (2) program director for the seminary's master of arts in pastoral ministry, and (3) directing the division's efforts to support local conferences in building a sustainable continuing education system for pastors. She has pastored for twenty-eight years in Illinois, Maryland, and Michigan. She and her husband, Ronald A. Knott, director of Andrews University Press, have a daughter and son-in-law—Olivia and Ivan Ruiz-Knott.

Evan Knott

Evan Knott is in the last year of the MDiv program at the Seventh-day Adventist Theological Seminary on the campus of Andrews University in Berrien Springs, Michigan. When he is not studying, Evan enjoys reading, writing, traveling, and spending time with his wife, Lauren. He will be returning to the Chesapeake Conference of Seventh-day Adventists to continue pastoral ministries in December 2015.

Macy McVay

Macy McVay, BA, is a recent graduate of Walla Walla University. Employed by the Oregon Conference, she feels privileged to minister in the East Salem Church. She enjoys working with all ages, but especially treasures moments when she can help build bridges between young and old. Her life goal is to bring people closer to Jesus.

Jiří Moskala

Jiří Moskala, ThD, PhD, is dean of the Seventh-day Adventist Theological Seminary and professor of Old Testament exegesis and theology. He joined the faculty in 1999. Prior to coming to Andrews University, Moskala served as ordained pastor, administrator, teacher, and principal in the Czech Republic. Moskala is a member of different theological societies and has authored or edited a number of articles and books in the Czech and English languages. He has enjoyed participating in several archaeological expeditions in Tell Jalul, Jordan.

Gary Patterson

Gary Patterson, DMin, has served in ministry as a pastor, evangelist, youth pastor, conference youth director, conference ministerial director, conference secretary, conference president, North American Division assistant to the president for administration, and general field secretary for the General Conference. Patterson began his ministerial employment in the Idaho Conference in 1960 and retired from the General Conference in 1999. Since retirement he has served as interim pastor of twelve churches. He is the author of three books and numerous articles.

Calvin B. Preston

Calvin B. Preston, MA, has served in ministry for the past thirty-nine years, pastoring in churches in Georgia and North Carolina. He also served as the secretary of the South Atlantic Conference of Seventh-day Adventists for six years. He is currently the senior pastor of the West End Seventh-day Adventist Church in Atlanta, Georgia. Preston has been married to Wynona, formerly Wimbish, of Akron, Ohio, for thirty-nine years. He and his wife have three adult children and one grandchild.

Stephen Reasor

Stephen Reasor, DMin, currently pastors the Bentley, Blackfalds, and Rocky Mountain House churches in the Alberta Conference of Seventh-day Adventists. Since 2001 he has served the Alberta Conference as a pastor, chaplain, and teacher. His wife, Pattie, teaches high school science, and they have two seven-year-olds, Aeden and Mackenzie (Sissy).

Ángel Manuel Rodríguez

Ángel Manuel Rodríguez, ThD, recently retired from the Adventist Church as director of the Biblical Research Institute of the General Conference of Seventh-day Adventists. At the present time he continues to work part-time for the institute. Rodríguez has published more than twelve books and pamphlets and hundreds of articles in books, journals, and magazines. He has participated in dozens of Bible conferences and theological symposiums around the world and in several interfaith conversations with theologians from other Christian communities. He and his wife, Guivi, are located in Texas. They have two daughters, Edlyn and Dixil, and two granddaughters, Maricelis and Ariela.

Nikolaus Satelmajer

Nikolaus Satelmajer, DMin, STM, started his ministry in New York City and has served the church as pastor, administrator, and, until his recent retirement, editor of *Ministry* and associate ministerial secretary of the General Conference of Seventh-day Adventists.

Since retirement he has continued lecturing to ministerial groups in various countries, taught at several higher education institutions, and edited and contributed to several books. He has also served as interim pastor of three churches—Atholton (two years) in Columbia, Maryland, Jackson Heights (one year) in New York City, and Frederick, Maryland. He and his wife, Ruth, live in Silver Spring, Maryland, and enjoy spending time with their children and grandchildren.

Rollin Shoemaker

Rollin Shoemaker, DMin, STM, is a doctor of ministry supervisor for Andrews University seminary. He enjoys holding revival and evangelistic meetings, reading, and writing, especially on the topic of New Testament writings. In addition to teaching, Shoemaker has pastored in the Greater New York and Southern New England Conferences. He has also worked as a parliamentarian. He resides in Berrien Springs, Michigan, and has three sons, one daughter, and nine grandchildren.

Diane Thurber

Diane Thurber is director of women's ministries and associate director of communication for the Lake Union Conference of Seventh-day Adventists. She has also served in family and shepherdess ministries, and in various other ministries in the churches and conferences in which she and her husband have worked. She is married to Gary Thurber, executive secretary of the Lake Union Conference. They are blessed with two adult sons, Ryan and Justin. On her ministry journey, she claims the promise "And I am certain that God, who began the good work within you, will continue his work until it is finally finished on the day when Christ Jesus returns" (Phil. 1:6, NLT).

Ivan L. Williams Sr.

Ivan L. Williams Sr., DMin, serves as the director for the Ministerial Department of the North American Division of Seventh-day Adventists. Williams sensed God's call when he was thirteen. He has worked in full-time ministry for more than twenty-six years in three different conferences. He also serves as a chaplain (lieutenant colonel) for the air force reserves, and had the privilege to serve for eight years as a chaplain for the California State Assembly. He enjoys media ministry, barbering, and landscaping. He has been able to be all he can be with the unconditional love and support of his Heavenly Father, wife, Kathleen, and their two children, Imani and Ivan II.